T0354727

I BELIEVE IN YOU

I BELIEVE IN YOU

THE INCREDIBLE JOURNEY OF R&B LEGEND

JOHNNIE TAYLOR

GREGORY M. HASTY WITH T.J. HOOKER TAYLOR

ARCHWAY
PUBLISHING

Archway Publishing books may be ordered through booksellers or by contacting:

Archway Publishing
1663 Liberty Drive
Bloomington, IN 47403
www.archwaypublishing.com
844-669-3957

ISBN: 978-1-6657-5876-5 (sc)
ISBN: 978-1-6657-5878-9 (hc)
ISBN: 978-1-6657-5877-2 (e)

Library of Congress Control Number: 2024906776

Print information available on the last page.

Archway Publishing rev. date: 5/16/2024

CONTENTS

PREFACE

Stumbling onto something good always seems to happen when you least expect it. Such is the case with Johnnie Taylor and *I Believe in You*. While working diligently on another book called *Oak Cliff and the Missing Pieces*, I was informed by my friend Ed Gray that Johnnie Taylor was a resident of Oak Cliff. The Oak Cliff narrative highlighted 150 years of the area's history and featured biographies on many of its well-known residents. It was in our conversations about notable individuals that Ed informed me Johnnie lived in Oak Cliff and had his business there. This revelation led me to include him in the book of the storied Dallas suburb along with its celebrated personalities. Photos were needed so Ed put me in touch with T.J. Hooker, who generously provided a photo of himself and his father that was used in the book.

T.J. and I discussed the Oak Cliff book and he mentioned how someday he wanted to have his father's biography written. After our talks, it became obvious that Johnnie Taylor lived a life worth covering. What was shocking was that no one had ever written about his life story in a book before. Thus the undertaking found legs and a massive research project began. The more I discovered about Johnnie, the more fascinated I became with his story and his legacy. I was confounded. Why had no one written about Johnnie Taylor before now? It was mind boggling in this day of biography excess that Johnnie's tale had not been told. T.J. was instrumental in putting all the pieces together for this book. He shared his personal experiences with his father, introduced me to Johnnie's former girlfriends, his daughters and other sons who were able to shed light on his life. T.J. also connected me to former associates and closest confidants of Taylor who provided unfiltered insight into his history.

Johnnie's circle of friends and family was essential in making this book accurate and enlightening. Thanks to T.J.'s vision, this story became reality, the biography of one of the most famous American soul, blues and gospel artists who's ever lived.

Growing up in Oak Cliff, I developed a fascination for music beyond what a normal kid my age would acquire. I had a small, cheap turntable sitting by my bed and I'd put on an LP, listen intently and mouth the words to my favorite artists. Some of my early preferences were the Four Tops, Aretha Franklin, Otis Redding and The Temptations. However, my parents didn't approve of the music I was listening to, and more than once told me to "turn off that racket." You can probably guess what happened next. I not only continued to listen, but I expanded my interest even further. Over the coming years, I would suffer several failed attempts to play in garage bands, but regardless of the washouts, the music fever remained engrained within my soul. One summer I began working at my father's cafeteria. I discovered I was the only White employee in the building. At first it was daunting and light years out of my comfort zone–cultural upheaval enhanced by the constant stream of Black tunes the employees kept blaring in the kitchen. Soon I was exposed to new favorites influenced by the listening taste of my fellow workers. Enter Bobby Womack, Albert King, Eddie Floyd, Al Green, the Isley Brothers, Marvin Gaye, B.B. King, Bobby Bland, Bill Withers, Johnnie Taylor and many more. Those months I spent working alongside my Black friends laid the important foundation for my appreciation of R&B and soul.

In high school, I worked for my high school newspaper. The editor knew my affinity for music, so whenever a concert or show took place, she always assigned me to the story. My second year in college led to an opportunity to work as a DJ for the campus radio station. There I played an unusual blend of rock, soul, blues and folk. I found my calling when it was discovered we could interview traveling musicians coming to town prior to their shows. I was fortunate to interview several high-profile artists, and my favorite was Freddie King. I had seen Freddie's shows several times and never quite got enough of his performances. He became a heat-seeking target to interview once the opportunity presented itself. One night he was playing at a club in Lubbock and I asked a member of his crew about the possibilities of interviewing Freddie. His associate said he would ask him, but it depended on how the celebrity felt after the show. Freddie laid his soul bare on stage. By the time he finished his performance he barely had enough energy to walk to the dressing room. I was doubtful. When approached by his crewmember, King rolled his eyes in exhaustion, looked at me and sauntered over to where I was standing. He said to follow him back to his hotel, let him shower and relax and then he'd think about it.

It was past midnight and the prospects of bringing Freddie back to the station were fading. I waited for nearly two hours in his hotel room with other members of the band and sat awkwardly until Freddie emerged. He was visibly exhausted, but to my surprise agreed to go to the station for a live interview. I called ahead and let the staff know we were on our way and to prepare the studio for his arrival. Freddie, followed by his entourage swept into the studios around 2:00 a.m. Eyes of the studio staff were wide with excitement seeing the oversized bear of a man shuffle into the control room and take a seat behind the mic. Tapes rolled and the interview began. Freddie was generous with his time, and even though he was drained, he spent almost twenty minutes answering questions. Toward the end of our conversation, we asked Freddie to play a tune. After all, he had brought an acoustic guitar to the studio, so it was a fair ask. He peeked over at the tape machine and noticed he was being recorded, and balked. It took us a while to finally persuade Freddie to play, and he hesitantly began Jimmy Rogers' "That's All Right." Sadly four years later Freddie passed away from severe stomach ulcers and pancreatitis. Fast forward thirty years and I came across the reel-to-reel tape I kept of Freddie's interview. It was then that I discovered Freddie had a daughter in Dallas who was playing the club circuit carrying on the family tradition of singing the blues. I met with Wanda King at one of her shows and informed her of the taped interview and the song Freddie played at the station three decades prior. She was amazed and excited, took the digitized version I gave her and put it on her next album adding me to the credits on the liner notes.

Once off to college, I tucked my musical tastes away and fused it with the new rock 'n' roll onslaught of the seventies bearing down on the listeners. After college and a short career as a disc jockey and music director at a local ABC affiliate, I left the world of entertainment and began a long career in business. However the fire that burned inside for music, especially soul and blues, remained. In later life I was hired to write music reviews for *Lit Monthly* magazine and the editor heard the account of my night with Freddie and was fascinated. A story ensued and memorialized the unforgettable encounter with Freddie. After many album reviews, serving as emcee for concerts, interviewing dozens of artists, and thousands of hours listening to music, I felt prepared to write a story on music, specifically on R&B and its history. Then Johnnie's opportunity surfaced which seemed to meet me at the crossroads. After reviewing Johnnie's music, I realized that several of his songs were familiar to me. Getting to know him through the various interviews with family members and friends brought his colorful character to life. I knew this was meant to be when I found out that Johnnie had lived only three houses down from me in Oak Cliff. This type of coincidence is stunning. I had vague memories of someone of his stature living nearby, but I didn't make the connection until I was knee-deep into the research for writing *I Believe in You.*

Johnnie's story begged to be told. His rich legacy will fascinate readers as much as it did me. This biography celebrates his achievements, his battles, and his many victories. He was loved by many and will always remain in the annals of music history as the "Philosopher of Soul." As I write these words, it's as if he's whispering to me from the heavens, 'I believe in you'.

INTRODUCTION

Some performers are immortal. Johnnie Taylor is one. The soul, gospel and blues sensation can be considered one of the all-time greats among his peers. For sixty years he graced the stage and traveled the country entertaining hundreds upon thousands of devoted fans. Johnnie often took his listeners to school on the ways of life. He was relatable and seemed not only to understand, but be understood by his audience. Taylor was adaptable, versatile and universal. When trends in music changed, he customized his course to meet the appetite of his fans. If you wanted the blues, he'd sing the blues. If you wanted gospel, he could lay that down too. Soul-funk with a pinch of pop? Well try on "Disco Lady." Johnnie Taylor, as the consummate entertainer, could do it all.

To many, Taylor will always remain a mystery. Little has been written about his life. *I Believe in You* was written to finally share the intimate story of his personal journey to stardom that touched generations of loving fans. What became evident to this author is that Johnnie Taylor was an extremely complicated man. This carefully researched account–this first written study of the man–shares with you his unique essence as a father, husband, friend, and other-world performer. *I Believe in You* captures thoughts and memories from his many children, former girlfriends, devoted friends and professional associates. Was he a saint? No. Was he a good man? Yes. This story sheds light on his many admirable qualities, despite the nature, degree and number of challenges he faced.

From his early childhood, he had developed a conflicted personality, held captive by two diametrically irreconcilable forces. His spiritual upbringing, knowledge of scripture and steadfast faith were locked into a continual life-or-death tug-of-war with his compulsive sexual behavior and drug use. Getting inside someone's head to understand why they did what they did is difficult even for the professionally trained. What makes this task more challenging is when a person like Johnnie has been deceased for two decades. Evidence to solve Johnnie Taylor's mysterious cold-case has become locked away; little information remains and is ebbing as years go by. When family members and colleagues slowly pass away, Johnnie's legacy becomes fainter by the day which calls for the important task of chronicling his biographical existence.

His children are his biggest fans. Several have followed in his footsteps to develop careers of their own. The lightning rod of the clan is T.J. Hooker. As an *unacknowledged* son for many years of his life, he understood his dad for who he was. T.J. knows full well his dad wasn't the best father he could have had, but he loved his father just the same. All thanks go to T.J. who personally took the initiative to have Johnnie's life recounted. Yes, T.J. grew up without a father, but despite Johnnie's absence, T.J. developed a love and fascination for his one true idol. Thanks, T.J., for your spirit, insight, perseverance and dedication to making the memory of Johnnie Taylor a lasting legacy.

CHAPTER 1

CRAWFORDSVILLE CONCEPTION

Johnnie Taylor was an enigma. Deep down inside he had two dynamic life forces, each battling for territory. He was a victim of the back-and-forth faceoff between his faith background in the church, and his prestigious occupation, overindulgent lifestyle, and unorthodox upbringing. Despite his inner turmoil, he grew into a consummate entertainer who dazzled thousands on stage and sold millions of records. Regardless of Johnnie's lifetime of turbulence, he somehow produced some of the most cherished soul and R&B music ever recorded. Johnnie Taylor confounded the most astute behavioral experts. Sharing his story reveals Johnnie's dual identities and brings some understanding of the impact the dualities had on his improbable life. Let the music begin.

Stationed at the convergence of U.S. Highway 64 and State Highway 50, a small rural burg emerged in Northeastern Arkansas pitched in the backswamp along the Aluvian Plains of the Mississippi River. Thirteen miles east of West Memphis, Adolphus Fountain Crawford pioneered the hamlet of Crawfordsville encased within Crittendon County. The small community was only spittin' distance from Tennessee, and the city of Memphis loomed less than twenty miles away, where it straddled The Big Muddy. Incorporated in 1912, Crawfordsville emerged from among the woodlands punctuated by oaks, hickories and bald cypresses. This was timber country. Trees fell, the wood milled and was hauled out by rail to parts unknown until the land gave up its plenty. After only a few decades, Crawfordsville transformed itself from forest land to farmland. The new king was cotton.[1]

Cotton fields fanned out in all directions, worked by descendants of former slaves, who eked out a living sharecropping on farms and plantations. Two of these field-workers were Willie Taylor and Ida Mae Blackman. The married couple gave birth to three children in Crawfordsville: two girls, Georgia and Addie Bea and the last child, a son, born May 5, 1934. His parents named him Johnnie Harrison Taylor. Here the kids spent their childhood in a segregated community. The Black kids couldn't attend school with White students in Crawfordsville, so if they wanted an education, kids had to trek outside the city to rural "wing" schools. Life was difficult for Black residents who hard-labored the fields. This often meant young people had to forgo school to help their families pick cotton. Johnnie looked on as his family whiled away the hours plucking the white, powdery fleece in the repressive heat and humidity of Northeastern Arkansas. As a youngster, he realized picking cotton was strenuous and grueling. Johnnie wondered whether he was cut out for pickin' and choppin' cotton, especially as he watched his family perform the back-breaking tasks. "I didn't want to pick it, man," he told Rashod D. Ollison in 1999. "You have to keep in mind that this was during a time and in a place where that was all folks did. My family picked it. I didn't want to."[2]

Johnnie dreamed about singing for a living rather than working in the fields. As a young kid, he hummed songs and hymns as his parents and siblings toiled among the row-crops. His vocal incantations led to chirping and chanting, and later to singing. The family recognized that Johnnie was a young man with an exceptional voice. "He figured out he had a voice that people responded to, that was sort of his ticket to a better life."[3] Rather than make him work alongside the others, his parents allowed Johnnie to make melody

JOHNNIE'S FATHER WILLIE TAYLOR
PHOTO COURTESY OF FONDA BRYANT

while they worked. This was agreeable to Johnnie since he wouldn't have to pick cotton. This demonstrated early on how Johnnie became proficient in exploiting his talents to enhance or improve his circumstance. As we will see, this methodology became a clever form of opportunism, a trait he would refine, enhance and incorporate into a permanent part of his identity.

In the 1950s, the town of Crawfordsville had approximately 400 citizens. The streets were, for the most part, named after early city residents. Church was an integral part of Black family life in Crawfordsville and Johnnie's clan partook, shepherded by his grandmother who made sure he was always present and accounted for in church on the Sabbath. Johnnie reflected on his past, "I'm from Arkansas originally." "West Memphis to be exact. I was born in Crawfordsville, but I have no memories of the place."[4] When Johnnie was six, members of the church became aware of his singing talents, and showcased the child marvel. He was performing in earnest in front of the congregation and God Himself. Not long after, Johnnie's parents separated, and his mother moved to Kansas City with her new man, Joe Jackson. However, Johnnie stayed in Arkansas. He moved in with his grandmother, down the road to West Memphis and started his new life without his parents. His grandmother inherited the task of raising the exceptionally talented young man. Johnnie sang gospel with the church choir and became the darling of West Memphis and beyond. Grandma was strict but godly as Johnnie would describe, "That woman didn't take no mess, but she was a loving woman."[5] Leaders of the church took Johnnie on the road all across Arkansas, Tennessee and even Illinois where churchgoers listened in awe to the gifted young prodigy. "They showed him off as a priceless little bauble, an adorable, pint-sized curio with golden pipes."[6] About this time, another personality characteristic may have developed, known as the "Child-Star Syndrome." When a young child grows up accustomed to adoring fans and constant admiration, they sometimes fail to grasp the serious magnitude of their situation. It can lead to emotional consequences brought on by stress, unpredictability and sometimes loneliness. Child stars, separated from their home, would work long adult hours, and suffer unhealthy time alone. Those who led the traveling gospel parade were not always above reproach. Often there were dubious circumstances involving members of the choirs, the pastors and entertainers. Dallas artist Bobby Patterson, a well-traveled young gospel vocalist himself, confirmed some of the carrying-on behind the tents was eye-opening and best not repeated.[7] It remained the secret of the traveling ministry. This complex can leave a child-star with deep-seated emotional troubles. With Johnnie's less than desirable upbringing, these characteristics evolved, and were similar to those of other child celebrities. Stars such as Michael Jackson, Shirley Temple, and Tiger Woods, reportedly experienced this manifestation. Johnnie's son Jonathan shared his thoughts about his father's experience as a child star. "It led to him growing up faster I think … [than] he obviously would of cause he was around adults a lot more and was on the road. I think that affects the rest of your life in a myriad of ways."[8]

In 1944, the US established a prisoner-of-war camp outside of Crawfordsville. Germans captured in North Africa who fought in World War II were incarcerated and contracted out to farmers for manual labor.[9] This was also the year that ten-year-old Johnnie left 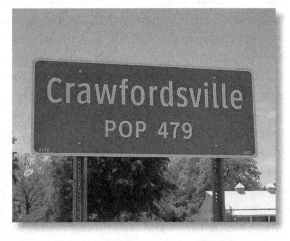 his grandmother's home in West Memphis en route to Kansas City to reunite with his mother and stepfather. There he started a new life in the 18th Street and Prospect neighborhood. In its heyday, 18th Street was immersed in musical performances and entertainment. Prior to Johnnie's arrival it was teeming with clubs, bars and juke houses up and down the streets. This area became a historical point of origin for jazz music. Although the area was beginning to decline, Johnnie took it on as a new stomping ground. He arrived in this musical hotbed, offering his raw talent developed in the church to the new distinctive environment of jazz and blues surrounding him.

CHAPTER 2

GOIN' TO KC

As Johnnie's talents evolved, he developed a tendency for being the center of attention. Johnnie liked the limelight. He savored being a virtuoso with *the* gift and the empowerment it brought. He sought out any opportunities to perform for audiences in the church. During his time in Arkansas, he had become a child phenom, idolized for his youthful vigor and gold-plated voice. Johnnie knew he had what it took to be an entertainer. Some would consider him a veteran performer even though he was only a teen. However, over the period of only a few years, fortune had dealt Johnnie setbacks in toxic, life-altering events. His parents separated, he was abandoned by his father and mother, and then dispatched to West Memphis to live with his grandmother. A few years later, he was sent 450 miles to live in Kansas City. There he reunited with his mom Ida Mae and new husband Joe Jackson. This unpredictability and chaotic home life would have undoubtedly made an impact on Johnnie's state-of-mind. The young Taylor, a church worship-leader and entertainer, eventually developed a unique self-sufficiency to endure these transitions. He also tasted life on the road, as he traveled the gospel circuit across state lines with ministers and other adults. Exposure to adult life and exploits on the road resulted in him becoming more worldly, cultured and street-smart. Experiences such as these seemed to be a catalyst for his precociousness and advanced maturity. Johnnie learned life lessons that few his age would have encountered.

The 18th Street neighborhood of his new home remained a hotbed of entertainment featuring gospel and jazz along with rhythm and blues. The crossroads of 18th and Vine was the urban center for Blacks in Kansas City who were forced to move from the rundown areas around the Missouri River. An autonomous Black neighborhood emerged amidst the area's oppressive segregation and evolved into a self-sustaining town within a town. It featured a robust business center and a fledgling entertainment mecca. Bolstered by the Musicians Local 627, union clubs such as Dante's Inferno, the 12th Street Reno, Cherry Blossom, The Blue Room, Gem Theater, and the Pla-Mor Ballroom sprang up in the new high-steppin' entertainment neighborhood of 18th and Vine. Sounds from Chicago and New Orleans began to filter into Kansas City. These new musical styles transformed into Kansas City's own brand of jazz. The Bennie Moten Orchestra exploded on the scene in the twenties and thirties, bringing with it an orchestral-jazz style they soon made famous. Moten's sound attracted the renown William J. (Count) Basie to Kansas City who led the band after Moten passed away unexpectedly in 1935 from a routine tonsillectomy. During this era, the music scene exploded in Kansas City, fueled by Thomas J. Pendergast. Pendergast was a subversive political boss who controlled Kansas City and much of Missouri from 1926-1939. His web of gambling, prostitution and bootleg liquor funded enterprises that imposed his agenda on political leaders, obligating them to cooperate. Law enforcement officials were persuaded to look the other way during Prohibition which allowed Pendergast to serve liquor in his clubs and dance halls and stay open around the clock. This ignited the proliferation of KC jazz and its first cousin, the blues. In the later part of the thirties, the KC native son and famed jazz saxophonist Charlie Parker also made his mark on the 18th and Vine landscape.

As Johnnie made his appearance in "The City of Fountains" circa 1944, his predecessors had blazed a new musical pathway and primed the pump, making the environment in Kansas City ripe for the young man's brilliance. Johnnie shopped his solo singing virtuosity and met contemporaries who shared his passion for gospel music and praising the Lord. Gospel itself had a long history in KC with the likes of Thomas A. Dorsey and the Whitney Singers paving the way for young up-and-coming artists like Taylor. Churches were known to feature young talent, and Johnnie became a regular on the local scene singing with his newly created quartet, the Melody Kings, (also known as the Melody Makers).

He was only around thirteen at the time. The "Gospel Highway" in and around Kansas City was soon the new traveling circuit and allowed the Melody Kings to mature and become an accomplished and polished ensemble. The group's reputation grew as they performed at area churches, parties and family gatherings. This organic growth fathered a close-knit gospel fraternity in Kansas City. This was especially true for youth who maintained a network of like-minded groups and vocalists. These vibrant circles of religious artists would also come in contact with gospel performers outside the state which provided inspiration along with fresh creative ideas. New York and Chicago had grown into gospel institutions that featured many emerging crusaders for the church. Chicago's Highway Q.C.'s was one of these jubilee quartets. The group was founded in 1945, when Johnnie was eleven. The founding teenagers ranged in age from thirteen to sixteen, and emerged from the Bronzeville neighborhood on Chicago's south side at the Highway Missionary Baptist Church. The company of singers adopted "Highway" from the church name and added "Q.C.'s" which some say was shorthand for "Quartet Crusaders". The Q.C.'s' neighborhood of Bronzeville was an African-American cultural center. It was known as the "Black Metropolis" and was a launching pad for golden-era gospel music in the Windy City. Early members of Bronzeville's Q.C.'s were brothers, Lee, Bubba and Jake Richardson, Creadell Copeland, and Marvin Jones. Bubba Richardson was a friend of Sam Cook, his classmate at Wendell Phillips High School. Cook would play a pivotal role in the Q.C.'s and the gospel uptrend in South Chicago.[1]

The Highway Q.C.'s' performances emulated the iconic Chicago gospel group known as the Soul Stirrers, which was established in 1926, in Trinity, Texas just north of Houston.[2] The Q.C.'s soon became known as the "Soul Stirrer Juniors." They modeled themselves after the acclaimed singers and collaborated with the older vocalists to refine their craft. R.B. Robinson of the Stirrers coached the young cantors on how to fine-tune their deliveries. In the spring of 1947, an epiphany took place when two of the Richardson brothers met Sam Cook. He was the young son of the Reverend Charles Cook, pastor of Chicago Heights Church. Sam began as many young gospel standouts did, by singing worship songs at church services. He and his siblings performed at his dad's church. Sam was asked to join the Q.C.'s and instantly elevated the group to new heights. The group caught their first break performing with a musical caravan that included the Soul Stirrers, the Fairfield Four and the Flying Clouds from Detroit. In the audience was promoter Louis Tate who was so impressed with the Q.C.'s that he excitedly commiserated with his friend and Soul Stirrer member, R.B. Robinson to develop a plan to take the Q.C.'s on the road to major venues. In 1949, the quartet played at Detroit's Forest Club. There they caught the attention of Reverend C.L. Franklin, Aretha Franklin's father. With the support of Tate, Robinson, and the Reverend Franklin, the singers landed a gig on Memphis radio station WDIA. The radio performance helped them market their skills and led to booking local live performances in Memphis. Ironically, the boys' sound was so much like the Stirrers, it actually limited their ability to make records and gain the notoriety they had been working so hard to achieve.

In 1950, Robert H. (R.H.) Harris, the Stirrers' lead singer for over a decade, unexpectedly shocked the gospel multitudes when he announced his plans to leave the outfit. This announcement left the group in disarray without his guidance to advance their careers. When he heard the news, Sam Cook jumped at the opportunity to audition for the vacant position. He was immediately accepted by the other members who were impressed with Cook's vocal characteristics and extraordinary style. By 1951 he was an integral member of the famed Soul Stirrers and a more-than-adequate replacement for Harris as their lead singer. However, Cook's departure to join the Stirrers proved to be devastating to the Q.C.'s. To replace the colossal loss of Sam Cook, the Q.C.'s enlisted the up-and-coming Lou Rawls, who was recruited from his former group, the Holy Wonders.

Meanwhile Johnnie had been sharpening his vocal and performance skills in Kansas City with the Melody Kings. His church-touring travels took him to many locations

SAM COOK

across the Midwest. It wasn't uncommon for young gospel singers to caravan their way across the countryside as guest performers, where they were enthusiastically received by each congregation. On these journeys Taylor met scores of other talented gospel singers and visited a continual string of tabernacles in the process. His wandering pilgrimage crisscrossed the Midwest from Kansas City to St. Louis, Springfield to Chicago and occasional performances in the Deep South, Memphis, Indianapolis, Milwaukee and Detroit. These expeditions called for grueling hours on the road where travel was arduous and accommodations were seldom available. The Jim Crow era forced Black pilgrims like Johnnie to secure lodging with friends, family members and church hosts. Motels and roadhouses were unavailable to the Black gospel performers. Johnnie's travels eventually led him to become acquainted with Chicago, the city where his aunt took residence. Since he was constantly on the road, he split his time in Kansas City with his mom and when traveling north, stayed with his aunt in Chicago. His nomadic way of life didn't offer a consistent lifestyle that most young people were accustomed to, and he wasn't able to attend school regularly. Johnnie's hard-nose education was all about learning the rules of the road, not what was taught in books. His social network included his song mates and musicians, gospel leaders, pastors, friends, families, and congregational celebrants. This unorthodox upbringing laid a foundation of self-sufficiency and forced him to scratch out an existence without the help or guidance of his family.

CHAPTER 3

LORD GET ME TO CHI-TOWN

As an early teen, Johnnie spent a great deal of time in the "Windy City" absorbing the local music scene. Taylor decided Chicago was the place he wanted to be, so he left Kansas City. He set off on his own, and left his mother Ida Mae in Missouri. In Chicago he befriended the Cook family, led by a Church of Christ minister who brought his wife and eight children from Mississippi to Illinois in the thirties. All of the children were musically gifted, and Reverend Charles Cook made sure they were front and center when the singing began at his services. Sam Cook was the fifth child of the family and sang tenor with his siblings in the church quartet. Sam first met Taylor when they were teens; and Johnnie spent many hours hanging around the Cook family home on Chicago's south side. Initially, Johnnie was probably closer to L.C., Sam's younger brother, who was about the same age as Johnnie. Sam, on the other hand, was three years Johnnie's senior, and Johnnie would have looked up to the older teenager. Cook was handsome, talented, and came from a solid, functional family that stuck together through trying times. Even at an early age Sam was charismatic, adventuresome and mischievous. For an adolescent young man with little or no parental direction, Sam served as Johnnie's circumstantial spiritual guide. Taylor's upbringing in a religious environment, as a traveling gospel singer and an aspiring artist, blended perfectly with the Cook family singers. As Taylor got to know the Cook family, he began hanging out at the house as vocal performers invariably do, harmonizing and honing their skills. Johnnie's gift became obvious to the family and struck an impression with Sam. Johnnie's lack of adult guidance imbued a tendency of insecurity which, in turn, produced behavioral traits of arrogance and brazenness. Sam was drawn to Taylor's feisty persona and allowed him into his sphere regardless of the age difference. These early days of getting to know one another set the stage for Johnnie's veneration of Sam Cook. Henceforth, Taylor would go about emulating his guru and soul educator.

On his recurrent trips to Kansas City, Johnnie met Ruby Richards. Ruby was a fifteen-year-old young lady who attended Lincoln High School. In the early years of Johnnie's formative career, he not only earned a reputation for being a standout vocalist, but was also known for his fastidious threads and immaculate appearance. He was always dressed to the nines and never went anywhere unpolished or unkempt. After meeting Johnnie, Ruby was dazzled by his presence and swept off her feet. Soon she would become his hometown girlfriend in KC. One thing led to another and Ruby became pregnant. Nine months later, Johnnie became a reluctant father when his first child, Anthony was born on October 21, 1953. Ruby was only sixteen. After becoming a father Taylor spent less and less time in Missouri as his singing career shifted into another orbit. His unexpected new role as a father may have caused his preoccupation with Chicago, or perhaps he saw more opportunities there.

YOUTHFUL JOHNNIE TAYLOR

The same year Anthony was born, Johnnie was involved with various gospel ensembles, and for the first time sang with secular bands. The effects of living in the fast-paced community of Chicago exposed Johnnie to other musical experiences and eclectic lifestyles. This led him to join a street-corner group named the Five Echoes, for which he replaced Tommy Hunt who was drafted to join US armed forces in the Korean War. Johnnie's new group performed doo-wop, a sub-genre of R&B, originating from Black communities in the forties. It featured melodic harmonies with an uncomplicated beat and virtually no instrumentation. In 1954, the Echoes struck a record deal and made their first recording on the indie label Sabre Records, which specialized in blues, jazz and doo-wop. After Lou Rawls departed the Q.C.'s and joined the Chosen Gospel Singers in 1953, his departure created a need for a lead vocalist. Johnnie more than amply filled the Q.C.'s need. While Taylor was performing doo-wop with the Five Echoes he maintained his gospel roots by moonlighting with the Q.C.'s. He was, Johnnie said, straddling two genres. "I was kind of back and forth there for a while. I kinda left and stopped singing with the Q.C.'s for a while and I went back to the Echoes and I stopped singing with the Echoes and I went back to gospel."[2] Taylor was a critical influence in the Q.C.'s changing record labels. The Echoes were brought in to cut singles, "Tell Me Baby" and "Evil Woman" with Vee-Jay Records (the first Black-and woman owned label in the US). Afterwards he introduced the Q.C.'s to Vee-Jay. That introduction led to the group recording four songs that same year, just before Johnnie turned twenty-one.[3]

It was in the realm of Chicago's Black music circles that Johnnie kept watch on Sam Cook in the early fifties. Johnnie had followed Cook from his early days with the Q.C.'s and had developed a pronounced admiration for Sam's singing talents and leadership. Taylor watched Sam from afar and slowly developed a musician's crush on the charismatic leader of the Soul Stirrers. He and Cook traveled in the same circles, and Sam would become Johnnie's confidante, mentor, supporter, and guide as Johnnie cut his teeth on the Chicago music scene. The young men spent many an hour sitting on Cook's back porch, talking, singing and daydreaming about paths they wanted to follow to stardom. The two were polar opposites, however. When it came to performing, Cook was pensive, creative, stylishly polished and more of a crooner; whereas Johnnie, although smooth at times, could be brash, audacious and rough around the edges. Peter Guralnick, in his book *The Triumph of Sam Cooke Dream Boogie*, described Johnnie as " ...an arrogant little fellow who strutted around like a banty rooster ..." and further described him as, "a feisty little man with a long, lantern-jawed face, full mustache, and high pompadour ...".[4] Taylor's time was split between the secular Echoes singing at places like the Squeeze Club and performing for the gospel-based Q.C.'s at local churches. Johnnie was being pulled in conflicting directions. These diverging interests produced a dissociative identity which developed within Johnnie's persona. The push and pull of polar-opposite forces left Johnnie marooned somewhere in between, with the dual personalities battling it out for a beachhead. The *Journal of Gospel Music* was spot-on when it portrayed Johnnie as sometimes being an "irrationally conflicted person."[5] While in Chicago, Johnnie met and became involved with Mildred Singletary. She became pregnant and Taylor's second son, Floyd was born on January 25, 1954. Floyd's arrival was only three months after J.T. had his first son Anthony, from his relationship with Ruby Richards in Kansas City. A few years later, Johnnie fell in love with Chicagoan Harriet Lewis, and they were married in 1956.[6] Johnnie was apparently a prolific womanizer and this behavior was exacerbated in his early twenties, leading him through a disturbing pattern of sexual exploits. It seemed that the more time he spent on the road amidst mature adult situations the more his fans adored him. Johnnie's indulgent tendencies were fueled by Sam Cook, who led a similar, less than chaste lifestyle. The bottom line was, "Both liked girls, enjoyed to party at times and behave recklessly."[7]

The Highway Q.C.'s group served as a springboard for vocalists that transported members on a trajectory to success, first producing Sam Cook, then Lou Rawls, followed by Johnnie Taylor. The Q.C.'s history of yielding star-material became an essential part of a singing "internship," or a farm club for the much-renowned Soul Stirrers. To the Q.C.'s credit, the Stirrers actually viewed the group as serious competition, as demonstrated by their repeated adoption of talent from the quartet.[8] According to vinylmeplease.com, Johnnie was first recruited when he was "plucked from a Chicago whiskey joint" by members of the Q.C.'s.[9] Once he started singing full-time with the Q.C.'s, the group coalesced and continued where Rawls and Cook left off. During the year 1955, Johnnie partnered with Q.C.'s co-lead singer Spencer Taylor (no-relation) to score a major recording of the passionate gospel tune "Somewhere to Lay My Head" on Vee-Jay. The song was so impressive, Soul Stirrers' guitarist Leroy Crume declared, "The Soul Stirrers were in New York riding down the street to the Apollo Theater, and Sam Cook and I were kidding around with each other. We heard this record come on the radio. Johnnie Taylor was singing 'Somewhere To Lay My Head' with the

Highway Q.C.'s, but at the time I didn't know who it was. I said, 'Sam, if you ever leave the group, this is the guy I'm gonna get.'"[10] This recording was followed by a handful of celebrated singles, one of which was "Pray, I'll Trust His Word." Johnnie's last recording session with the Q.C.'s in March 1956 ended his short three-year tenure with the group. He performed, "I'll Trust His Word," singing a-cappella and demonstrating his trademark vocal runs, patterned after his inspiration Sam Cook.

CHAPTER 4

GOSPEL TRAITOR

A decade earlier in 1944, Specialty Records was established in Los Angeles by its founder Art Rupe. He was also creator of the recognizable labels Atlantic, Chess, Savoy, King, and Modern Records. Specialty had, in its stable, artists like Little Richard, Lloyd Price, the Pilgrim Travelers featuring Lou Rawls, and the Swan Silvertones. Rupe was very selective in the genres his company recorded, most notably jazz, R&B, gospel and some rock and roll. However, Rupe's top-billing client was the Soul Stirrers. Robert "Bumps" Blackwell was a producer who worked at Specialty. Blackwell, groomed many of the label's top-tier performers and also produced their records. In 1956, while Cook was still with the Soul Stirrers, Blackwell started arranging recording sessions in New Orleans with the intent of producing more secular music on an experimental basis.[1] The objective allowed Sam to break free from his gospel roots and pursue a more lucrative career, using the thinly veiled name of Dale Cook for anonymity. Specialty's owner Rupe, begrudgingly went along with the scheme. He was fearful Cook's crossover would detrimentally impact the sales of the Stirrers' gospel renditions and damage their credibility with dedicated supporters. When the material was released, discerning fans and radio stations immediately saw through the smokescreen of the fabricated character known as Dale Cook.[2] Blackwell and Cook arranged to have a follow-up session in order to finish the project they had begun in New Orleans. However, Rupe mandated that if there was to be another session it would have to be in L.A. This way he could keep a watchful eye on the proceedings and apply his idealistic approach to maintaining

Cook's gospel framework.[3] In the midst of the next L.A. sessions, Blackwell, Cook and the musicians were knee-deep in recording when Rupe unexpectedly made an appearance in the studio. Upon seeing that Sam and Bumps incorporated White, secular back-up vocalists called the Lee Gotch Singers, he flew into a rage, chastising the two. Rupe's public tirade created an irreconcilable falling-out between the owner, Sam and Blackwell, Sam's producer at Specialty.[4] After considerable negotiations, a settlement agreement was reached ending Blackwell's association with the company. The stipulations assigned Sam's recording contract to Blackwell along with four secular recordings that he and Cook completed in New Orleans. Rupe's offer also included assigning Bumps the rights to four of Bump's own instrumental masters. For his part, Blackwell gave Rupe a full release of all future financial obligations that included his past due bonuses and royalties, which were substantial.[5]

In the negotiations both Rupe and Blackwell made calculated risks. The gamble hinged on Cook's future prospects and whether his entry into the popular music field was successful. Hindsight showed Rupe's wager was a major misjudgment, giving Blackwell Sam's recording contract. Cook sensed Rupe was in a tenuous position. His notion was  based on Rupe's distaste for the industry's commonplace, but illegal payola, his concern regarding the future of gospel music, added to the effects of a contentious divorce with his wife. These issues were a forewarning that Specialty's long-term viability was uncertain. The perplexing release of Cook and Blackwell from their Specialty obligations was an indication of the company's distress and enabled the two to make a convenient departure.

In 1957, Blackwell took Sam's material to a newly formed label, Keen

Records and hit the jackpot with "You Send Me", which became Cook's biggest selling single. Keen also gave Blackwell and Cook more recording freedom and enhanced their royalty payouts. These events earmarked the demarcation line between Cook's past gospel career and his exploitation of secular soul, rhythm and blues.

J.W. "Alex" Alexander, was once a tenor with the Pilgrim Travelers in Art Rupe's stable at Specialty. After his singing career, Rupe used Alexander to cultivate new artist opportunities as an A&R man (artist and repertoire). During their time at Specialty, Alex and Sam developed a close friendship. Alexander was fifteen years his senior, and began to mentor him as a young artist. J.W.'s guidance was instrumental in steering Sam through the maze of the recording business during his early days at Specialty. Following Cook's, and Blackman's departure from Specialty, they were joined by Alexander in their new venture.

The year 1958 turned out to be a volatile period for Chicago gospel after Cook abandoned the fellowship. He did so with the prospect of cutting a new career path that could generate more notoriety, fame and bigger paydays. Cook's initiation to secular R&B represented a shift from the church to nightclubs and his influence began to permeate the sobersided gospel ranks. He was taking a leap into the great unknown relying on blind faith and self-confidence. Sam thoughtfully added an "e" to the end of his name at the suggestion of Blackwell to distinguish himself as a classy, new R&B celebrity, leaving behind the simpler "Cook" from his former gospel days.[6] The name Dale Cook used in the New Orleans sessions was lost to anonymity.

Cooke's jump to R&B disappointed and angered gospel fans. The first bluesmen were descendants of illiterate slaves who chose to play music, some out of necessity. They didn't have any skills to obtain higher level jobs and scorned the idea of working in the fields. Thus, the blues genre developed an unsavory reputation and was considered seedy especially after the bluesmen began to play in sleazy juke houses, brothels and bars. The bluesmen played music to dodgy characters who frequented these establishments, and performed songs their listeners could relate to. Drinking, womanizing, lust, and down-on-their-luck stories became a common theme among blues performers. Churchgoers felt blues music was evil, and those who performed it lived in sin. In their mind, blues was devil's music.[7] Well known bluesmen didn't dispel the notion as Son House and Leadbelly were both convicted killers and the mythical Robert Johnson was poisoned. Blues singers would also modify well-known Christian hymns into their own renditions adding insult to injury with the righteous.

CHAPTER 5

SHAKEN AND STIRRED

The Soul Stirrers left Texas in the thirties seeking an escape from the oppressive racial barriers of the South and to introduce themselves into the mainstream of Chicago gospel theater. The group ranged from a true quartet to five or six singers, but regardless of members, the contingent was always called a quartet. The Stirrers went on to sustain astounding longevity, retaining their relevance at the forefront of American Black gospel music for decades. When Sam Cooke left the Highway Q.C.'s in 1951 and joined the Soul Stirrers at age twenty, he immediately had an undeniable impact. He held the lead-singer role for six years before electing to change course into the uncharted waters of secular music. Over this time, Cooke helped the Stirrers build a loyal following and become the gold standard for modern-day gospel. After his departure in 1957, the group scrambled to find a suitable replacement. This was not easy given Cooke's popularity and superlative talent. The Stirrers were on tour in Augusta, Georgia and met Little Johnny Jones, the youthful lead singer for the Swanee Quintet. Jones was recruited by the remaining Stirrers where he assumed the unenviable task of filling Sam's shoes. Little Johnny's addition appeared to be a perfect fit. He knew all of the Stirrers' material and had a singing style similar to Cooke's. However, it didn't last. Only two months after joining, Jones departed the group, homesick after an exhausting tour, and missing his girlfriend back in Georgia.[1] In need of an immediate replacement, the group approached Q.C.'s co-lead Spencer Taylor. Taylor balked due to prior commitments, so they pursued former Melody Kings and Q.C.'s vocalist, Johnnie Taylor as the next heir apparent.[23] There were false reports that Johnnie was handpicked by Cooke to be his replacement in the Soul Stirrers. According to sources close to the matter, this was clearly not the case.[4] Sam could have made a recommendation, but after the sting of his abandonment, the Stirrers undoubtedly made their own independent decision. Johnnie did mention that Sam came by his place to suggest he join the quartet, but in reality, it was up to the remaining members to decide.[5] Stirrer guitarist Crume went to recruit Johnnie. He said, "I went by his apartment about two or three o'clock in the morning …" Crume went on to say, "He was living on the South Side. We sat out on the steps of his apartment-he was living upstairs on the second or third floor on the South Side. We sat out on the steps of his apartment and we talked about him coming with the Soul Stirrers. Johnnie asked 'How much time I got?' I said, 'You got time enough to get your clothes and let's go.' He got his clothes and we went to Atlanta, Georgia. That was our first date with him."[6]

In the beginning, Johnnie sang co-lead with Paul Foster, but soon after took over the role, and led the fivesome going forward. At first, the other Stirrers weren't overly enamored with Johnnie. His insecurities and arrogance rubbed a few of the members the wrong way. "Paul Foster in his 1981 interview with Ray Funk, expressed his own reservations about Johnnie Taylor, which included sending him back to Chicago to learn a little humility shortly after he joined."[7]

In 1957, Taylor and his wife Harriet had their first child together, Johnnie Jr. The newborn was Johnnie's third son and would be brought up in Chicago. Throughout his early career, Johnnie was focused on gospel hymns, church choirs, and studying the Word. As a child and during his young adulthood, Johnnie maintained a measure of righteousness. He memorized scripture, practiced his faith and grew to become an authority on the Bible. These early influences inspired Johnnie to develop an objective to preach the gospel and be a church and faith leader. To do so, Johnnie set his sights on becoming a Baptist pastor. In 1958, Johnnie accomplished this goal, ordained as a minister appointed by nationally recognized Baptist ministers from Chicago Rev. Clay Evans and Rev. S.M. Hart.

While Johnnie was being ordained and performing with the Soul Stirrers in '58, Cooke continued making records. He carried out his plan, and abandoned gospel music to concentrate on the more lucrative and popular secular domain. His interest in music however, became more profound than merely performing and recording. Sam wanted to create a new cultural environment for Black recording artists by providing first-rate production and publishing. In the predominantly white-run record business, Sam's venture as a young, Black entrepreneur was unprecedented. Owning his label, he could retain the rights of his music and assist other artists in protecting their catalogs. Additionally he would mentor young Black recording artists and give them opportunities to grow and flourish. Cooke's departure from Specialty Records was behind him, but his association with Keen Records took a turn for the worse when the company failed to pay royalties in a timely manner.[8]

Now as a member of the Soul Stirrers, Johnnie had ascended to the pinnacle of the gospel hierarchy. His climb began with the Melody Kings, followed by the Highway Q.C.'s; then Johnnie worked his way up the ladder to join the Stirrers, considered the most illustrious gospel group in the nation. "I was singing in this little group, and here was this big star asking me if I'd join the biggest gospel group around. Man, I thought I was on easy street," Taylor recalled.[9] However filling Sam Cooke's shoes in the Soul Stirrers would prove to be a tall order. It took time for Johnnie's vocals to resonate with the group's faithful followers. Johnnie would later describe his first year as a Stirrer, and how the audiences responded: "[It took] a while to get used to me. At first, they were kind to me, but it took them a minute to kinda get with me. Once I started recording [with the Soul Stirrers], people started to accept me because of the records."[10] Although there were similarities in style, Cooke's silky, polished dexterity overshadowed Johnnie's granular crooning and took time for some to adjust. Their voices and delivery were described by Stax co-owner Al Bell; "They sang alike, yet they didn't sound alike."[11] As co-lead vocalists, Taylor and Paul Foster guided the Stirrers to lay down tracks for a number of singles on Specialty Records. Johnnie's occasional personality quirks surfaced at times as related by Leroy Crume. "Johnnie was high-strung. He wasn't a real easy guy to get along with because he had a big ego. We let him go one time because he was kind of difficult to get along with." Taylor could be abrasive, and the other Stirrers warned Johnnie about conflicts with other touring performers: "If you can't get along with the other groups, you gotta go."[12] As the discord still hung in the air between Art Rupe and Sam over recording secular music, the Soul Stirrers continued recording gospel with Rupe and Specialty. Notwithstanding his difficult personality, Johnnie and the Soul Stirrers were successful in releasing new material after Cooke's acrimonious departure. They released 45s over the next several months featuring Johnnie singing lead. This included the single, "The Love of God", and on side B, "Out On a Hill" released in mid-1958.[13] Johnnie injected spirituality in the process of making music as Al Bell described, "He was a free-spirit as a human being. He'd take a lyric and say, 'I'm going back to the hotel and put this under my pillow, and the Spirit will tell me whether or not I should sing this song.' Then he would come to the recording studio, and whatever came out on that take was what came out. He didn't try to do it in the same way twice. He just sang, and you didn't know what was gonna come out of his mouth or how he was gonna do it or what he was gonna say."[14]

CHAPTER 6

SAM AND SAR

The wind of change began to sweep into Los Angeles, carrying with it monumental implications caused by the rise of R&B at the cost of the dying gospel sector. After the Keen royalty debacle in 1959, Cooke and Alexander joined forces and created their own production company, and the natural outgrowth was to form a label. They would call the new company SAR Records. The name SAR, was an acronym for Sam, Alex and Roy Records. Cooke included his mentor, founder and former manager of the Soul Stirrers, S.R. (Roy) Crain as a contributor.[1]

In 1959, Rupe made the shocking decision to dump Johnnie Taylor and the Soul Stirrers from his label due to flagging sales. The group's last session produced such favorites as "When The Gates Swing Open," and "The Lord Laid His Hands On Me," released in February of that year.[2] The group had been a staple of Specialty for many years and Rupe's announcement came as a jolt to the gospel world, especially to the Stirrers. Their parting was not as much an indictment on Johnnie as it was the critical loss of a beloved Sam Cooke whose importance to gospel music was now evident. Once Cooke officially crossed-over into the orbit of soul and pop music, gospel fans seemed to sense a monumental shift on the horizon. Gospel had become lukewarm, while popular music was on fire, especially with Sam Cooke leading the charge.

During this season of change, a performer named Lou Rawls emerged as a critical postscript to Cooke's first year as a secular artist. The year following Sam's departure from the Stirrers, he and Lou Rawls, another former Q.C.'s member, embarked on a tour together. Rawls had just returned from active duty in the Army as a paratrooper and joined Sam's shows as the opening act with the Pilgrim Travelers from Houson. On the Southern leg of the circuit, the car Cooke and Rawls was riding in was involved in an accident running into a truck. Cooke sustained only minor injuries, but one of their passengers Eddie Cunningham was killed. Rawls himself was pronounced dead en route to the hospital. However, after remaining in a coma for nearly a week, Rawls did slowly recover, finally gaining his memory after months of rehab. This undoubtedly shook up Sam.[3]

During this stormy period, Sam Cooke remained in Johnnie's headlights. Taylor watched his mentor and good friend very closely, intrigued as Cooke set sail for the choppy waters of popular music on the West Coast. J.T. followed in Cooke's shadow, first to the Q.C.s and then to the Stirrers. He even patterned his singing style after Cooke, often being mistaken for Sam, Johnnie's principal inspiration.

When Johnnie was with The Q.C.'s, they occasionally opened for the Stirrers. They featured Taylor as some sort of Sam Cooke facsimile and the same held true after he joined the Soul Stirrers. Even though Johnnie lacked Cooke's charisma, he was still able to captivate fans with his stage presence and energy. This allowed him to carve out his own identity. Johnnie Taylor was nobody's fool. He was shrewdly opportunistic and took advantage of any situation that could further his own career. When it came to Sam's notoriety, Johnnie wasn't ashamed to ride on Cooke's coattails. The two stayed in close contact, fostering an inseparable bond they sustained over the years. They communicated, they commiserated and they communed. Cooke was an astute, highly savvy individual who saw Johnnie for what he represented. He understood Taylor's potential and knew Johnnie would be a star someday. Cooke wanted nothing more than Johnnie to succeed and savored the opportunity to mentor the untamed mustang.

In 1958, Taylor had a circuit tour across the Southeast. There he met Arona Phillips Bryant, a gospel promoter in Gastonia, North Carolina. Her business was to arrange and promote performances at various venues, including local churches and high schools. Her own home served as a way-station for artists to hang out since Blacks weren't allowed to patronize local hotels or restaurants. Sam Cooke and The Soul Stirrers, the Mighty Clouds of Joy and The Staple Singers all stayed at the Bryant home while passing through. It was at the Bryant's where Johnnie first met Arona's daughter Peggye, just fifteen at the time. Peggye saw Johnnie occasionally when he came to town in what began as an innocent platonic relationship. Peggye was young and naive, and was ultimately seduced by Johnnie on one of his visits to Gastonia. Months later when Peggye's sister Martha went to attend Johnnie's show at the Apollo Theater in New York, she met with Taylor afterwards and told him Peggye was pregnant. In 1960, Peggye delivered a daughter and named her Fonda. Peggye was only seventeen at the time. Peggye recounts Martha's conversation with Johnnie after he heard she was pregnant. He told her, "we only did it one time," and Martha replied, "That's all it takes." After hearing the news, Johnnie never returned to visit the Bryant's or make an attempt to see Peggye or his daughter Fonda.[4]

On the West Coast, Sam Cooke and J.W. Alexander began the task of locating and signing new talent to the SAR label. Interestingly enough, the first group they signed was the Soul Stirrers who had just been dropped from their label in 1959. Jilted by Specialty, The Soul Stirrers were in need of a record company and Cooke desperately needed to sign talent to the fledgling SAR label. Ironically it was the Stirrers that Cooke abandoned a few years prior, and were now suddenly signed as a new client. The Stirrers' prior relationship with Alexander at Specialty had to be a benefit for joining SAR and offset any hard feelings they may have had with Cooke for deserting them. Sam and J.W. continued recruiting and used their influence within the gospel ranks to sign other performers like Johnny Morisette, The Sims Twins and the Womack family quintet known as the Valentinos. The Stirrers' first single on SAR, "Stand By Me Father" was released in September 1959. In the studio, Sam was a perfectionist and worked diligently with the artists as a producer as much as a pit boss. He was strict, demanded buy-in and commanded the utmost effort. He even implemented a SAR drug policy. If you were caught high at the sessions, you'd be fined $50. Bobby Womack was said to be a frequent violator.

CHAPTER 7

HARD TIMES

The year 1960 was a dismal year for both the Stirrers and Johnnie Taylor. After their gig, the Stirrers were driving on the roads of Chicago when a little girl moved in front of the car and was hit. Johnnie was behind the wheel of the Stirrers' vehicle when the accident occurred. Although she had been run over, the little girl wasn't fatally injured. Johnnie was questioned and taken to jail, while authorities attempted to determine the circumstances of the accident. Soon after, a story was published in the local paper about the incident giving the Stirrers unwelcome negative press. A police investigation of the incident concluded Johnnie was under the influence of marijuana at the time; and remained in custody.[1] The members of the Stirrers bailed him out, and upon his release, Johnnie admitted to his drug use. In fact, he acknowledged smoking weed for over ten years.[2] Soul Stirrer member, Leroy Crume described the scene: "J.J. Farley (bass player) and myself went down and got him a lawyer, and he got out of it." Crume went on to say, "That's when we dropped him. We didn't know he was using that stuff."[3] A separate account indicated Taylor was without shame or remorse and immediately resigned from the Soul Stirrers before the other singers had a chance to render judgment. The incident left Taylor distraught from the near tragedy, and was exacerbated by the blowback from the quartet over his illegal drug habit. Regardless of whichever story is accurate, he left the Stirrers and decided to devote his life to a career as a full-time minister. "God Is Standing By" was Taylor's first song written for the Soul Stirrers, but after his untimely departure, Johnnie wasn't able to participate. His replacement and new lead vocalist,

Jimmie Outler sang in his place. Not long after his ouster, Taylor arrived to preach in the pulpit at Fellowship Baptist Church in Chicago. This would begin Johnnie's abbreviated service as a man of the cloth. He immediately set out as a traveling pastor. "He was astonishing in his knowledge of the Bible," expressed Wolf Stephenson, VP and engineer at Malaco Records. "He could converse with anyone about the Bible. His knowledge of Scripture was encyclopedic. If you didn't think he could preach, you let him get started and he could go. If he'd stayed a preacher, he would have been one of the top ones around. He had the spirit."[4]

Another setback for gospel music occurred when Art Rupe became disenchanted running Specialty. According to *The Specialty Records Story*, Rupe decided to phase out the label in 1960 due to what he deemed was the crooked business of payola, being obligated to pay radio stations to play his records.[5] During this period of the music business, the recording industry was flush with cash. Shady DJs, who had control of which songs to air, began accepting kickbacks from the bloated, fat-cat, record labels. To the recording companies, payola was a minor promotional expense and a mere line-item in the accounting department. The disgusting business of payola had unfortunately become a necessary evil to ensure the label's material was promoted on the airwaves. Rupe didn't want to play the game any longer. He wanted out.

With the occurrence of these two crucial events, the world turned upside down for both Johnnie and the Stirrers. Devastation set in when Johnnie's negligence threatened the life of a small child. He certainly must have questioned whether the accident would have occurred if he'd been straight. According to his son, T.J. Hooker, despite his life as a part-time preacher, his drug use became excessive at this point.[6] Overcome with guilt after the near fatal accident and his sudden departure from the Stirrers, he undoubtedly fell into a soul-searching state of mind, and his ego must have been bruised. Johnnie's flight from the Stirrers and his uncertain future lured him deeper into a shroud of darkness triggered by drugs. It's amazing how much had occurred during the preceding, short three-year period. Cooke left the Soul Stirrers. He became a secular artist with Specialty. Cooke, Bumps Blackwell and J.W. Alexander abandoned Specialty. Johnnie replaced Sam in the Stirrers. Then Specialty dumped the Soul Stirrers and they were left without a label. The quartet opted to sign with SAR Records. Next, Johnnie left the Stirrers after the driving mishap. In the wake of all of this turmoil, the Stirrers found themselves without a lead vocalist. Cooke and SAR were left with remnants of the Stirrers, now a fractured gospel quartet. Lastly, Johnnie seemed stuck in ambiguity as a minister on the road.

Johnnie was obviously shaken by his driving accident and retreated to his faith, becoming a full-time minister. During this time, Harriet, his estranged wife in Chicago, delivered a baby girl she named Sabrina Norvell in 1960. Johnnie accepted the baby into the splintered family as his own. In a cryptic state of spiritual awakening, J.T. suddenly felt a calling to go west, so he redirected his path to California. On his way, Johnnie stopped by a girlfriend's house in the old haunts of Kansas City. There, Mary Hooker consoled him and gave Johnnie $38, all the money she had, for bus fare to L.A.[7] Why Los Angeles? It's possible he was seeking comfort from Cooke, his good friend and supporter. Or he may have been attracted to L.A. which had become the recording epicenter for gospel music. Only Johnnie would be able to reveal the true reasons, if he even knew himself. Once Johnnie arrived in L.A. he became a traveling minister. Much like serving a penance for the Chicago incident, he set-aside his hopes of becoming a star and went out to spread the good news of the Lord. However, it wasn't long before Taylor realized preaching wouldn't sustain him financially. So, he sought out Sam. The old friends met and talked about Johnnie's life and future as an entertainer. Cooke believed in Johnnie's abilities and shared the benefits of becoming a secular artist. It's where the money was, Sam told him. Johnnie was then faced with a difficult decision. Should he abandon the work of the Lord and sell his soul to secular audiences? Or should he continue the ministry, bringing others to Christ, saving His lost sheep? The clash within his consciousness was certain to have caused deep reflection and self-examination. Johnnie's residual guilt from the accident in Chicago grappled with his temporal yearning to chase the almighty dollar.

Taylor ended up doing both. He traveled across L.A. to preach; at night he'd sing in clubs, at house parties, or hotels, beginning the slow evolution of becoming a solo secularist. This bifurcated lifestyle was further evidence of his conflicted identity mentioned earlier. Johnnie was a young man trying to resolve his inner demons while doing everything he could to maintain his faith and righteousness. One evening in 1960, Johnnie served as host and entertainer for a friend's house party. He invited a young lady he had met briefly who sang with the Los Angeles Community Choir that was an opening act at some of the local venues. Her name was Helen Myles and she was sixteen at the time. Their rendezvous that night at the party developed into a special romantic relationship which would endure for years to come. After Taylor went solo, Helen would attend Johnnie's shows across L.A. at places like the California Club on the old Santa Barbara Boulevard or the Clark Hotel. Other venues where audiences might have caught his shows were the 5-4 Club, the Oasis or the Waikiki Club. He typically made use of small house bands to provide rhythm, and occasionally horns were featured. Helen described Johnnie as being kind and considerate and very funny. He was always very personable and to the ladies he was the ultimate charmer. "He was a man most women would want," Helen explained. "Johnnie was romantic and intimate and always knew the right words to say. He was very 'touchy-feely,' brushing or caressing your arm when he spoke, which made you feel special."[8] Over the years he showered Helen with attention and was mild-mannered and low-key when they were together.

According to Helen, Johnnie was intent on giving his audiences a good time. He would carry on conversations and tell stories during a performance, and it was obvious he enjoyed himself as much as the crowd. Taylor was a perfectionist and always wanted to be at his best. Johnnie was an immaculate dresser and wore a suit wherever he went. Helen and Johnnie once talked about marriage, but Helen's parents wouldn't allow it, insisting that he was too old. Knowing how so many musicians struggled with unpredictable paydays and living above their means, they feared she would end up supporting him. After Johnnie's career began to flourish, he made a point to contact Helen's parents. Johnnie proudly described his success and asked whether they thought his singing career could now support their daughter. Their reply was, "If you really loved our daughter, you'd have run off with her."[9] He couldn't win. During this period, Johnnie, and Sam stayed in close contact. Cooke was well aware of Johnnie's growing popularity and appeal in the L.A. area. When asked if Johnnie and Sam were close at the time, Helen said laughing, "They were more than close" and added, "They were best friends."[10]

CHAPTER 8

SECULAR SHIFT

Sam began to pursue Johnnie to join SAR Records. In 1961, after lengthy discussions, Cooke finally convinced Taylor to cross over, and accomplished the feat of signing the young up-and-comer. It was a difficult decision but Taylor ultimately decided to leave his gospel roots and follow Sam once again. After leaving the Soul Stirrers, Taylor was in need of financial stability and needed a place to call home, so Johnnie agreed to join SAR. After Cooke's persuasion, Taylor took on his ambition to be a star and entered the dog-eat-dog world of popular rhythm and blues. "In gospel you start off with a cold audience and work them into an emotional state," he explained. "It's pretty much the same (in R&B). People feel what you do, and they automatically get with you. It's kind of like the old saying, 'That from the heart which is the heart,' because you can always tell when you're in the pocket in their groove."[1] Many years later, Johnnie recalled, "[It] took me and Aretha a while to switch tracks and catch on, but soon as we hear [Sam's] "You Send Me" we knew we weren't long for the gospel world. Wherever Sam was going, we was following."[2] Rodgers Redding, Otis's brother summed up Johnnie's transition, "It was a money thing. He admired Sam, Sam was his idol, so you go."[3] Radio personality David Washington shared, "[Johnnie] said, Yo, this preachin' ain't making no money and Sam said, 'Use your voice, use your voice, don't go back to gospel, come over the the pop field and make more money."[4]

SAR Records gained momentum by assembling a unique collection of bedfellows. Sam signed the Stirrers to the label despite leaving the group and spurning his fellow singers. Johnnie Taylor was then signed, although recently fired from the Stirrers. Cooke was the common denominator to both developments, and used his influence to bring the artists together and to put their differences aside.

Johnnie conducted his first pop session with SAR in 1961, recording "Never, Never" written by Ed Townsend and produced by Sam. However, the release would be delayed. It was disappointing for Johnnie, but Sam convinced him the song should be held back in order to create space between the "Never, Never" release and Johnnie Morrisette's forthcoming single. Morrisette was Taylor's labelmate at SAR, and his song "Meet Me at the Twistin' Place" was completed before "Never, Never" hit the finish line. Sam elected to stagger the two releases in order to maximize the impact on the listening public. "Alex stayed in Los Angeles to promote the new Johnnie Morrisette release (they had decided to hold back Johnnie Taylor's single until the beginning of May to give "Meet Me at the Twistin' Place" some breathing space).[5] In anticipation of Johnnie's milestone recording, Cooke and Alex held a release party for Taylor at the California Club with some of the other SAR recording artists. The festivity was described as "one continuous floor show, featuring many top-flight performers …"[6] J.T.'s release of "Never, Never" wasn't a big success, although it did introduce Taylor to producing a secular-styled song. "After Sam Cooke signed me to sing R&B on his label I wanted to have a hit right away. When I didn't, I kept asking Sam 'What's wrong? How come I'm not going anywhere?' He told me to relax. He said I was talented and that things would take care of themselves if I'd just let my career build. He was right."[7]

"Never, Never," was a representation of Johnnie's capabilities with his smooth delivery and meticulous phrasing. The song featured Edgar Redmond with a short sax interlude and finished strong with Johnnie's emphatic promise to never quit loving, wanting or needing. J.T. developed a style that was instantly recognizable, and there was never a doubt as to who was singing. "He would caress one song with consummate grace, then apply the grit with riveting rhythmic drive to the next, but the listener could always tell it was Johnnie Taylor."[8] Taylor's early influences were said to be R.H. Harris, the well-known Soul Stirrers' lead vocalist for over forty years; Archie Brownlee of the Five Blind Boys of Mississippi,

Junior Parker from West Memphis, Big Joe Turner of KC and bluesman Louis Jordan from Brinkley, Arkansas. Johnnie spoke about his sound, "We don't want to change it too much," Johnnie said, "We want people to know it's me. We just try to keep it simple, earthy and good."[9]

Johnnie and his first wife, Harriet Lewis divorced in 1961. The former Mrs. Taylor was mother of their two children, Johnnie Jr., (a.k.a 'Spud'), the eldest, and Sabrina, his younger sister. The couple split after Johnnie began spending more time pursuing his career in California. The kids were four and one respectively. Johnnie's traveling and the responsibilities of two young children laid a heavy burden on Harriet to raise her children. Johnnie accepted his obligation to be a supportive father and spoke of his responsibilities in an interview several years later: "Divorce", Taylor maintains, "Should not cut-off anyone from the responsibility."[10] "Daddy Taylor" as he was known by the two children, remained dedicated, even though he was on the road a better part of the year. They grew up in Chicago and attended public schools in the city.

Occasionally Johnnie would return to his home in Kansas City and play at the Ivanhoe Masonic Temple, a Chitlin' Circuit favorite; or the 9th Street Missionary Baptist Church led by Pastor Isaac Hooker. Rev. Hooker was a pioneer who arranged the first live radio broadcast of the church's services on KPRT, which featured gospel music and worship. When he was with the Q.C.'s, Johnnie was invited to sing one Sunday at the 9th Street Church. There he met Rev. Hooker's daughter Mary, who was always in attendance. Mary was a single mother at the time, a hairdresser

REV. ISAAC HOOKER
PHOTO COURTESY OF T.J.HOOKER

and also worked for the U.S. Post Office in Kansas City. When Johnnie and the Q.C.'s arrived at church one Sunday, he was introduced to Mary, and a relationship soon developed.[11] Not long after, she became pregnant and in November of 1962, she had Johnnie's son, Tyrone (T.J.).

Afterwards, Taylor's visits to the Hooker household would be infrequent which resulted in little time for Johnnie and T.J. to establish a father-son relationship. Johnnie's absence robbed T.J. of a male role model and father figure.

MARY HOOKER
PHOTO COURTESY OF T.J. HOOKER

CHAPTER 9

WHICH IS WHICH?

Little Johnny Taylor was born February 11, 1943, in Gregory, Arkansas. His actual name was Johnny Lamont Merrett (also known as Johnny Lamar Young in some circles). He devised his name by adding the moniker "Little" from his reverence for a chief influencer, R&B singer, Little Willie John. Little Willie was yet another Arkansan from Cullendale and six years Johnny's senior. The Taylor name was used in honor of soul and gospel vocalist Ted Taylor of Okmulgee, Oklahoma. Little Johnny migrated to California in his teens and sang with gospel outfits such as the Stars of Bethel and Mighty Clouds of Joy. In the early sixties he shifted and began performing secular music, much like J.T. During this time, he covered the L.A. club scene playing blues at various venues trying to build a following. After limited success releasing singles on the Swingin' label, in 1962, he collaborated with producer Cliff Goldsmith and arranger Ray Shanklin at Galaxy Records to produce "Part Time Love."[1] This song was the title track on his album of the same name and was his most successful hit lasting thirteen-weeks on Billboard's Hot 100 Chart. The song peaked at number 19 in October '63. It also found its way to number 1 on Billboard's R&B chart.[2]

Meanwhile, the other Johnnie Taylor had been on the national club circuit for many years, diligently chopping his way into the spotlight, gaining notoriety with the Q.C.'s and then the Soul Stirrers. After arriving in L.A., he initially struggled to make a name for himself before he elected to go solo with Sam Cooke into the soul/R&B market. Johnnie began touring on the Chitlin' Circuit, singing his way across the country, much like he had done on gospel tours. He made lifelong friends in the process and most likely spent more time on the road than at home. Music artist Bobby Rush said: "So artists like me, Tyrone, Denise LaSalle, Johnnie Taylor, Millie Jackson, Little Milton, Bobby "Blue" Bland, Shirley Brown, Latimore and others became more glued to this Chitlin' Circuit with its Southern soul/blues sound. The Circuit was compact, but its fans were loyal. And it's not that we retreated from anywhere that would buy our records or our tickets, it's just that gradually, year after year, Southern blues became more and more under the radar of where popular R&B stood. Blues/soul just petered out—by the taste of the times."[3]

Just as J.T. was getting on his feet with Sam's SAR label, Little Johnny Taylor came along with his smash hit "Part Time Love." Not only was LJT nine years younger, but in Johnnie's mind, he had copied his name. Adding insult to injury, Little Johnny came up with a big hit which was far more successful than anything Johnnie had ever released. Johnnie took exception to the perceived invasion of his personal celebrity. An excerpt from *The Triumph of Sam Cooke Dream Boogie* put this dynamic into perspective. "The next night there was a Johnnie Taylor SAR session at the RCA studio, but he didn't bother to attend. Johnnie had gotten even more of an attitude since his namesake (and he would argue his rank imitator), Little Johnny had enjoyed a smash hit with "Part Time Love" the year before. At first Johnnie wanted to call out the other guy, whose real name was Johnny Young: "I was the Johnnie Taylor that everybody knew, but then he began getting gigs on the basis of name confusion, and he adapted his own repertoire to the kind of Bobby "Blue" Bland-style blues that Little Johnny Taylor specialized in."[4] "Johnnie knew he had to survive one way or other so he started billing himself as Little Johnnie Taylor. During this time entertainers were not readily recognized because they didn't appear on TV much, so nobody knew their faces."[5]

Years earlier, Johnnie finessed his way into riding the groundswell of Sam Cooke's popularity to make a name for himself as a Soul Stirrer. When Little Johnny Taylor arrived on the scene causing confusion among the two, J.T. seized the opportunity and exploited the ambiguity. Johnnie began adding "Part Time Love" to his playlist at performances and began referring to himself as Little Johnnie Taylor. Handbills and posters advertising his shows were also printed, adding "Little" to Johnnie's name. He used the uncertainty to his advantage and rode it all the way to the bank. So much confusion resulted that a good many R&B listeners were certain "Part Time Love" was Johnnie Taylor's song. As one might expect this didn't go over well with Little Johnny and created a deep-seated animosity between the two entertainers. Little Johnny also used the confusion and benefited from being mistaken for the up-and-coming SAR artist. This discord lasted decades. Louisiana R&B legend Ernie Johnson knew Little Johnny before moving to Dallas. After Johnson's move to Big D, he met the other Johnnie, then attempted, on multiple occasions, to get the two together to bury the hatchet. Unfortunately the pride of the two stars was too great. Johnson shared, "they talked a lot of noise and couldn't stand each other."[6] Neither one was amenable to meet, and they refused to discuss it. They never reconciled. Some years later, Johnnie reflected, "Yeah, I made gigs back then doing 'Part Time Love,' and people thought that it was my record. But when I started having hits, Little Johnny Taylor started doing my songs and telling the public that those were his records."[7]

Johnnie cashed in on the benefits from copycatting Little Johnny's "Part Time Love." The needle was starting to move on J.T's fame, but he remained frustrated that his career had been stuck in neutral ever since he signed with SAR. Even though Johnnie had a close relationship with Sam, he continued to have misgivings about signing with Cooke, as related by Peter Guralnick in his book "The Triumph of Sam Cooke," Guralnick wrote: "Johnnie had listened to friends tell him over and over that Sam had only added him to the SAR roster to ward off direct competition, that he would never promote a rival who sounded so much like him—and the sales of his one SAR release to date only went to prove those friends right."[8] Cooke sensed Johnnie's frustration and came up with an ace. Betty and Beverly Prudhomme were soul and R&B writers and singers who wrote the original version of the song called "Rome Wasn't Built in a Day" in 1957. Because of Beverly's pregnancy, the duo offloaded the song to producer Fabor Robinson who in turn gave it to Johnny Russell, a teenage country singer from Mississippi. He recorded the tune on the B-side of his first single, but it went nowhere. Cooke heard the song and asked the Prudhommes if he could tinker with it to liven it up. After getting Robinson's approval, he went about reworking the song and when finished he had a winner. Betty and Beverly were ecstatic about the prospects of how Cooke breathed life into the weary ballad, making it into a glossy, new upbeat version. However, the two ladies were flabbergasted when they found out that Sam had given the song to J.T.[9]

Sam went all out with the preparations and focused on making "Rome Wasn't Built in a Day" a hit. The song was released in 1962. "Sam worked everybody hard, but no one harder than Johnnie. He stayed on Johnnie about his pronunciation, his emphasis, and his meaning. And he kept checking with Johnnie to make sure he understood, showing him exactly how he wanted it done, but urging everyone, always to keep it funky."[10] Sam perceived Johnnie's frustration with the SAR experience and wanted to throw his friend a meaty bone in the form of "Rome." Even if this was the case, Cooke worked diligently to make sure it was the best record it could be so Johnnie could benefit from their collective effort. "'Rome Wasn't Built in a Day' was a perfect example of the Sam Cooke influence on Johnnie Taylor's delivery. You can even hear Johnnie doing the same kind of vocal runs that Sam was known for in his songs," recalled Marcus Chapman, music historian.[11] "Rome" became a knockout. "It just fit Johnnie and Johnnie would always say, that was one of his favorite songs," commented L.C. Cooke, Sam's brother.[12]

The love song written by the Prudhommes, refined by Cooke gave Johnnie the much needed spotlight he was seeking. The lyrics of the tune told of the patient pursuit of a full-fledged relationship that wasn't quite mature and the possibilities of how it might grow someday if given time. Love would overcome, just give me time, Johnnie crooned throughout the refrains. "Rome" was the B-side of "Never, Never", but it soon became evident that the Prudhomme tune was the bigger hit. The upbeat arrangement was paired with precise horn play and rhythmical chanting in the background underscoring Johnnie's soulful vocals. "Rome Wasn't Built in a Day" didn't chart, but it turned the heads of listeners and influenced the public to acknowledge Taylor as a soon-to-be rising star. As one who chose to crossover with "Rome," Taylor finally and successfully navigated the divide between gospel and R&B. Along with Sam, J.T. became part of the first generation of gospel performers who transformed their work, entering into the secular hemisphere of

R&B. Otis Redding's younger brother Rodgers recalls the first time he met Johnnie in 1962. Rodgers had just performed and was outside the venue when Johnnie's car arrived, slowly rolling up to the club. Inside were four young ladies accompanying the singer. There was a line out the door to enter the club for his performance. When Johnnie arrived, the female driver hopped out and opened the back door to let Johnnie out. He emerged from the backseat wearing a full-length mink coat, dressed like he had just walked off the showroom floor. Fans waiting outside turned to watch his arrival, Rodgers remembers, "The people that was coming in, they broke the line, got out of line and ran out to that car to see Johnnie."[13] Rodgers didn't know much about Johnnie, and this was his first encounter with the popular vocalist. Inside, Otis Redding introduced his little brother to Taylor. Johnnie asked him, "Hey little brother have you got your money yet?" [for the gig he just played]. Rodgers told him no. Johnnie was incensed and went up to the club owner yelling and cursing ordering for the man to pay the young Rodgers. The shell-shocked owner reached down and the "money came out of his pocket so fast it was ridiculous."[14] Rodgers was paid in full on the spot. Back in the dressing room, Johnnie told Otis, "Don't worry, I'll take care of little brother."[15]

The same year of 1962, T.J. Hooker was born. His mother Mary, who lived in KC, had an ongoing relationship with Taylor whenever returning to his hometown. In the studio, Johnnie recorded two more singles, "Dance What You Wanna" and "Baby We've Got Love," both on Derby Records, a subsidiary of SAR created especially for pop music. "Baby We've Got Love" was Sam's composition and "Dance" was written by Sam and his business partner J.W. Alexander along with Clifton "Clif" White, a SAR session musician and associate of Cooke. Clif White was one of the passengers who survived the fatal auto accident mentioned earlier, that seriously injured Lou Rawls and took the life of Sam's chauffeur, Eddie Cunningham.[16] Both of the 45s were released in 1963, but neither achieved the acclaim "Rome" received.

CHAPTER 10

CAUGHT IN NEUTRAL

The end of 1963 was a tumultuous period underscored by the assassination of President John F. Kennedy in November. The Vietnam War was escalating and young men across the country were being drawn into the conflict. At home tensions were high because of the Civil Rights Movement. Rosa Parks' arrest in 1955 was a tipping point for race relations when she violated the Alabama state law requiring Blacks to relinquish seats to Whites on public transportation. In the sixties, Cooke became heavily involved in racial injustice initiatives. In 1964, he wrote a powerful anthem, "A Change Is Gonna Come" seeking an end to segregation and discrimination. The political climate in the US was chaotic and turbulent with hostilities on a number of fronts. During this tumultuous period, Johnnie was busy touring the countryside on the soul circuit promoting his new R&B tunes. He spent endless nights on the road staging shows in juke joints, churches, clubs and homes of friends. It was inevitable, given Taylor's charisma and romantic tendencies, that he would attract many female admirers. His performances showcased him as a talented, good looking, sexy young man who kept an active, vigilant eye for the ladies. Rodgers Redding recalled, "I had met him in March of '64. My brother Otis was working Kansas City and there was this car creeping down this street, and there was a lady driving it, a lady on the passenger side, a lady in the rear on the left, a lady on the right and Johnnie sitting in the back in the middle."[1] "Women loved Johnnie Taylor. And he loved women," noted Laura Lee, Chicago gospel and soul singer interviewed in *Unsung 818*.[2] Taylor was no doubt a virile man. There would never be any doubt about his fertility. It was during this time Johnnie was on a West Coast tour and noticed a young lady dancing in the audience at one of his L.A. shows. He arranged for a meet-up later that evening. This led to a romance with the teen who asked that her name not be used. In April of 1963, she had a baby girl. The youthful mother named the newborn, La Shawn. Later in August 1963, his other lover from Los Angeles, Helen Myles, now twenty-years old, had a baby girl herself, only months after La Shawn was delivered. Helen named her daughter Shaquanta–Shaye for short. J.T.'s relationship with Helen lasted nearly four years, and they stayed in constant contact. One evening after Johnnie finished up a show, Helen made her way back to the dressing room. The space backstage was jammed with bodies and no one could make it in or out. From the corner of his eye, Johnnie saw Helen outside the door trying to make her way inside. He promptly ordered those around him to bring her in. The only way she could get her past the throngs was for the men to lift her above the crowd. As she lay flat on her back, the men shuffled her mosh-pit style to where Johnnie waited.[3] J.T. loved people and looked forward to connecting with his fans. This is why he had an open-door policy to his backstage dressing room and gave instructions to his tour manager to allow anyone who wanted in free access. Taylor loved the crowds, the excitement, the animated conversations, "It's what he enjoyed."[4]

Johnnie had a girl in every port and as he made his way across the country, he visited them when in town. Another romance developed in 1963, this time with Susie Smith Jackson of Los Angeles. Susie, only sixteen at the time, delivered Johnnie a fourth child in the short two-year window between 1962-1963. Susie's daughter was named Schiffvon.

Johnnie released three singles in '64, "Oh How I Love You" written and produced by J.W. Alexander with "Run (But You Can't Hide)" on the flip side, penned by Johnnie himself, again produced by Alex. This record was released on SAR whereas Taylor's next single was dropped on SAR's Derby Records. There's probably a viable reason why Cooke and company chose Derby for some of Johnnie's releases and SAR on others, probably related to marketing or perhaps a strategy to sustain Derby revenues. The second release was "Get Married Soon," composed by R&B musician and vocalist, Charlie Julien. On the flip side was "Need Lots of Love" written by J.T. Lastly. "Keep On Lovin' You," his third release, was also authored by Julien. On the B side was Johnnie's previously recorded "Run (But You Can't Hide)." Both songs on the last record were produced by J.W. Alexander. Over the preceding years, Johnnie had steadily developed his own style. Initially he tried to imitate Sam and his vocal attributes, then carved out his own identity and vocal personality. Taylor took the many lessons and techniques he learned from Cooke, blended them with his own recipe and added his larger-than-life vibe. Johnnie longed to be his own man, to break free from the shadow of Sam Cooke, which he did over the succeeding years. Johnnie's need to separate himself from Sam and how he felt his career was being restrained is described by Peter Garulnick in *The Triumph of Sam Cooke*, " ...but that didn't stop him [Johnnie] from running off his mouth about how Sam was holding him back. 'Sam always trying to tell me how to sing a song? I know how to goddamn sing a song. That's one thing I know how to do'".[5] Later in 1989, Johnnie voiced his disappointment about how he was being handled by Sam in an interview with John Broven and Cilla Huggins: "Bobby Robinson told me, 'He ain't gonna promote you.' And he was right about that."[6]

Johnnie's frustration became evident about how Sam was handling his progress. Cooke and Taylor were considered best friends by some, but when it came to business, they each had their own inspirations which led to moments of discord. Further complicating the relationship was frustration on the part of J.W. Alexander and SAR over Johnnie's lack of commitment to his trade. J.T.'s priorities were at times conflicting with his career aspirations. It was widely known that Johnnie not only made a living as a soul and R&B singer, he supplemented his income overseeing a group of L.A. call girls. According to the *Los Angeles Sentinel*, Johnnie "was cruising around town in the new Buick Rivera he had gotten as a gift from one of his female 'admirers,' still unable to choose between the life of a singer and the life of a pimp."[7] He had not only created a reputation for being a lady's man, but was also known as a nookie-bookie for his ladies-of-the-night. His illicit activities weren't the best kept secret in L.A.

CHAPTER 11

BIG DIP INTO BIG D

On one of his many trips through the Deep South, Johnnie spoke about how he was summoned 'for a weekend engagement' in Dallas in 1963, "and I wound up just staying. There was lots of work here, and I needed a good place to bring up the last two of my six children."[1] In a 1976 *Dallas Morning News* article, Taylor commented on how he was attracted to Dallas, "I came here the first time to do a two-week engagement and wound up staying two years. Then I moved back to Kansas City where me and my wife got married, and, somehow we wound up back here. Then we started having a family and we started buying property. So I just said 'this town's been very good to me and they've always supported my shows.' I was probably one of the only artists who could live here and pack the Longhorn Ballroom on any given Monday night. A town that supports you like this is kind of hard to leave. I left on seven occasions, but I always wound up back here. The people here have been really wonderful to us. My wife is from California, and I'm from Missouri and Illinois, but we just found a bunch of friends here. So, we just said, opposed to living where you like, it's better to live where people like you."[2] "Dallas accepted Johnnie in a big way," noted friend Bobby Patterson.[3] Johnnie who had been anointed as the 'Blues Wailer' developed a healthy fanbase in Big D and, he established a number of friendships in the area. One of Johnnie's first shows was at the Empire Room within the Hall and Thomas neighborhood. Before gentrification wiped out the historic district, the area was a hotbed of entertainment and indulgent activity. Plush hotels, speakeasies, restaurants and doojee shacks lined the blocks attracting Black patrons from all walks of life. There they mixed and mingled in an atmosphere of amusement, entertainment, and pleasure. Johnnie liked the city's hospitality, with its down-to-earth character and saw the potential in Dallas as a possible homebase. Over time, he had grown weary of the L.A. scene and began contemplating a change. Taylor discussed his decision to operate from Dallas. "I'm a family man and I think it's better for the kids to have this type of environment as opposed to say, a Los Angeles kind of environment. I've lived in Los Angeles and it's not that hard when you can go to Los Angeles when you want to." He continued, "But I think I would lose my sanity if I had to stay out there all the time because you don't meet that many real people. Everybody's constantly on the make. If you go to a party, everybody's looking around to see who's the biggest name in the room. Down here you can kind of keep your sanity about you." That same *Dallas Morning News* article stated, "Taylor said it has not created any hardships on his professional life living in Dallas instead of say Los Angeles or New York."[4]

City of Dallas

CHAPTER 12

INSPIRATION-EXPIRATION

In November of '64, Johnnie returned to the studios to lay tracks for some new material. He and Sam worked together on the numbers, fine-tuning the rough edges into workable melodies. Only a few days later, Sam was with friends at Martoni's Italian Restaurant on Cahuenga Boulevard adjacent to Sunset Boulevard. He met friends for drinks and dinner, and became surrounded by songwriters, musicians and hangers-on at the bar. Cooke pulled out a wad of bills from his pocket and waved it around in plain view of the crowd. After having several cocktails, he noticed an attractive young lady nearby and asked to be introduced. Once acquainted, he and Elisa Boyer paired off and proceeded to get to know one another better while they continued pouring drinks. After midnight they left together and made one other stop at PJ's, a club nearby about closing time. From PJ's, Sam drove his pretty companion toward the airport in search of a quiet, out-of-the-way motel where they could avoid crowds and on-lookers. By this time Sam was quite inebriated and had a single focus, to get Boyer in bed. Cooke pulled into the Hacienda Motel on Figueroa Street, checked in and the couple went to his room. According to the young lady's testimony, Cooke got overly aggressive and began tearing off her clothes. She tried to slow him down and broke away so she could go to the bathroom. Upon her return, Sam decided it was his turn to visit the toilet. While Cooke was indisposed, she hurriedly grabbed his money, wallet, and clothes, and escaped out the front door. When Sam noticed she was gone, he burst outside, dressed only in his sports coat which was all there was left in the room for him to wear. In a rage, he made a bee-line to the manager's office where he assumed she had sought shelter. Sam was intoxicated and agitated. He banged on the office door demanding to see the girl. Since the manager on duty hadn't seen the young lady, she tried to brush him off, but Sam wouldn't have it. He kept pummeling the door and finally broke his way into the office where Bertha Franklin, the night manager, stood in fear. A struggle ensued and they fell on the floor in a tangle. Bertha out-scrapped the severely plastered Cooke, broke free, got to her feet, and went for a pistol she had nearby. By the time Sam got to his feet, Franklin had the weapon in hand and took dead aim at her attacker. When Cooke came forward, Franklin got off three rounds which reverberated loudly in the small office. One bullet penetrated Cooke's chest, piercing his heart. Sam took a step or two toward Franklin and in apparent self-defense, she began beating him with a broomstick. His bullet wound turned out to be fatal, and, moments later, he fell to the floor where he died. His last words were "Lady, you shot me!"[1]

In an instant, the life of Sam Cooke was erased. Shot dead in a seedy motel. When news about Sam's death broke, there was an outpouring of grief and disbelief. There were questions about the night with Boyer, his confrontation with Franklin, and whether the stories circulating about the case were true. Boyer was a known prostitute and considered a "professional roller." A roller attempts to have their subject go into the bathroom after they arrive at a motel. Once alone in the room, the roller would take the unsuspecting customer's money and belongings, including his clothes. The heist was designed so the victim couldn't pursue the perpetrator since he didn't have anything to wear. Once outside the room, an accomplice would be waiting in a vehicle to pick up the roller, (in this case Boyer) and the two would escape before Cooke came out of the bathroom and realized what had happened.[2]

A trial was held after the incident and testimony from both Boyer and Franklin were heard. The two ladies also passed polygraph tests. After a short two hours of testimony, the jury was released to consider Franklin's fate. A mere twenty-minutes later, the jury returned with a verdict of "justifiable homicide" for Franklin. The motel manager was exonerated and neither she nor Boyer were implicated in the matter any further. Friends of Sam and those familiar with the case were perplexed about how LAPD's seemingly superficial investigation was conducted. Many thought the police wanted to brush off the matter and not waste any further manpower on a case they considered closed. Cooke, being a Black man, raised more questions about the lack of a thorough investigation. Due to what some considered a slipshod investigation, speculation grew of a cover-up. After all, Cooke was seen at the club with a bundle of cash. His bankroll was never recovered at the scene or with Boyer or Franklin after they were detained and questioned. A Netflix presentation, *The Two Murders of Sam Cooke* explored Sam's killing and the possibility of such a conspiracy.[3] The case was never reopened.

The most logical scenario was that Boyer rolled Cooke for his cash. However speculation arose as to whether Sam was set up by co-conspirators of the crime, possibly Franklin and Boyer. Or perhaps pros were involved in some type of sophisticated scheme to dispatch the young, vocal Black activist. Cooke had more than a few enemies, especially after he took a prominent role in the civil rights movement. Over the few years preceding the incident, the famed singer had entrenched himself among civil rights leaders. He boldly and publicly campaigned for racial justice. There were many radicals who weren't fond of Cooke, similar to the feelings they had for Malcolm X, Stokley Carmichael and Martin Luther King. Many White conservatives considered Cooke to be too outspoken. Therefore, like Malcolm X and Dr. King, Sam was eventually taken out. A second consideration was raised in a Netflix special that posed other possibilities.[4] There were suspicions that Cooke's downfall was due to the lucrative financial arrangement he signed with manager Allen Klein. Cooke's team established a holding company to own and produce Cooke's recordings. In the music industry, the label typically owns the masters and rights to the material. When Cooke's holding company was set up, he took ownership of his own recordings, in essence extracting revenues from the label. In Cooke's situation, this would have been a substantial loss for the record label. Individuals familiar with the circumstances called into question the ownership of the label and who had control. It was presumed the label was run or influenced by, organized crime. If this was true, it presented a valid argument as to why disgruntled ownership might choose to have Cooke taken out.[5] Whatever the true facts of the case, Cooke's homicide was swept under the carpet, and very little was done to get additional facts or evidence to determine what really happened that night.

Johnnie was crushed when he heard about Cooke's death. Although they had their differences in the studio, Taylor considered Sam his best friend. Cooke had mentored Johnnie from his teenage years and was his primary musical influence. As Johnnie's Svengali, Cooke blazed a trail for him with the Highway Q.C.'s, then the Soul Stirrers, and eventually recruited him to join the SAR roster. Sam coached, taught, enlightened and led Johnnie along the road to success. It was clearly obvious Taylor's achievements were tied directly to Sam Cooke. There's no doubt the question arose in Johnnie's mind as to how he would continue without his long-standing personal bond with Cooke and the loss of his friend's leadership. The devastation caused by the tragedy immediately altered J.T.'s direction. Johnnie realized his extracurricular activities within the L.A. sex trade held similar dangers. Cooke's homicide made these risks very real to Johnnie. A disgruntled hooker, an unhappy John or rival competitors could pose a threat to his very existence. Taylor armed himself at all times to protect himself from these threats. Sam's death may have been viewed as an omen, especially just four years after Johnnie nearly killed the young lady who ran in front of his car in Chicago. Taylor had been commuting back and forth on tours between his Dallas home base and L.A, but considered leaving Los Angeles permanently while he still could. It stands to reason; after all, he had enemies too.

SAR folded soon after a dispute arose between Barbara, Sam's wife and heir, who tangled with co-owner, J.W. Alexander and manager Allen Klein. Barbara didn't trust either man, resulting in a hostile disagreement, so she decided to shut down the business. This series of events not only left Johnnie without his best friend and guide, but now he found himself without a label. His performing livelihood now faced critical challenges, as Johnnie was forced to find a new label.[6]

As a postscript to the Sam Cooke debacle, more distressing events occurred. Cooke's viewing was arranged at the funeral home. The crush of fans pushing and shoving to see the open casket created a near-chaotic situation. The crowd wishing to see Sam's body was disgruntled when they discovered his casket was covered with protective glass. As one of Sam's best friends, Johnnie served as a pallbearer at the service. Only days after Sam's funeral, Sam's widow Barbara was seen publicly with R&B singer Bobby Womack in an intimate setting. Only three months after Cooke's death, Barbara and Womack were married, raising questions about when their relationship actually began. Womack had been a protege of Cooke's for many years, and had become an artist among SAR's stable of talent. The timing of their relationship and the imprudent public display didn't sit well with Sam's friends, associates or fans. Meanwhile, Bertha Franklin, the woman who pulled the fateful trigger that killed Sam, sought punitive damages and restitution from his estate for what she claimed were traumatic mental and physical injuries. She filed a $200,000 lawsuit against the Cooke estate. The courts decided in her favor, but only awarded Franklin $30,000. Barbara Cooke then countersued Bertha Franklin for the cost of Sam's two funerals, but the court dismissed the case in Franklin's favor.[7] After the trials, both Franklin and Elisa Boyer were forced to move from their homes due to threats of violence.[8] Sam's closest brother L.C. put his loss in perspective, "We all took it real bad, you know, imagine, this our idol and all our hopes and all our dreams."[9]

CHAPTER 13

Johnnie had a hard time putting his life back together. Without the encouragement and counseling that Sam provided, his life was stuck in neutral. Making matters worse was the immediate concern of not having a recording contract. Taylor found himself back where he started. After many hours touring on the road, the hundreds of performances and days spent in the studio, he had little to show for his efforts. After Sam's passing, two memorial tours were scheduled in Cooke's honor. The first, held in mid-January of 1965 featured Jackie Wilson along with Sam's brother L.C., who looked eerily like his sibling. The second was a fusion of pop, soul, and gospel performances highlighted by Jerry Butler, The Impressions, The Soul Stirrers, The Highway Q.C.'s, The Upsetters, and J.T. Johnnie celebrated Sam during his tribute, singing his biggest hit to date, the Prudhomme song Cooke gave to Johnnie, "Rome Wasn't Built in a Day." Organizing and carrying out the tour had a strange feel for the entertainers. Sam's loss created a void hard to fill, but they came together and paid homage to their fallen brother.[1]

After the memorial tour, Taylor regrouped. Though difficult, he made an attempt to put the Cooke turmoil behind him. "That was a huge blow for him personally and businesswise cause he sorta didn't know where to go next after that. Sam was sorta everything," said Johnnie's son, T.J. Hooker.[2] Johnnie went back to what he knew best, the road circuit. There he continued to take advantage of the momentum generated from Little Johnny's infamous "Part Time Love." His intentions were to keep a presence in the eyes and ears of his fans and at least maintain the popularity he had built to that point. The grind of traveling back and forth from Texas to California began to wear on Johnnie. Especially since he lost his primary reason for being on the West Coast with Sam now deceased and his record company defunct. L.A. had become a grind. Johnnie set sights on approaching other recording companies to see if he could engage some interest with their R&A men. He considered the famous Motown label or Stax Records, a soul/R&B company out of Tennessee. When Johnnie was in St. Louis on his road tour, he decided the only way to choose between the two: "I flipped a coin to decide whether to go to work for Motown in Detroit or Stax in Memphis. Tails came up, and I headed straight down to Memphis. They said, 'Glad to have you man. Where have you been? You shoulda called us a long time ago. Here's your contract.'"[3] When Johnnie signed in 1965 he arrived about the same time as Al Bell. Bell was a former DJ and assistant station manager at a radio station in Little Rock. Bell would become the label's national director of promotions and was later promoted to executive vice president, eventually ascending to chairman of the board. Bell was sitting in his office one Saturday in early January 1966, when he received the call from J.T., who was visiting relatives in West Memphis. Bell had been a Taylor fan since his days as a disc jockey, having played Johnnie's Highway Q.C.'s and Soul Stirrers' songs on KOKY in Little Rock. Later playing "Rome (Wasn't Built in a Day)" at WUST in Washington, D.C. He'd been to one of J.T.'s shows in Chicago when he sang with the Q.C.'s and recalled him as having been "electrifying and charismatic."[4] Al Bell contributed his thoughts, "I was honored that Johnnie Taylor would call me, because I loved his singing." Bell added, "He came over that afternoon, and we sat and talked." Bell remembers Johnnie saying, "Man you know, I've been traveling across the country singing 'Part Time Love.' I've been doing fine with it, and it's gotten me hot, really hot in the marketplace. I'd like you guys to take me as an artist and record some songs on me like 'Part Time Love.' If you'd put that in the marketplace right away, then I'd get me a hit and be able to go on and build my career.' I called [Isaac] Hayes and [David] Porter, and the next day I believe they brought in 'I Had a Dream.' It became a hit, and he never looked back."[5]

Stax already had an impressive lineup, maybe not as glitzy as the Motown roster, but the Stax label featured the likes of Otis Redding, Sam and Dave, Booker T. & The M.G.'s, The Bar-Kays, Eddie Floyd, Isaac Hayes, Albert King, Little Milton and The Staple Singers. If Motown was uptown, Stax was downtown. Stax Publicity Director Deanie Parker shared some insight about first meeting Johnnie. "My first memory of Johnnie was that we had this guy who had been on SAR Records and had been with The Soul Stirrers and who everybody thought was a hellacious singer. He had this little hat sitting on the side of his head. He kind of walked with a swagger. His torso kind of went out first and he kind of glided into the room. He was really cool. He had a very cool walk, and he had a cool talk. He had a nasal tone, and he referred to everybody as 'Pete' once he got to know them. He was just an easygoing person. He was like no other artist that had come in there. He wasn't hyper. He wasn't anxious. He was really laid-back. Every day almost that he came

STAX HEADQUARTERS MEMPHIS, TENNESSEE–SOULSVILLE USA

in, he had a quart of beer in a brown paper bag. He kept it in his hand." About Johnnie covering Little Johnny Taylor's "Part Time Love," Parker explained, "There was a great deal of confusion about Little Johnny Taylor and Johnnie." Parker added, "One of the greatest difficulties that I had publicity-wise was getting people to understand that this was not Little Johnny."[6]

CHAPTER 14

STAX AND THE DALLAS DANDY

Taylor finally decided to leave L.A. and lay down permanent roots in Dallas in the early sixties. Growing weary of the West Coast scene and possibly trying to escape the many vices that had possessed him there, he chose to establish himself in a more accommodating city. To Johnnie, Dallas seemed to feel right. Johnnie saw leaving L.A. as an escape from a place where he was a small fish in a big pond. In Dallas, he would be a big fish in a small pond where it would be easier for him to make a name for himself. The unpretentious pond in Big D welcomed Johnnie. He moved to a large Dallas suburb south of the Trinity River called Oak Cliff. The area proved to be one of the most scenic parts of Dallas and had a strong Black presence. It was also home to a number of famed musicians and bluesmen. T-Bone Walker, Z.Z. Hill, Bobby Patterson and Al Green were all from the area where music and entertainment were at the forefront. There were a number of venues in Dallas that provided Johnnie a hospitable platform to "tread the boards." The Empire Room and the San Jose Hotel, tucked away in the Hall and Thomas neighborhood, became his familiar haunts. Aside from performing in Dallas, touring the countryside had always been Johnnie's calling card. He put more miles on his vehicle in a year than some would accumulate in a lifetime. As Johnnie made his way around the country, he would call or stop by to see his various girlfriends. Helen, or perhaps La Shawn's mother or Susie in L.A., Mary or Ruby in Kansas City, Val in St. Louis, Peggye in North Carolina and others who may never be identified.

Once settled in Dallas, Taylor continued his philandering with young

Irma Jean Parker. Irma's brother was a musician and made the introduction one night when she was in the audience at the Empire Room. Irma gave J.T. her number and they began dating. Taylor had a personal driver named Gertrude who would take Johnnie and Irma all over town to clubs and parties. Johnnie always looked "dressed to kill" riding in his sleek Lincoln Continental. Irma's first impression was that Johnnie was just another wandering musician. As she got to know him, her impression changed, and their relationship soon blossomed. Irma recalls an unusual practice on their drives through Dallas. Whenever he

was playing gospel music on the radio, he'd turn it off for certain people and play popular music. It was apparent Taylor was selective to whom he exposed his love for religious melodies. Irma would frequently accompany J.T. on tours around Texas to attend his shows. Their budding romance led to her pregnancy and Irma, consequently had a child

IRMA JEAN PARKER
PHOTO COURTESY OF RAHEEM MACKEY

named Rodney in 1965, who goes by the name of Raheem Mackey. As time went on Johnnie didn't get around to seeing Irma as often as she would have liked, but Johnnie kept in touch to see how she and Rodney were getting along.[1] For the most part Johnnie was diligent about staying in touch with lovers regardless of his visible absence. Whenever J.T. made his pleasure-seeking drop-ins, he took after the character portrayed in the song "Papa Was a Rollin' Stone." The tune was written by Motown writers, Norman Whitfield and Barrett Strong, and made famous by The Temptations in 1972. Truly, "wherever he laid his hat was his home" could most certainly have served as Johnnie's catchphrase.

Johnnie shared stories with Rodgers Redding about his days as a young entertainer, one in particular served as a humbling experience. He and a number of musicians and celebrities had assembled at a party. The group of who's who sat around philosophizing about life and their careers. Brook Benton, a well-known soul singer and songwriter from South Carolina, brought Johnnie along to meet some of the guys. Meadowlark Lemon, the famous Globetrotter who had made a name for himself on basketball courts around the world, was speaking in an authoritative manner. He thoughtfully expressed his feelings about life while everyone in the room listened politely. Johnnie was younger than the others and listened for a moment, and attempted to add his two cents. As Johnnie began his response, saying, "I think ..." Lemon abruptly interrupted, "Who said that?" Johnnie identified himself. Lemon asked who he was and who brought Johnnie to the house. J.T. pointed to Brooks. Lemon replied sharply, "You need to learn when to talk and when not to talk. Once you learn something, then you can talk. Until then, sit back down on the couch and shut up." Johnnie felt like a young child who had just been scolded. He was embarrassed and ashamed. Later Johnnie tried to explain to Brook what he was trying to say and asked why he didn't come to his defense. Brook told him, "in this world you had to make your own way. You have to figure out things on your own cause no one's gonna help you out of some situations." Brook's tough love taught Johnnie a lesson that day, one he never forgot.[2]

J.T.'s career with Stax Records was off and running. The company was founded in 1957 by siblings Jim Stewart and Estelle Axton in Memphis. Originally its name was Satellite Records, then changed to Stax in 1961, taken from the combination of the first two letters of each owner's last name. Stax made its way to becoming one of the foremost record companies in America, famous for its raw, gutbucket-soul sounds.[3] In 1962, Stax stumbled upon a new artist who, for a time, was chauffeur for the group, Johnny Jenkins and the Pinetoppers. Jenkins had come to the studios to record, but the session went poorly and ended prematurely. The chauffeur had been sitting nearby continually asking for an opportunity to sing, annoying the Stax production team. After Jenkins finished his session in frustration, the tall strapping chauffeur was finally given a few minutes to sing. He stunned the studio technicians who listened. What chauffeur Otis Redding sang that day was his rendition of "These Arms of Mine." Within four days, Stax signed Otis to a contract; and the young man, barely twenty-one would become the label's biggest star.[4] After Otis had been with Stax for only three years, he racked up a dozen hit singles and became the Stax bell cow. Three years later Johnnie arrived. "He [Johnnie] wanted to be the number one artist of Stax after Otis, that's for sure, and I think he had accepted the fact that Otis was gonna be number one as long as Otis was there you know," said former manager Alan Walden.[5] After Al Bell's arrival in 1965, "Things only got better in the new year, with the company signing in quick succession Johnnie Taylor, Eddie Floyd, Albert King, and Mable John, with all four artists immediately enjoying chart hits.[6] Taylor had a unique strategy pertaining to White listeners. Many R&B artists performed for White audiences, but were forced to accept less pay. This was an attempt by Black artists to attract new record buyers outside of their customary fanbase, broadening their appeal. Otis ascribed to this philosophy and, according to his brother Rodgers, he played the 1967 Monterey Jazz Festival for next to nothing. Johnnie didn't agree with this approach. He had many opportunities to perform for White audiences, but refused to play for less than his going rate. For this reason he rarely performed at White shows. Rodgers presumes this is why he was never fully embraced by the White music fans, because he had less exposure than those who played the game.[7]

OTIS REDDING

CHAPTER 15

SOUL PHILOSOPHY

On August 11, 1965 following a drunk driving traffic stop in the Watts neighborhood of L.A., a scuffle ensued with police officers and Marquette Frye who resisted arrest. Frye and his brother, Ronald who intervened, (both Black men), were beaten then arrested in front of a crowd of onlookers. Their mother was also arrested after she arrived at the scene and joined the fray. By this time, the Civil Rights Movement was well underway. The excessive force used by the police ignited a series of riots by Watts residents that expanded into other parts of the city. It was the heat of the summer, tempers were short and Sam Cooke's killing and possible cover-up was still fresh on the minds of Black Angelenos. Black citizens maintained that L.A. police authorities had glossed over Cooke's killing and should have performed a more complete investigation. With Black frustration building, the beating and arrest of the Frye brothers set off six days of rioting in L.A. The riots continued until the California National Guard was finally summoned to quell the disturbance. After the dust settled, over thirty people had died and property damage totaled in the tens of millions of dollars. The Watts Riots became a demarcation line for civil rights and a rallying cry by Black Americans. In the coming years the Watts riots would serve as a catalyst for one of the most historic music festivals in California history.

"I Had a Dream," was Johnnie's first single with Stax. It was written by Isaac Hayes and David Porter and recorded on January 8, 1966. The tune was originally penned for Bobby "Blue" Bland, but when Porter shopped the song with Duke Records, Bland's label–Porter and Don

Robey, owner of Duke Records, couldn't agree on a reasonable price. So Porter gave it to Johnnie.[1] The B side was "Changes," co-written by Johnnie, Hayes and Porter. Under the new Stax regime Johnnie was able to escape the critical scrutiny of Sam Cooke, and enjoyed recording freedom in the Memphis studios. "Dream" had a crisp, earthy sound, complemented by a full-backing band and off-mic coaching from songwriter, musician and vocalist David Porter. In the studio were Isaac Hayes and Booker T. Jones on keys, Steve Cropper on guitar, Donald "Duck" Dunn on bass, and Al Jackson Jr. on percussion. With this high level of supporting musicians, Johnnie's first single turned out tight and sultry, tapping new territory within the blues arena.[2] This adagio number creeps along, punctuated by the in-and-out cadence of horns penetrating Johnnie's soul-dipped vocals. J.T.'s lyrics recall a dream about going to his on-the-job graveyard shift and leaving his wife asleep in bed. After getting sick, he left work and returned to an empty house finding no sign of his woman. Was it a dream or a premonition of what the future might hold? The listeners are left to decide for themselves. One should take note of a few lines in the song where Johnnie establishes a conversation, with the listener. In essence saying, " ...that's why I'm telling *you* ..." and, '*you* see ...". Taylor used second person personal pronouns like *you* as a foundational approach on many of his tunes. This concept served as teaching moments, where Johnnie shared his wisdom and experiences to help unsuspecting men deal with similar situations. Al Bell came up with a nickname for Johnnie. "Word twists and provocative lyrics suited Johnnie, and as his career unfolded he'd adopt the moniker of 'The Philosopher of Soul.' The nickname was another reflection of his dual personas, evoking the gritty and the smooth, the simple and the complicated."[3] Ian McCann said it this way: "Stax had dubbed Taylor the 'Philosopher of Soul,' but his kind of philosophy was strictly down-home, barroom, over the back fence, and sometimes downright no good. All the same, he was a fine singer, capable of a creamy smoothness you might expect from someone championed by Sam Cooke, and also possessed a sneaky funkiness, adjusting his approach according to the topic he was singing about."[4] Johnnie expressed his thoughts about his nickname, "Stax came up with that, ('Soul Philosopher' nickname), but it fit me.

Most of the songs I was doing had a piece of advice in them that people picked up on."[5]

Taylor released two singles following "Dream". The first, "Little Bluebird," was composed by Booker T. Jones, Hayes and Porter. "Bluebird" was another slow blues number that had suggestive undertones, although sufficiently disguised for radio play. Taylor sang about cutting his lover's wings so they could be together in his nest. Gospel listeners who sampled the song probably cringed when they heard Johnnie's seductively-coded messages. "Toe Hold" another song written by Hayes and Porter was on the flipside. J.T's third single "I Got to Love Somebody's Baby," also written by Hayes and Porter, was a slurry-dripped soul outcry seeking somebody to love. Johnnie painted aural images describing his roving eye and unfed love which underscored

JOHNNIE TAYLOR

JOHNNIE
PHOTO COURTESY OF THE STAX MUSEUM
OF AMERICAN SOUL MUSIC

his need for intimacy, no matter who she belonged to. Somebody was seeing his baby so why couldn't he do the same? The adept piano intro and Johnnie's repetition of the word 'somebody' at the opening, is classic. The B-side was "Just the One I've Been Looking For." All Bell described Johnnie's singing virtuosity: "There was something about his singing style that held throughout his career. There was so much passion in his voice. In addition to the passion, he could treat a melody with the greatest of finesse when he wanted to, and then when he thought to put the pain and anguish in it, he could do that also. I loved that about him."[6] The three singles were part of Johnnie's inaugural Stax album, *Wanted One Soul Singer* which also included his cover of Herbie Hancock's "Watermelon Man." Also featured on the LP was an old classic entitled, "Sixteen Tons" made famous by Tennessee Ernie Ford, who was a renown baritone singer and one-time actor in the "I Love Lucy" TV series. The *One Soul Singer* album released in early 1967 showed clear evidence how Stax painted Johnnie's vocals with a distinctive, unmistakable Memphis sound. "[*Wanted One Soul Singer*] paved the road to success for Johnnie. The next year he released the single 'Who's Making Love,' which became Stax's biggest selling single to date (even more than Otis Redding's 'Dock of the Bay').[7] "In a couple of years Johnnie would become one of Stax's mainstays, enjoying an incredible run of hit singles for the label from October 1968 through September 1975 under the production auspices of Don Davis.[8] In 1966, Al Bell dispatched Stax performers to the weeklong "Rocky G's Boogaloo Spectacular," (promoted by local disc-jockey Rocky G). The Stax Revue played at the Apollo Theater in New York and boasted a star-studded lineup consisting of Sam and Dave, Otis Redding, Carla Thomas, Rufus Thomas, the Mad Lads and Johnnie. The Reuben Phillips Orchestra, Apollo's house band, provided backup throughout the event which also included a teen fashion show unveiling boogaloo threads and boogaloo dance lessons for the audience.[9]

CHAPTER 16

STAX'S COLLAPSE-MAKIN' A BREAK

On December 10, 1967, a plane left the Cleveland Hopkins airport headed for Madison, Wisconsin. The night before, its passengers had enjoyed a show featuring the O'Jays and the Temptations at Leo's Casino in C-Town. An inexperienced pilot, inclement weather, and a faulty battery affecting the instrument panel caused the twin-engine Beechcraft to crash into Lake Manona only a few miles short of the runway. The plane slammed into the water and crumpled. All, save one of its eight passengers, perished in the frigid waters. Otis Redding and four members of his teenage backing band, called The Bar-Kays, were killed, along with Otis' valet and the pilot.[1] Ironically the accident happened three years and a day after Sam Cooke's murder on December 11, 1964.[2]

The news of Redding's death sent shockwaves across the nation, especially with his fans and those in the music industry. Employees at Stax Records were dumbfounded and searched for meaning in the loss of such a great friend, performer and flagbearer of Stax. Once the numbness subsided, Al Bell and his team began to comprehend how Otis's tragedy would impact the company. Redding was the main attraction, the headliner, the iconic celebrity who represented the foundation of the label, and his loss was a devastating blow. Johnnie and Otis had become friends when J.T. joined the Stax team. The two co-existed at Stax with mutual respect and regard for each other's talents, although some friendly competition existed. Otis' funeral was held at the Macon Municipal Auditorium in Georgia, where an overflow crowd of almost 5,000 attended the service. Not only was Johnnie a pallbearer, he sang a heart-wrenching "I'll Be Standing By," bringing everyone to tears. In the contingent was also James Brown, Wilson Pickett, Isaac Hayes, Joe Tex, Arthur Conley, Solomon Burke and Don Covay, a complete array of soul royalty. "Otis's 'Respect' had become an anthem of hope for people everywhere. Respect is something that Otis achieved. Otis sang, 'Respect when I come home.' And Otis has come home," expressed music journalist and famed producer Jerry Wexler after the funeral. "I only wished that Aretha had been there to sing that song."[3] Apparently Aretha was so shook up over Redding's death that she couldn't bring herself to attend.

Now that Otis had been lost, Al Bell and the Stax management turned to Johnnie and put all their chips on the young man who held the keys to the label's future. Their focus and priority were to build Johnnie into a star, and the team began grooming him to somehow fill Redding's shoes. The pressure on Johnnie to succeed must have felt heavy on his shoulders. Whether he was up to the task, only time would tell. "What Steve (Cropper) is saying is that we realized we could never replace Otis, so we spent all the time we can really trying to make a William Bell, trying to make a Johnny Taylor, to take up the slack and all that we lost in Otis and, I must say, the Bar-Kays," Stax session drummer Al Jackson said in his interview with *Rolling Stone Magazine*.

For the second time, J.T. was forced to climb out of the shadow of a superstar. The difference this time would be his access to the Stax recording mystique that included its talented management and the exceptional group of studio musicians who supported the artists. To help Johnnie achieve the levels needed to succeed, Bell brought in Don Davis from Motown Records in Detroit. Davis was a musician and first-rate producer who cut his teeth in the studios of the legendary Motown sound machine. Al Bell's ingenious move to bring Davis in was designed to add an element of Motown polish into Johnnie's repertoire. This was a game-changer. "Al Bell wanted to create sort of a combination of the Memphis sound and the Detroit sound by bringing Don Davis into the picture, he was able to create a whole new sound for Stax that Johnnie Taylor was able to take advantage of," reflected Marcus Chapman.[4]

Another memorable event took place in 1967 when Johnnie's daughter Crystal was born after his romance with St. Louis girlfriend, Val Wilson.

Crystal would grow up to be one of Johnnie's closest children. Soon after the time of Crystal's birth, and following Rodgers Redding's brother's tragic airplane crash, Rodgers returned from the armed services. He had been friends with and familiar with many of the gospel and R&B performers during Otis' days as an entertainer. Johnnie and Rodgers were acquainted, but weren't close friends at the time. Out of the blue, Rodgers received a call from J.T. wanting to meet him in Atlanta to help him conduct some interviews while he was on tour. In the middle of an interview, Johnnie introduced Redding as his booking agent. This was news to Rodgers, for they hadn't discussed this beforehand, and Taylor's statement took Redding by surprise. Later Johnnie took him aside and explained how he liked the way Rodgers handled his business and felt he would be a good fit for the PR role, if he was interested. Redding accepted the position that day in Atlanta launching a partnership that would span decades.[5] As it turned out, Rodgers was the perfect man for the task and was praised for his many connections and relationships: "If Rodgers Redding doesn't represent you, you don't work. If he does represent you, you work all the time."[6]

In early '68, one of Johnnie's friends and fellow Arkansan singer from Cullendale passed away at the early age of thirty-years old. William Edward John, a.k.a. Little Willie John, was a talented youth who sang gospel and R&B. Willie's song "Fever" sold over a million copies, but before his career elevated to the next level, alcohol wrapped its death grip around the young artist. One night, after Little Willie's performance in Seattle, he was arrested after killing a man. He was convicted and sentenced to prison. He never made it out, and it was reported the five-foot-four brawler died from a heart attack while still incarcerated. Johnnie was honored when asked to sing a tribute at Little Willie's funeral.[7] Following Little Willie's demise, James Brown released an album later in 1968 by the name, "Thinking About Willie John and a Few Nice Things."

The added pressure Johnnie felt by becoming the face of Stax Records was overshadowed by the startling news of Dr. Martin Luther King's assassination in April. King was shot shortly after 6:00 p.m. while standing on the balcony just outside his second-floor room at the Lorraine Motel in Memphis. His assassin was James Earl Ray, an escaped fugitive who was captured, confessed and sentenced to a ninety-nine-year prison term. The Black public was incensed and began a series of protests that led to violence and significant property damage. The man who preached "love thy neighbor" and abhorred violence had met a violent end. King's [passing] changed the trajectory of civil rights in the United States. Without Dr. King, racial injustice and civil unrest may never have started down a path to resolution. Many of the Black performers, including Johnnie, mourned his death.

When Don Davis arrived at Stax, his first duties were to work with Carla Thomas to produce a hit record. After their first effort was released, it became a Top 20 R&B success. With their notable achievement, Bell assigned Davis to work with Johnnie. "Al believed there was untapped appeal in Johnnie Taylor, and wanted Davis to expand his audience. 'I knew Johnnie could be in that arena with Marvin Gaye,' exclaimed Al Bell, 'if he was produced in that fashion.' When Davis expressed an interest in Taylor, Al leapt at the notion; Hayes and Porter had been producing him, and so had Cropper and Al Jackson. Johnnie's voice was warm and wistful, attractive enough to be steadily hovering inside the R&B top forty, but unable to find that breakout song or style."[8]

When Johnnie walked into the Stax studios to record, there was no way to know he'd be surrounded by session players who would become famous on their own accord. Steve Cropper got his start as a young guitar player for the Mar-Keys, and upon arriving at Stax played with the critically acclaimed Booker T. and the M.G.'s, (short for Memphis Group). The band was led by Booker T. Jones on keyboards, Alan Jackson Jr. on drums and Lewis Steinberg (later replaced by Donald "Duck" Dunn) on bass.[9] The M.G.'s went on to achieve major success, both as a session band and as a popular group that charted several songs. Booker Taliaferro Jones Jr., born in Memphis, started his employment at Stax as a teenager and worked his way up to a session musician extraordinaire. Jones and his band were well known for their "Green Onions," "Hip Hug-Her," and "Groovin" songs. Playing alongside the M.G.'s, in the studio was the distinguished Isaac Hayes who would contribute his self-taught keyboard and sax talents to Johnnie's sessions. Hayes would go on to forge his own massive success as an actor, vocalist and musician, highlighted by his legendary album and the movie *Shaft*. These fine musicians created a backdrop that splashed the Memphis trademark onto Johnnie's songs.

With Davis on board, he worked with Johnnie to refine his craft, and they focused on his strengths to produce quality recordings: "Everybody knew that Johnnie Taylor was a talent," songwriter Bettye Crutcher commented. "But they just were not getting him right. So Homer Banks had started a song. He's the kind of guy who would come up with a line. They're looking at somebody's girl, and Homer goes, 'Well, who's making love to your lady–while you're out making love?' And I said, 'You really got to tell this story in a way that women are going to listen to it.' And so, the song gave the guy a thought that his girlfriend might be playing with somebody else while he's out. And Don Davis recognized that. He said 'I want this to be an anthem for women.' And I would have guys who would stop me and say. 'Why did you write a song like that? You had me going back home, checking to see if my wife was leaving with somebody!'"[10] The song written by Homer Banks, Bettye Crutcher, and Raymond Jackson was first heard by Davis when it was played in the Stax studios. Banks provides insight on the tune's inception which began after he heard Frank Sinatra on TV, "I heard him on television," Banks remembers, laughing. "He had a song entitled 'Who's Taking Care of the Caretaker's Daughter While the Caretaker's Out Taking Care.'"[11] This sparked the concept for "Who's Making Love." "He took the material, reworked it for Johnnie and presented the song for him to record. When he (Davis) started to produce Johnnie, it just, I mean it was like magic. The two of them together it was like magic."[12] Davis contributed guitar play on the cut and also produced the effort both in Memphis and Detroit. "Who's Making Love" would soon change the course of Johnnie's career, and with it, elevate Stax to new heights. "Interestly, Johnnie Taylor hated 'Who's Making Love,' referring to it as the "the boogity boogity song." He thought it was too fast. Davis bullied him into recording it. "Johnnie bitches about doing the song," explained Davis. "I just kept telling him he wasn't singing the song. I just kept harassing him, really. I said, 'I'm just going to give the song to Sam and Dave, you can forget it.' That was a big challenge to his ego."[13] He begrudgingly went on to record the song. "'Who's Making Love' is a bold statement, more overtly sexual than anything Stax had done, and musically it fulfilled Al's vision: Rooted in gospel–it has a sophisticated sound that takes Stax into yet more new and fresh territory. In spirit, it captures the humor, the fun, the love that permeated so much Stax material, but its drive and modernity draw heavily from northern polish."[14] "We had a ball working with Don Davis," remarked guitarist Steve Cropper, "'Who's Making Love' is one of the most fun sessions I ever played on. In the old days, there was one guitar player because we couldn't afford but one …" Cropper continued, "That [song] had three guitars on it. Raymond Jackson, one of the song's writers, he laughed so hard he fell backwards out of the chair." Wayne Jackson who played trumpet, chimed in, "'Who's Making Love' was a step off the curb for all of us," "because it was such a sexually charged song. It was perfect for Johnnie Taylor, because he's so good looking. People started fighting when they heard him sing, 'cause their girlfriends started lifting that dress, and Johnny'd be on the stage and just destroy all of them."[15]

"According to engineer Ron Capone, Taylor was uncomfortable with the then-new concept at Stax of wearing headphones and overdubbing the lead vocal on a finished vocal track, claiming that he could never cut a hit record that way. After "Who's Making Love" turned his career inside out, he decided headphones and overdubbing weren't so bad after all."[16] "The popular broadcast media was not ready to accept 'Who's Making Love' at that point," Stax owner Jim Stewart contended, "This was an ongoing battle all through the sixties and early seventies. Pop stations said, 'It's too funky,' but we knew they meant, 'It's too black.' They wouldn't admit they didn't play Black records. They didn't consider Motown Black records, but Stax was Black. 'Who's Making Love' sold close to half a million copies before we could get it onto pop radio." Executive Vice President Al Bell added, "After they recorded it, they were saying, 'Well, we can't release that. That's a little too risqué. What are you talking about, too risqué? This is an automatic record here. It sells itself."[17] "When I first heard 'Who's Making Love' it was like, hmmm, is this song not supposed to be played on the air? But then once you listen to it, its life, its everyday life."[18] Bettye Crutcher saw it somewhat differently, "I like writing songs that people relate to and actually it wasn't like a song about sex or anything, it was about reaping what you sow."[19] Crutcher later added, "Sometimes we hit it just right and 'Who's Making

Love' was one of those just right songs."[20] Johnnie claims he had a good feeling about the song and asserted, "I knew right away it was a great song. But I had no idea that it would be that big of a hit."[21] J.T. commented further, "Having a big record is a great responsibility. An artist has to be able to entertain in person as well as on records, however. The years of struggling I went through before *Who's Making Love* broke it for me are my dues. I learned to be an entertainer long before I had a hit record and became a star. Now I can afford the extras, like having my own 15-piece band; this all helps me put on an even better show."[22]

The song, barely out of the gates, featured Taylor's wail *'a la* James Brown that immediately demanded the ear's attention. J.T. began giving advice, asking listeners to consider who *might* be making love to your woman while you're out doing the same? The song's subject matter exposes a what-if situation that alerted men to be cautious if they're out carousing. "He gave a lot of advice in his songs and warned guys of what they should and should not be doing with their women and did the same thing with women too," Marcus Chapman related.[23] The lyrics tiptoed on a tightrope between the FCC's permissible subject matter and crossing the line into what was considered risqué. There were stations who believed it fell into the latter category and were hesitant to play the song. This made "Who's Making Love" more sought after. Behind Davis' chord stroking on guitar and Jack Ashford's tambourine, the horn section lay in wait and would bray occasionally between lines. On the second half of the song, the driving rhythm built to a climax before the horn section belted out rigorous notes for effect. The lack of an audible drum cadence didn't seem to hinder the song's impact, which featured delicate but sassy female background vocalists. Framed by Johnnie's leering voice, this danceable tune captured the listener's attention, causing folks to tap their foot and snap their fingers. The song had all the perfect ingredients, which can sometimes be mysteriously elusive. For Johnnie, his world had changed. "Who's Making Love" sold over a million copies and earned him his first gold record. Ian McCann said this about the song in his udiscovermusic.com article: "I've Got To Love Somebody's Baby" and "Somebody's Sleepin' In My Bed" cast him as someone who realized love was a cheatin' thing, but the "Who's Making Love" single practically defined the 'can't trust a lover strain of soul.'"[24] Marcus Chapman stated in his *Unsung 818* interview, "He could deliver a lyric in a way that made it relatable to the common man."[25] Sam Cooke's brother L.C. added, "God gave him a good gift and he know how to use it."[26] The ultimate compliment would be paid to Johnnie and the songwriters when Dan Aykroyd and John Belushi, comedians of Saturday Night Live fame, formed the Blues Brothers and covered Johnnie's "Who's Making Love". For two White guys, they came up with a respectable rendition performed by the Jake and Elwood characters. The Blues Brothers' single was released in 1980.

Later in life, Johnnie shared his observations about the song's message, "While you're lyin', cheatin' on your woman, there is something you never thought of–now tell me who's making love to your old lady while you were out making love?" Taylor goes

THE BLUES BROTHERS–PAINTING OF DAN AYKROYD AND JOHN BELUSHI

on, "I'm just tellin' it like it is ... I could sing songs that in the end condone adultery or playing around with someone's feelings. I have done it in the past but that's not where it's at today. So, I'm just acknowledging that such situations do exist. But like a preacher, I guess I'm tellin' folks that bad will come out of not playing the game right."[27] "Who's Making Love" was the title track of Johnnie's second album which was pieced together to accompany its hit song. The LP contains several slow-moving blues numbers that fixate on Johnnie's familiar down-on-your-luck plots that dispatch a message to the listeners. He cautions, advises, and guides them through the complications of heartbreak, cheating, and trusting, earning his reputation as the Soul Philosopher. Taylor instills gospel roots into a new soul identity; when the vinyl spins, it jells into a work of fusion. "'Who's Making Love' captures some of the high points of Taylor's career as a Southern soul man, and finds him nodding to his past as well as his future in his search for inspiration."[28] J.T. reflected further on the song: "Well, these are songs about everyday life. All the tunes are what actually happens. A dude thinks he can run around and win 'em all and lose none. His old lady is at home. Hey man! She's thinking too. Women, especially, bought "Who's Making Love", by the way. They were teasing their husbands with it a lot. Some of them may not have been teasing. Who knows? But, at any rate, I like to pick a song that says something about life and about the human condition, especially one that says something about relationships between man and woman. This is always fascinating, for it is a relationship that has its tensions, joys, and its ups and downs."[29] The single, "Who's Making Love" was certified gold in 1968 and "would prove to be Stax's biggest record to date, selling 850,000 copies before the end of the year, and two million copies before its chart run was over! It would be the first of eight straight singles Davis would produce with Taylor that would break into the R&B Top 10."[30]

As Johnnie's booking agent, Rodgers Redding shared a tale about a gig he and Taylor lined up in Houston. It was a large venue, expecting a sellout of 3,000 fans. Rodgers always kept a close eye on Johnnie, as his drinking habits required constant vigilance. Before they arrived, Rodgers cautioned the venue manager, known as "Big Bopper" to keep Johnnie away from the booze if he wanted a successful performance. Ignoring Rodgers' instructions, Bopper took bottles onto

SOUL BROTHERS TOP 20
Title, Artist and Label

1. LOVE CHILD . . . . Diana Ross & Supremes (Motown)
2. WHO'S MAKING LOVE . . . . Johnnie Taylor (Stax)
3. SOULFUL STRUT . . . . Young-Holt Unlimited (Brunswick)
4. I HEARD IT THROUGH THE GRAPEVINE . . . . . Marvin Gaye (Tamla)
5. CAN I CHANGE MY MIND . . . . Tyron Davis (Darkar)
6. I'M GONNA MAKE YOU LOVE ME
    Supremes & Temptations (Motown)
7. MY SONG . . . . Aretha Franklin (Atlantic)
8. GOODBYE MY LOVE . . . . James Brown (King)
9. COURT OF LOVE . . . . Unifics (Kapp)
10. EVERY DAY PEOPLE . . . . . . Sly & The Family Stone (Epic)
11. SOUL SISTER, BROWN SUGAR . . . . . . Sam & Dave (Atlantic)
12. THIS IS MY COUNTRY . . . . The Impressions (Curtom)
13. TOO WEAK TO FIGHT . . . . Clarence Carter (Atlantic)
14. MALINDA . . . . Bobby Taylor & Vancouvers (Gordy)
15. CALIFORNIA DREAMING . . . . Bobby Womack (Minit)
16. PAPA'S GOT A BRAND NEW BAG . . . . . Otis Redding (Stax/Volt)
17. MESSAGE FROM MARIA . . . . Joe Simon (Sound Stage)
18. HOW YOU GONNA GET RESPECT . . . . . Hank Ballard (King)
19. FOR ONCE IN MY LIFE . . . . Stevie Wonder (Tamla)
20. SOUL LIMBO . . . . Booker T. & M.G.'s (Stax)

Hit of the Week SOULFUL STRUT . . . Young-Holt Unlimited (Brunswick)
Artist of the Week WHO'S MAKING LOVE . . . Johnnie Taylor (Stax)
Album of the Week TCB . . . Supremes and Temptations (Motown)
Honor Roll Hit SAY IT LOUD . . . James Brown (King)

Young and Holt   *Diana Ross & Supremes*   *Taylor*

PHOTO COURTESY OF T.J.HOOKER

Johnnie's tour bus and they spent all afternoon draining three quarts of liquor. By showtime, Johnnie was so intoxicated, that he was only able to perform for fifteen minutes, then had to be carted off. Management of the club was incensed. The next day, Johnnie apologized to Rodgers, admitting, "I messed up." He regretted the ordeal and told Redding to call the owner and schedule a make-up performance. Rodgers assumed they'd return in a few months to finish the show, but the club wanted him to play the next weekend. Johnnie agreed, so they made their way back to Houston and played to another sellout crowd. This time his show was so successful the club scheduled a second show the very next night which also sold out. Rodgers described Johnnie's performances as "awesome" and the club forgave Taylor for his earlier blunder.[31]

Ollie Walter (O.W.) Gates Sr., is a Kansas City restaurateur and businessman, owner and president of the Gates Bar-B-Q restaurant chain in KC. He opened the first Gates & Sons restaurant at 12th and Brooklyn in 1958. Gates was an influential Black leader in KC and periodically organized shows and concerts. On one occasion in 1957, he hired Johnnie to play Gates' Club OG. Taylor had just begun his career and was excited to play for the local crowd in his hometown. Gates only paid him $100 for his show. After Taylor's performance dazzled the audience, Gates was asked what he thought of Johnnie's performance. Acting as if he wasn't that impressed, Gates half-heartedly admitted, "he's awright." Ten years later in 1968, after Johnnie's smash hit, "Who's Making Love" charted, and his popularity soared, Gates booked him again. This time the show was held outdoors at Parade Park. In another sellout, Johnnie's growing acclaim drew thousands who cascaded onto the grounds for his performance. City officials erected a fence around the park to manage the crowds and were forced to close off several streets around the venue. Upon his arrival, Johnnie made his entrance driving a vintage Model-T Ford and wearing a full-length white fur coat and matching fur hat. How things had changed from the last time Gates hired Taylor to perform. It goes without saying, Johnnie's payday for the Parade Park performance far surpassed what Gates paid him a decade earlier and Johnnie required Gates to pay him in advance.[32]

JOHNNIE SHOWING OFF HIS GOLD RECORD
PHOTO COURTESY OF STAX MUSEUM
OF AMERICAN SOUL MUSIC

CHAPTER 17

REPROACH AND NOTORIETY

At the end of '68, Janis Joplin's fame was on the rise. She and the Kozmic Blues Band were touring the country promoting their new rock and roll album *Cheap Thrills*. Janis and Kozmic were unexpectedly booked by Stax Records to play at the "Stax/Volt Yuletide Thing" holiday party in Memphis at the Mid-South Coliseum that December. It was unusual from the standpoint that Stax was a predominantly Black recording company stocked with mostly Black talent. Joplin wasn't signed to Stax. She and her band were White and were asked to play at what was advertised as a Soul and R&B event. Al Bell's strategy was to attract members of the rock audience to the Yuletide Thing by featuring a high profile name like Joplin. This theoretically would entice the rock press to cover the event. His maneuver was genius as the rock magazine *Rolling Stone* gave the show prime coverage, something they had never given Stax in the past.[1] Turns out that Bell inserted Joplin as the headliner over all the great Stax artists. This created a bad feeling in the air. There was a lengthy delay getting Janis and her band set up and the crowd grew antsy. When Joplin finally took the stage she and the band performed songs that were unfamiliar to the crowd. The songs weren't well received by the audience who were still disturbed by Janis and Kozmic receiving top-bill. The spectators listened politely but had little appreciation for the music, or how Janis had swooped in as the headliner. After a ho-hum performance, Janis and the band left the stage waiting for a curtain call. It never came. In the awkward moment, Johnnie was immediately rushed on stage with hopes of recapturing the show's momentum. He won the audience back as he closed out his performance with "Who's Making Love."[2]

Back in Dallas, Johnnie was setting down roots. His fame from "Who's Making Love" unfurled a red carpet to places seeking Johnnie to perform at their establishment. He continued to play at the Empire Room or the Hill Smith, a New Orleans-styled hotel across the street. Also locations in South Dallas like the Blues Palace owned by R.L. Griffin near Fair Park or D.G. Clark's place in South Dallas at Spring and Lagow. "He was very, very important. He kept the trend going for about three decades,' says singer and bandleader R.L.Griffin, whose nightclub in South Dallas was a place Mr. Taylor would frequently drop by. 'He was one of our leaders.'"[3] North of downtown in the Hall and Thomas neighborhood, Johnnie resumed his temporarily dormant activities in a side hustle with ladies of the night. According to the Dallas Police Department, Taylor was a known pimp and had a gaggle of escorts who attended clubs with him. According to a Dallas undercover narcotics detective, Johnnie would schedule a performance at a particular venue and bring several escorts with him. Once the show got underway, the ladies would filter through the crowd looking for johns, then service their clients. After his performance, the ladies and Johnnie would reconvene and Taylor was not only paid for the show, but collected his cut from the ladies. They'd then depart together in a limo or in one of Johnnie's expensive rides.[4] Because of his side business and involvement in drugs, he always carried a piece. "Johnnie always had a little thug in him."[5] "You know there was a side of Johnnie that had nothing to do with the recording business but he was making money, if you can read between the lines, from the ladies side too."[6]

Ernie Johnson is a famed bluesman from Winnsboro, Louisiana. He moved to Dallas in the early sixties. While performing across the city, he and Johnnie eventually met and slowly developed a friendship. At first, Ernie didn't take to Johnnie. If Taylor didn't know you, it was hard to penetrate the protection of his well-guarded exterior. He was savvy, street-smart, and a very distrustful person. If you were on the outside, he didn't want anything to do with you. Ernie observed, "Hardly anyone could get along with Johnnie, he was just one of those guys. He was very arrogant at first, and when we first met, I thought he needed a whoopin'."

Johnson, a large man, around six foot five, dwarfed Taylor who was only five foot nine and weighed 155 pounds. But Johnnie had a brashness that commanded respect and required a person to earn their way into his trust. Johnson and J.T. would become friends over time and Ernie's first impression wasn't an indication of what the true Johnnie Taylor was all about. Even today, Ernie imitates Johnnie's frog-like voice he used whenever he wanted to make a point. After his first few years in Dallas, Johnnie began to date a long-time companion, Gerlean Rockett, a beautiful young lady who captured his fancy. Rockett would become a serious relationship for Johnnie in the months to come.

Johnnie's third album, *The Johnnie Taylor Philosophy Continues*, falls a notch below the two previous efforts. The tracks felt a bit diluted and didn't capture the effervescence of Taylor's vocal potential. Releasing three albums in thirty-six months gave one the impression Stax was in a production-line mode, feeding as much material into the market as quickly as possible. The strategy lacked the sometimes essential element of building the fan's anticipation. Judicial timing on

DALLAS BLUES ICON ERNIE JOHNSON
PHOTO COURTESY OF ERNIE JOHNSON

when to release an album is an art form in the marketing and promotion business, and astute marketers typically avoid product saturation. *Philosophy Continues*, seems to violate these laws of inundation. That said, "I Could Never Be President" from the album made the charts with "Love Bones" and "It's Amazing" drawing respectable attention from listeners.

In February 1969, Johnnie received the much anticipated Grammy nomination in the "Best R&B Male Vocal Performance" category for his monster hit, "Who's Making Love." Several other Stax artists were also nominated. Otis Redding was nominated as Best R&B Male Vocal for his hit "(Sittin' on) The Dock of the Bay." Redding's tragic death was still fresh in the minds of NARAS (the National Association of Recording Arts and Sciences) voting members which may have persuaded them to award the Grammy to Otis, although it was well deserved.[7] The accolades were a seminal moment for the Stax label, given the hard work they put forth to achieve their collective success. Despite flooding the market with music, Johnnie's career was trending upward and his stardom continued to float on the success of "Who's Making Love." Stax maintained the momentum following a televised promotional event and scheduled the "Gettin' It All Together," production in April held two weekends in May at the Holiday Inn Rivermont in Memphis. The event was designed to bring in the press, retailers and distributors to enjoy performances by the Stax stable of thoroughbred entertainers. The shows were highly successful and drew big crowds. Johnnie was featured on the first weekend along with Rufus Thomas, Eddie Floyd, Isaac Hayes, the Bar-Kays, Carla Thomas, pop group Knowbody Else and others. As host, Stax showcased their R&B hitmakers and received great acclaim from the many professionals who attended.[8]

In December 1969, Johnnie was summoned to Washington D.C. as a guest of President-Elect Richard Nixon. J.T. was honored to perform at Nixon's celebratory inauguration ball held at the National Museum of History and Technology. Also, in 1969, Johnnie released yet another album, the second of two in the short span of twelve months. It was obvious Stax never received the message about oversaturation. *Raw Blues* was in fact bluesy material although the songs weren't any more raw than his previous efforts. "You Can't Win With a Losing Hand," was Johnnie's attempt to sing a song he wasn't accustomed to pulling off. The Joe Tex, up-tempo beat didn't play to his strengths and came across as pedestrian. The tune certainly wasn't a blues number and must have snuck onto the album while no one was looking. However, "Hello Sundown" did match the disc's title, and Taylor's unhurried, poignant delivery hit the eight ball in the corner pocket. Johnnie's ability to occasionally bend syllables reminded listeners of the finessed style he honed over the years from his gospel days. Even though the enthusiastic clapping and jeering in the background was a plus, the horn play, at times, seemed to overwhelm the song, calling to mind images of a Las Vegas floorshow. Although the song was poorly produced, the renowned Memphis Horns ensemble was impressive whenever they didn't overshadow the rest of the arrangements. J.T. and his team also poured salt in Little Johnny Taylor's wound when they included "Part Time Love" on the *Raw Blues* LP. By adding Little Johnny's song, it further misled listeners as to who the rightful owner of the song was. Overall, the album was a success, but didn't achieve the desired goal of competing for Grammy hardware.

CHAPTER 18

EGO CHECK-TIE THE KNOT

Johnnie would never forget the year 1970. He and Gerlean (Geri) Rockett were married on January 25, 1970, in Dallas. Taylor was intent to start a new life with his bride and build a comfortable home they could both be proud of. The year would also be remembered for other reasons. Johnnie took some time off and traveled to the Bahamas seeking a peaceful respite on the out-of-the-way island. What was designed as relaxing time away became a sudden nightmare when Johnnie was arrested for possession of marijuana, and for carrying a revolver and brass knuckles. For his offense, Taylor spent three months in a Nassau jail until Geri could bail him out. When Al Bell heard about Johnnie's dilemma, he commented on the arrest, "That didn't affect us at Stax. That was Johnnie Taylor. Whatever that was in the Bahamas, it didn't matter."[1] Taylor's momentum after "Who's Making Love" never missed a beat and wasn't impacted by the Nassau bust. He kept on working as if nothing had ever happened.

No matter how good Johnnie's albums turned out to be, the vinyl couldn't compare to his live performances. Being on stage was Taylor's wheelhouse. He was a born entertainer. Performing in front of a live audience was his epicenter, the command post for everything Johnnie accomplished. Interacting with the crowd allowed him to feel what he was delivering. There were no restraints, no retakes, no guidance and no input from anyone other than his emotions. Candi Staton shared, "When he walked out on the stage, it was like, he just lit the place up."[2] "There was no other entertainer like him on stage," recalled radio personality

David Washington.[3] Gregg A. Smith added, "Johnnie Taylor was one of the greatest soul singers that ever picked up a mic and graced the stage."[4] "Johnnie always had his greatest moments on the stage. That's what he lived for," Don Davis said of his close friend and colleague.[5] Johnnie sold records by touring non-stop. When on the road, there wasn't a performer who promoted himself more effectively or worked harder than Taylor. Johnnie contrived a formula to his success on stage. Taylor had been performing since he was a kid and this early experience taught him how to charm the crowd and provide the entertainment they were seeking. He was a veteran of live performance and felt as comfortable as anyone could be in front of fans. As girlfriend Helen Myles noted, "Johnnie wanted to please the audience. He saw to it that they had a good time and he'd have a good time himself. They paid good money for the show and Johnnie made sure they got what they paid for. He talked a lot on stage, had conversations with the crowd and moved around telling stories."[6] Taylor was meticulous in preparing for a show, from choosing his own threads to the wardrobe of the band, the playlist and progressions throughout the performance. He wasn't bashful flaunting his moves in front of the shimmering spotlights. Johnnie would bob his head, gaze at the audience with mischievous eyes, and unfurl a smile that could melt the most hardened listener. When Taylor was supported by his horn section and backing vocals, the shows became a spectacle–no longer a concert. There were very few shows like it. Johnnie was, "a salesman of songs," and "had remarkable consistency and breathtaking authority."[7] "Johnnie Taylor was among the rare artists who seemed to perform better before a live audience than in the seclusion of a recording studio."[8]

As a long-time smoker, Johnnie had a gravely, throaty voice that accentuated his tenor inflecions used to deliver sexy, promiscuous concepts. J.T. could sing in a whisper, or belt out a holler with equal effectiveness. The range of tools in his arsenal was endless and Johnnie could deliver notes that transcended description. He refined his skills by using the vocal techniques learned from Sam Cooke and added his own brand of crooning to fuse a flawless end product. All Bell commented, "First time I heard it, I said, wow. This Johnnie Taylor is awesome. He sang it in such a manner, but not in a manner that knocked you out, but penetrated gently into your being."[9] "We never had a release on Johnnie Taylor that was not a hit record."[10]

Johnnie was the best dressed performer in the music business. The motivation for dressing-up was developed in his early years singing at the church. All the entertainers wore their Sunday best and if someone served as a worship leader they would have to bolster their appearance. When Johnnie went on tour with the early gospel groups, they would be singing in church sanctuaries, so he'd always dress to the nines. As Sam Cooke's understudy he came to understand how looking your best scored with the audience. Sam set an example, so Johnnie followed suit. That never changed. His fastidious, fashionable dress looked as if he just left the dry cleaners. But Taylor's wardrobe wasn't worn solely for the stage, he wore a suit everywhere he went. "…

Johnnie would be so sharp sometimes we just go out to maybe one of our friend's

JOHNNIE TAYLOR FOLLOWING HIS HIT,
"WHO'S MAKINGLOVE"
PHOTO COURTESY OF THE STAX MUSEUM
OF AMERICAN SOUL MUSIC

birthday parties or something you would think he was getting ready to perform."[11] Singer-songwriter Candi Staton shared, "Johnnie was always fine. He always dressed in the latest styles, the biggest cars, the limos you know, he had it all."[12] He typically wore knit suits for business and velvety outfits for the stage. Bernard Jenkins, a former bandleader, expressed the strict guidelines Taylor required of his band, "He always wanted us to have shiny shoes, you know pressed everything, you know everything there, everything had to go together it was a package."[13] A big part of Johnnie's wardrobe was his jewelry. He loved wearing bling and would always have rings on multiple fingers, some with diamonds the size of quarters. He wore gold watches, bracelets and medallions, always sporting generous amounts of glitz and glitter flashing in the spotlight. Taylor's fellow Chitlin' Circuit rider, bluesman Bobby Rush, commented on the dress of their time, "With our tailored rhinestone-covered outfits, jewelry, and well-groomed hair, it kinda put some of us Southern blues/soul artists in a trick bag. We didn't look like the "authentic blues artist," at least the way they thought the authentic blues artist should look. Guys on my circuit like Little Milton, Johnnie Taylor, Tyrone Davis, Bobby "Blue" Bland, and others ain't going onstage in a white T-shirt and blue bib overalls so folks can feel like they done seen the real Black/blues experience. Fuck that. We had earned our stripes. We didn't have to prove that we were the real thing–'cause we knew we were. And our audiences were mostly Black."[14]

Putting it into perspective, Johnnie's success as a live performer was based on his stage presence, charisma, professional delivery, comfort in front of a crowd, confidence in his abilities, singing experience from his childhood, and discipline on stage. Taylor also set himself apart by showcasing his immaculate appearance. Johnnie's daughter Sabrina summed it up, "He could sing the phone book and it was great."[15] And his son T.J. added, "He was just a total package."[16] "He lived like a superstar's supposed to live. He loved being the main man."[17]

CHAPTER 19

CHURNIN' VINYL

In the first year of the seventies, Johnnie released another album, *Rare Stamps*. Stax went over the top again, releasing an additional album in less than a year. *Raw Blues*, the fourth album, wasn't even fully cooked before *Rare Stamps* hit the market. Stax appeared to be more interested in quantity versus quality, eager to keep the cash register churning. *Stamps* was a compilation of Johnnie's bestsellers and served as a semi-camouflaged greatest hits record. With songs like "Who's Making Love," "Little Bluebird," "Just The One I've Been Looking For," and "Take Care of Your Homework," the LP showcased Johnnie's recent achievements. As for "Take Care of Your Homework," Johnnie's vocals were described as "a man lyrically unloading his personal burdens, perhaps hoping the listeners will take heed and take care of their own homework."[1] Johnnie's impressive body of work solidified a reputation for producing reliable, quality sounds. The release of the collection gave Taylor some time to tour, offering a break from the grind in the studio. In 1971, the Beverly Hills/Hollywood branch of the NAACP bestowed honors on several Stax performers for their achievements. Isaac Hayes was named Male Vocalist of the Year and Producer of the Year and Stax won Record Company of the Year. The National Association of TV and Radio Announcers (NATRA) also awarded Johnnie the honor of R&B Vocalist of the Year, and Al Bell as Man of the Year.[2]

Taylor's stablemate Isaac Hayes was once a session musician at Stax working with Johnnie. He began recording his own material, and by the early seventies, had released four albums, the first completed in 1967.

Hayes slowly grew his dedicated fan base, and in 1971 he experienced a meteoric rise when the movie *Shaft* and the accompanying soundtrack were released. The movie was filmed in Harlem and other boroughs of New York, and explored themes of salaciousness and machismo amidst the era of Black Power. The action thriller starred Richard Roundtree, who played a private detective named John Shaft. Hayes wrote the score for the soundtrack, featuring one of the most popular lines found in a song, "They say this cat Shaft is a bad mother … (Shut your mouth)." Not only was the movie successful, but Hayes won three Grammys, one of which was "Best Original Song" making Hayes the first Black man to win the award. Isaac's breathtaking rise to fame began to overshadow Johnnie's hard-earned, blue-collar efforts scratched out in the studio and on the road. Although the men were friends, "Shaft" undoubtedly prompted competition between the two behind the closed doors at Stax. Each wanted to be the main attraction.

Johnnie was suddenly forced to cancel some appearances in the middle of a regional tour. He developed some dental complications and had to interrupt his schedule of shows. It may have been at this time in 1971 when Taylor underwent dental surgery to enhance his appearance, which was always a concern for him.[3] Johnnie was able to perform at the February Auditorium Theatre in Chicago on East Congress. He headlined a line-up featuring Curtis Mayfield, Chairman of the Board, Marjorie Joseph and Syl Johnson.[4] Also in 1971, Johnnie released another album, *One Step Beyond*. Stax continued to persist in pushing out his material on an annual basis, bordering on what could have been too much of a good thing. Yet *One Step* turned out to be one his best albums to date, featuring the extremely popular "Jody's Got Your Girl and Gone." "Jody" was another one of Taylor's prophetic tales where he warned men that another guy could be at their house, and soon their girl would be gone. The song hit home for many men who heard the tune on the radio and made unexplained side-trips to the house to check on their lady. Jody became the catchphrase for a backdoor man who secretly sought out women without the knowledge of their boyfriends or husbands. Other artists began to use 'Jody' in their songs, based on lyrics from Taylor's song; and it became an expression listeners understood and part of the present-day vernacular. Johnnie's invention of the fictitious Jody gave rise to its use in some of the most unexpected places. "In the US military, cadences sung by marching or running soldiers are often dubbed "Jodys" or 'Jody calls'. "This name "Jody" refers to a recurring civilian character, the soldier's nemeses, who stays home to a perceived life of luxury. Jody stays home to drive the soldier's car, date the soldier's friend, hangs out with the soldier's friends, and eats mom's great cooking."[5] Harvey Scales, a studio collaborator with Johnnie pointed out, "That's basically telling the fellas you better hurry up and get home cause somebody else is wearing your pajamas, you know."[6] The longer "Jody" was out, the more the song expanded its popularity because of its real-life application and colloquial folklore. Johnnie, himself, rationalized the Jody phenomenon. "A lot of men bought that record, I guess they saw themselves as Jody–as a player with a lot of money who could get lots of women, even their best friend's girl."[7] Johnnie's son Anthony said, tongue-in-cheek, "You know he probably meant to say Johnnie got your girl and gone. But it probably wasn't best to use his own name in there so he's kept the Jody in there."[8]

Also found on the album are favorites like "I Don't Want to Lose You, Parts 1 and 2" written by Melvin Davis and Van McCoy, a songwriter, producer and arranger who recorded the famous, "The Hustle", a disco-era instrumental. Johnnie's double-edged song began with a chanting dialogue asking his lover to listen. Then he told the story of a trip he made to the doctor because of an aching heart. The physician expressed that it was no heart attack, but a love attack. The pulsating bass lines channeled Johnnie's slow entrance into the song asking his lover for another chance. "Don't Take My Sunshine" and "A Fool Like Me" were honorable mentions and quality tunes in their own right. Overall, *One Step Beyond* was a classic record, surpassing previous efforts. The *Chicago Tribune* weighed in, "Other notable releases include Johnnie Taylor's *One Step Beyond* [Stax]. A six-minute version of "Time After Time" opens this platter with an extended display of Taylor's husky-mellow vocals laid over skillful Muscle Shoals sidemen. The extended play, backed by a prominent strings section, smacks of the psychedelic soul sound that Isaac Hayes has turned into a bundle of loot under the label "hot buttered soul." Perhaps the influence of Hayes' success has pervaded the rest of the Stax lineup."[9]

CHAPTER 20

The year 1972 marked the seventh anniversary of the Watts Riots in L.A. Wattstax, "The African American Woodstock" as some called it, would be organized to commemorate the loss of life, a response to police brutality and the possible turning point in racial equity. Based on riot history, Stax decided to organize an outdoor music festival. Plans were to feature the label's artists which would not only honor the occasion, but promote its bevy of Memphis recording stars to the West Coast. "It was a celebration of the African-American experience and a testament to the transformative power of music."[1] Al Bell and his staff, supported by the event sponsor Schlitz Beer, secured the venue and organized the festival, planning the details for every phase of the outdoor exhibition. The name Wattstax was cleverly formulated to include 'Watts,' the neighborhood being celebrated and 'Stax,' the record label name. The date was set for August 20, and the event would be held in the cavernous Los Angeles Memorial Coliseum. When passing the Coliseum that morning, "Al saw all those empty seats and wondered how they could possibly fill it up. But promotion was his specialty. The morning kicked off with a parade through Watts, Stax stars riding in open Cadillac convertibles, waving and basking in the California clime, so unlike the swamp back home. Isaac was the grand marshal (it was his thirtieth birthday). He wore an African striped tunic, riding alongside Johnnie Taylor, Luther Ingram and David Porter."[2] The Wattstax lineup was impressive, including The Staple Singers, Eddie Floyd, Albert King, Carla Thomas, The Bar-Kays, Rufus Thomas, The Soul Children and the indomitable Isaac Hayes.

Initially scheduled to perform, Taylor chose not to participate. The official version of why J.T. didn't play was due to the recurring delays from earlier performances that continually pushed the schedule back throughout the evening. Word circulated there was not enough time for Johnnie to perform. "The day had drawn well into the night before the show's finale. There was disappointment backstage as the set changes and other delays inherent in such a massive event caused the cancellation of several key acts. Luther Ingram, Johnnie Taylor, The Emotions, Mel & Tim, and Little Milton all were ready and willing and present but there were not enough minutes in the day. Filming of some was rescheduled. Anticipation was high as MC Rev. Jesse Jackson revved up the crowd for the climax."[3]

However, sources close to Taylor said the real story was that Johnnie was told to take the stage before Isaac Hayes who had been chosen to close the show. Although Johnnie was the label's most successful artist, Isaac was chosen to be the final act. Hayes was riding high from the fame generated by his movie *Shaft* along with his award-winning soundtrack. Stax had no other choice but to climb on his white-hot popularity and insert Hayes into the clean-up role. It was also Isaac's birthday. Johnnie was incensed, having been assured he would be the one to close the show. His frustration was understandable, Isaac had been only a session musician for Taylor in the early days at Stax. In Johnnie's mind, Isaac was usurping his position as the label's superstar. Johnnie sold thousands of Stax records long before Isaac Hayes had a hit, so he had a legitimate beef with Bell and the organizers. Rodgers Redding shared this about Johnnie and Wattstax: "I remember him [Johnnie] telling me once, he said that your brother's [Otis] gone. The only two people I let close the show behind me is, Aretha Franklin and Bobby Bland."[4]

<small>PHOTO COURTESY OF GREGORY M. HASTY</small>

The seven-hour Stax event came off without a hitch, save Johnnie's exasperation. Al Bell was successful in filling the stadium, over 110,000 spectators arrived to experience the all-day show. The music festival was later made into a film and was released the following year. Even though Taylor wasn't part of the Wattstax line-up, he did make it onto the documentary directed by Mel Stuart. A month after the festival, Johnnie had a gig at the Summit Theater in Los Angeles. He performed in the "red velvety club, and he's owning the place, with the camera tight on him."[5] Johnnie's hit, "Jody's Got Your Girl and Gone," was filmed at the show. The song was incorporated into the movie, even though he didn't make an appearance at Wattstax. This was an indication that Stax included his performance in the film to placate Johnnie and his fans. A month after Wattstax, in September 1972, Johnnie performed at Jessie Jackson's annual PUSH (People United to Serve Humanity)

Expo at Chicago's International Amphitheater. PUSH attracted as many as a million visitors to the expo and raised in excess of $500,000. The show supported initiatives for hiring and promoting Black employees and encouraging the use of Black suppliers. Taylor was joined by Isaac Hayes, the Staple Singers, and Luther Ingram, all of whom, donated their standard paycheck to the cause.[6]

Taylor continued to tour, tracking areas wherever his fanbase was concentrated. Because of his days as a Soul Stirrer, Johnnie would always spend significant time in Chicago. One such date was the Super Soul Bowl in January of '72. The venue was at the historic Arie Crown Theatre on Lake Shore Drive. The theater could seat as many as 5,000 concertgoers and was adjacent to the McCormick Place Convention Center. He had two performances and shared the stage with Al Green, The Chi-lites, Delfonics, Otis Clay and Rufus Thomas.[7] *Tailored in Silk* was Johnnie's seventh album, released in 1973. His two years off from recording gave him renewed energy to make a hit record. It was evident in the results. The album revealed how Taylor had matured as an artist, and also allowed time for his other LPs to season within his circle of fans. His daughter Sabrina commented, "I've had promoters tell me he's changed, he's a lot calmer. And my response would be because he has the one he loves and trusts, [and] is gonna look out for him,"[8] Songs on the album showed a shift from Johnnie's customary stories about who's cheatin' who, and settled more into the sedate, enlightened character of a wiser, smarter middle-aged man. He was now thirty-eight, married to Geri and had settled into his cozy permanent life in Oak Cliff. Geri and Johnnie were expecting their second child, who would be named LaTasha. Before she was born, Johnnie beamed, "She wants a girl, but it doesn't matter to me," he laughs. "I'll take what I can get."[9] The year before, he and Geri brought their son Jonathan into the fold. The newborns added stability and a more balanced life between he and Geri. Family life appeared to finally domesticate the feral road traveler. The song "Cheaper to Keep Her," is a good example, where Johnnie admitted the revolving door of lovers may seem attractive, but how much easier was it to keep a good woman … and cheaper. The composition's sage advice, along with a taste of humor directed to male listeners, is evidence of Johnnie's effort to impart more responsible life lessons. He also mentioned leaving behind five children and having to pay alimony, perhaps expressing some measure of guilt from his own narrative. The songs were primarily down-tempo renditions that took a page from the rhythm and blues discipline and pioneering his groundbreaking shift into pure soul. The album featured a hard-core, gut-busting blues ditty, called "Doing My Own Thing," produced by Don Davis. The cut served as the only song on the LP that departed from the overall vibe Taylor maintained throughout *Tailored*. Beyond other treasures on the record, like "Starting All Over Again," "One Thing Wrong with My Woman," and "I Can Read Between the Lines," "I Believe in You (You Believe in Me)" stood out as an enduring anthem. The tune "was the first record on which Don Davis constructed the track via layered riffs instead of functional chord changes. Davis referred to this as the 'monolithic approach.' The net result was a more melodic, Sam Cooke-influenced Johnnie Taylor."[10] The lyrics mention faith and trust in his lover, revealing a side of Johnnie unseen to that point. It's evident he sang the song for Geri. "In 1965, songwriter Don Davis began writing "I Believe in You" when he discovered he was two songs short while working on one of Johnnie Taylor's albums. It became one of the songs that would find its way on *Taylored in Silk* in 1973."[11] It was an important time in Johnnie's life, and he was admitting how important it is to support and nourish your wife and partner through thick and thin. Johnnie and Geri had just delivered their first child Jonathan that year and their lives were to change now that a newborn had joined the household. The sweet melody with such heartfelt lyrics serves as a memorable guidepost for those who grew up hearing this beautiful arrangement. "I Believe in You" may be the most underrated song Taylor had ever produced even when compared with smash hits like "Who's Making Love" and others. The song is forever enduring and should remain relevant indefinitely. "I Believe in You" duly earned gold record status, certified in 1973. "That was a pure love song and a beautiful melody. And Johnnie sang it, Johnnie said it, Johnnie told it."[12]

CHAPTER 21

PLAYIN' THE LAST HAND

Johnnie's life took a bittersweet turn in 1973. He had just released *Tailored in Silk*, had his second child LaTasha, and was living a charmed, comfortable life in Big D. His pristine lifestyle was abruptly interrupted when his mother, Ida Mae Jackson suddenly passed away. Johnnie's most important lifeline that connected him to his childhood, upbringing, and family lineage had departed. The sadness had a profound effect on Taylor, and he sought the best ways to honor Ida Mae for her positive influence on his life. Johnnie saw to it that she was interred in a comfortable resting place at Forest Hill Calvary Cemetery in Kansas City. He had her remains placed in a granite-clad niche in the tranquil Forest Hill mausoleum as a final resting place. Johnnie's son, T.J. Hooker recalls the day of the funeral, "It was a sad day when my dad finally came into town. You could tell he was a different person than what I ever met before the service." After the funeral, "Me, my dad and my brother Anthony were upstairs getting acquainted at Uncle Willie's house after the service. I remembered we stayed up all night and talked. We talked about life and love."[1]

Later that year, Johnnie had the opportunity to perform for WFLD-TV's "Merv Griffin Presents Isaac Hayes," also known as "Isaac Hayes and the Stax Organization Presenting the Memphis Sound," which was taped at Caesar's Palace in Las Vegas. The Fox affiliate aired the program which documented over 200 years of Black history. The program featured Albert King, Carla Thomas, The Emotions, Luther Ingram, the Staple Singers, and Johnnie, with Isaac Hayes as the MC. Hayes was still floating on the success of *Shaft* and was the network's choice for heading up the special program. Once again Taylor found himself looking up to see Isaac Hayes in the spotlight.[2]

Tragedies seemed to define Johnnie's life. Early on his dad and mom left and he was sent to live with his grandmother. In the years that followed he accidentally ran over a little girl, his best friend was murdered, he lost his recording contract, then his mom passed away. His phenomenal success with Stax was the single most positive experience Johnnie enjoyed after the many setbacks and harsh realities of life. Stax Records took him beyond his wildest expectations. He was now a bona-fide, legitimate star and his new-found fame led to international acclaim. Johnnie was held in high esteem by his peers, had forged a loyal fan base from coast to coast and had become one of the foremost entertainers in the music business. The dependable foundation he built at Stax helped Taylor chart a course to become an R&B legend. Then it happened. Stax Records folded.

Stax and its demise began over disputes with Columbia Records. The circumstances warrant a look-back at the events that unfolded. Columbia Records was founded in 1929 and was originally called the American Record Corporation. It was acquired by Columbia Broadcasting System in 1938 and was renamed the Columbia Recording Corporation. In 1966, the company reorganized to become CBS Records. The corporation was sold to Sony in the early nineties. The first signs of a crack in the infrastructure of Stax were tied to getting their product to market. Columbia/CBS Records, whom Stax used as a distribution partner, had received large quantities of records from the Memphis outfit. For whatever reason, CBS declined to deliver the albums to the marketplace. One could speculate why Columbia refused to push the merchandise to market, but the end result was a significant backlog of vinyl being returned to Stax. This was a huge blow. Not only did CBS return merchandise that was once considered sold, they withheld 40 percent of what was owed to Stax for the returns. It was obvious Columbia and Stax "could never get on the same page,"[3] asserted Stax owner Jim Stewart, who went on, "From the beginning of the argument over who would control the branch distributors, record sales started dropping."[4] Following this grave disappointment, another distributor, Polydor Records decided to forgo the renewal of their existing European distribution contract. During the period, energy prices soared and Stax, who relied on petroleum and its by-products for operations, began to feel the pinch. As expenses rose and their music wasn't being distributed, Stax's cash flow began to evaporate. The unfortunate by-line of the Stax financial problem would be that the label never stopped recording top-rate music. The distribution issues however resulted in making it harder for buyers to obtain their product. Added to the company's woes was the watchful eye of the feds who were beginning to monitor payola infractions and had also begun to scrutinize Stax's tax returns.[5]

One of Stax's local Memphis distributors noted they were unable to get Stax products "almost from the day the Columbia deal began," which added insight to Stax's inability to disentangle itself from Columbia's necktie. "We couldn't buy the records to distribute them. It was clear Columba was trying to put Stax out of business."[6] Matters got worse when Columbia's alleged backlog of Stax music resulted in the CBS powerhouse withholding $1.3 million owed to Stax. Meanwhile Stax's Memphis lender, Union Planters Bank, had been practicing liberal lending practices and came under fire from the Securities and Exchange Commission and banking regulators. Besides issuing non-collateralized loans, the bank was being investigated for kickbacks and embezzlement. Stax was one of Planters' largest lending customers. As a result, Planters fell under heavy pressure to accelerate the Stax loan repayments due to the risk the bank faced without collateral. Planter's poorly managed loan portfolio subsequently attracted the attention of bank examiners who came knocking on the door. This led to their bank president resigning.[7]

The avalanche of financial woes led to Stax delaying payments to vendors, employee's payroll, and royalty payments to artists. Lawsuits followed. This included litigation initiated by Isaac Hayes who sued Stax for $5.3 million in a federal civil suit for amounts owed to him. In an unending barrage of misfortune, Columbia sued Stax, accusing the company of violating their distribution agreement. Stax countersued. Stax's litigation contended that Columbia had breached its distribution agreement in an attempt to force Stax out of business. A heated discussion between the company leaders ensued. During a contentious meeting between the two companies, Al Bell threatened World War III on Columbia. Unfortunately for Stax, the CBS corporate giant began to exert its wrath on the smaller Memphis company. Bell shared insight: "After that, I grew to appreciate the power of a corporation like CBS. I didn't realize that they could reach into offices that one would never have thought they could reach into. And they cut off the spigot. They said, 'We don't owe you any money because here's the product that didn't sell that we had in our warehouse.' Several eighteen-wheelers came back to where we housed our goods, returning a substantial portion of all the inventory they had purchased on the same skids they were shipped out on. No more cash flow. We couldn't pay many of our artists and other obligations. They were knocking us to our knees, breaking our back."[8]

At this point, Stax found its company in dire straits. Planters' new leadership became more aggressive and called the Stax loans. Stax defaulted. Without the ability to pay, Union Planters took control of the Stax crown jewel, the publishing company. In a flurry of other developments, Stax payroll checks bounced leaving employees in a lurch. The former Union Planter banker under investigation was indicted on charges of embezzlement. RCA then sued Stax when Stax was unable to pay for record blanks used in their pressing plant. An out-of-court settlement was eventually reached between Stax and Columbia which temporarily eased the pressure from the record giant, but Stax was still bleeding profusely. In a desperate attempt to right the ship, Al and Stax management approached King Faisal of Saudi Arabia with hopes of securing a last-minute investor to rescue the failing company. The king was very interested in exploring the opportunity so Al and his attorney flew to Saudi Arabia in hopes of consummating the deal. Unfortunately Faisal was assassinated by his nephew while at his home on March 25, 1975, before agreements could be executed. The deal fizzled.[9] Bad news didn't end there. Al Bell was charged in a federal grand jury indictment on fourteen-counts of conspiracy to obtain fraudulent loans from Union Planters. UP bank manager Joe Harwell was charged with taking kickbacks and bribes as well as an all-expense-paid trip to L.A. for the Wattstax movie premier. Amidst the fracas, the IRS continued its investigation implicating Stax employees who were allegedly distributing payola to radio stations. The foreboding demise of Stax was punctuated in mid-December, when three creditors filed a petition sending Stax into involuntary bankruptcy.[10] During the ensuing chaos, the company was closed and Al Bell escorted out of the building by gunpoint. Bell, however, was successful in his defense and was acquitted of all the charges, but the damage to his reputation was irreparable. Thus, the Stax era had officially ended and as a result, Johnnie was left without a record deal for the second time in ten years.

Johnnie's last album recorded at Stax was *Super Taylor*, issued in 1974. The initial track featured "It's September." The song was an upbeat number that curiously belied the lyrical message of a departed lover who was called back home for the holidays. The forlorn lyrical message is supported by an easy cadence, friendly rhythm, and equates to a feel-good sound written by Irish folk musician, Dennis Gilmore. "Try Me Tonight," another happy-go-lucky tune, took Don Davis' penned song surrounded by Johnnie's relaxed and appealing tenor, which materialized into an exceedingly pleasurable melody. Other cuts deserving acknowledgement are "Darling I Love You" and "Just One Moment." The collection of new material on *Super Taylor* was clear evidence of a more accomplished Johnnie Taylor, especially with Don Davis at the helm. It was evident the two, along with the studio musicians and engineers had arrived at a high threshold of professionalism and musical integrity. Johnnie was at the top of his game. As life lessons tend to teach, just when you start to get things right, things change. The team at Stax, who Johnnie had grown so attached to, was now splintered by the demise of their label. As it turned out, Taylor was Stax's last charting artist when he released "Try Me Tonight." The tune only made it to number 51 on the R&B charts, but provided Stax-a much needed stream of revenue that had virtually trickled to a halt. On August 15, 1975, Stax agreed to tender Johnnie's contract after he demanded it be terminated. This allowed him to sign with Columbia.[11] With all the success at Stax in the rearview mirror, Johnnie seized on the new opportunity, but was forced to start over once again.

CHAPTER 22

HOME SWEET HOMEY

In 1975, Taylor attended his daughter Sabrina's cotillion, where she was formally presented to society. Even though she had lived the majority of her life without Johnnie, when Sabrina turned sixteen, he joined the family to celebrate the momentous occasion. J.T. had remarried and took up residence in Dallas. Even so, he didn't hesitate to be involved with his daughter's coming out ceremony in Chicago. He and his first wife, Harriet were on good terms and planned to celebrate Sabrina together along with friends and family. This event shed some insight on Johnnie's character. Taylor wanted to treat all of his children equally he told *Jet Magazine*. Her cotillion was something he felt any parent with a girl Sabrina's age should do, "if they are in a position to do it," he declared. About being a good dad said, "You can be just as good a father with this type of work, maybe better. There is no different context because I'm an entertainer. I don't think that has anything to do with it. It's just the love you have for your offspring." To Johnnie, this love was essential in protecting his children's future. Taylor told *Jet Magazine* he had established trust funds for the kids. "That was taken care of a long time ago," he mentioned. "All they have to decide is whether they want to use it for education or not." Taylor goes on, "See I found there are three things you can't buy, time, health and experience. It doesn't matter how you try to talk to your children. They must live their own lives. You are only there as a guide to instill in them the better things and make an example of yourself. Then they must go their own ways." Insightful advice, but his words sound a lot like the old adage, 'live like I say, not like I do'. Even Johnnie's best intentions couldn't escape the hypocrisy of saying one thing and doing another. His son, Anthony Arnold, now deceased, spoke of his dad in 2018, "He was torn between knowing what was right then knowing what's wrong, and doing the latter."[1]

About his daughter growing into womanhood, Johnnie remarked, "I wouldn't be in favor of her, at her age, being serious (with boys). But I think she has plenty of time to think of becoming serious. I would rather have her think in terms of a lot of fellows, to meet them and just look around." He shares his thoughts about Sabrina entering into a serious relationship, "I would take it like anything else," he expressed. "I'm not used to thinking of her in that way yet. But, after all, they do grow up; they don't remain babies. I would just like to know that he had the right thing in mind as far as she was concerned."[2] On one hand, these statements reveal a mature, paternal perspective, but on the other it was common knowledge Johnnie had romantic relationships with fifteen-and sixteen-year olds and got them pregnant.

Young, inexperienced adults tend to make mistakes, and perhaps Johnnie used the evils of his past to guide his children. "I give them the benefit of my experience and I try to break it down to where they can understand it, and then they think it over for themselves. I like for them to have their own minds,"[3] Johnnie was surprisingly noncommittal about his faith, "But I don't advise them about religion. No one told me what religion to follow," although he did follow his father's footsteps into the Baptist ministry. Of course, Taylor dropped his robes and pulpit for tuxedos and microphones more than 10 years ago."[4] Sabrina spoke about Johnnie's constant traveling before and after her parents were divorced and recalled "wanting to be with him like other girls and their fathers. I'd wish he'd be home when I got there." She was regretful when thinking about her friends having fathers in their lives, they'd say, "my father and I did this when we went to this place' and 'we do that when he comes home,'" which made Sabrina feel left out. She added, "It's just the fact that I can't do that when I come home." Given Johnnie's hectic schedule and the demands on his time, the entertainer still made an effort to be there for his daughter. Celebrating her cotillion was an indication of this commitment. He also made himself available when Sabrina called, "I get disgusted about problems in school. I write him when I have a whole lot to say." According to Sabrina, they would stay in touch by phone at least once a week. Even though Johnnie didn't express it earlier, as the interview with *Jet* came to a close, he quoted scripture from the Gospel of Luke, 6:31. Talking of his children, he recommended, "Keep a strong belief in God and do unto others as you would have them do unto you."[5]

Taylor had become a very successful entertainer by this time and had earned substantial sums of money from his live shows and record sales. Further insight into Johnnie's personal philosophy on wealth was reported in 1973, again by *Jet Magazine*, "If you get up in the morning and eat garbage, you're gonna be sick at your stomach." Likewise, if you feed your mind negative thoughts, you're gonna poison your mind. A lot of being rich depends on your attitudes. Richness is a state of mind." Johnnie grew up with very little and was forced to scuffle and scrap to gain success, "Why shouldn't Blacks want the good things? They've never been able to have them before now." In a later edition of *Jet*, Johnnie's financial success became a topic. "He became very wealthy in short order and sported the accouterments of that wealth: a $6,000 fur coat, a $14,000 sports car (Excalibur), big diamond rings, jeweled watches and took out a $100,000 insurance policy on

JOHNNIE TAYLOR

Johnnie at His Best
Photo Courtesy of Stax Museum
of American Soul Music

himself so that 'my kids will be protected if something happens to me.'" He doesn't want them to experience the poverty and want he suffered as a youngster. So he works hard to pass on security to them."[6]

Johnnie's second wife, Geri gave insight about his married life in Dallas, "He was a homebody a lot of the times especially in the early years. You know he'd come home and read a lot. The first thing he would do, he would come home and rest, and he would read for about three days."[7] His daughter and youngest child LaTasha in Dallas, shared her memories, "He loved to clean the pool, it was like a tranquil thing for him to clean the pool. We had a great backyard and had great birthday parties and great 4th of Julys; and when he was around he was on that barbeque, hooking it up." LaTasha elaborated further, "We'd take the Winnebago out to the lake, we'd go fishing, we would take family vacations, we could be normal sort of 'ish' people without it being so nuts all the time." Others provided a glimpse of Johnnie's identity and life away from show business; "He loved his home, loved his kids, you know he had his faults but he had a good heart," said his son Jonathan.[8] His oldest son Anthony added, "The personal side of him and his personal relationship with his wife irregardless of what might have happened on the road, he believed in her and she believed in him."[9]

The definition of a paranoid personality disorder is: a mental health condition marked by a pattern of distrust and suspicion of others without adequate reason to be suspicious. People with PPD are always on guard, believing that others are constantly trying to cheat, harm or threaten them.[10] Johnnie exhibited some of these traits. He called into question people's motives and treated those he didn't know with judicious doubt. The entertainment business attracted individuals who were always looking for a way to borrow, steal, mooch or leech their way into a performer's life. Singers and musicians like Taylor were the head of the snake, keeper of the abundance and the target for plunder. Johnnie undoubtedly faced these encounters and his natural tendency was to safeguard his money and protect himself from being hoodwinked. His attitude was a result of the business he was in. Taylor was frugal, cautious and watched his back at all times. Johnnie "dedicated himself to maintaining a relatively low profile around the media. Mr. Taylor did most of his speaking on stage ...,"[11] and "is reluctant to talk about his personal life and he rarely grants interviews. It's an attitude he developed years ago to create a certain mystique, Black male artists didn't let their fans know they were married. The artists were also generally distrustful of the press."[12] When Taylor did grant interviews: "He answers questions tersely but without evasion, like a man used to being in charge."[13] Stax's publicist Deanie Parker added, "I took him to Chicago to meet with the *Chicago Sun-Times* and other media," she remembered. "He had not had any kind of organized media effort before. I got a suite in the Continental Plaza on Michigan Boulevard. I got the accommodations that were befitting his being a star and for him to feel comfortable dealing with the media. This was new to Johnnie. He was not at ease doing this. He was ill at ease. He wanted to be at his very best, and it was my role to help the artists think in advance about some questions that they might be asked so that they could respond in a way that was a marketable answer, but also an honest answer. He did quite well, but as soon as those interviews were done, he invited me to join him and friends picked him up. We went over to the South Side of Chicago where his friends–the everyday people–had killed the fatted calf. He pulled his hat and coat off, and he was very much at home with the guys."[14] Since Sam Cooke shaped a good deal of Johnnie's career, he's had to answer his fair share of questions about his mentor. Johnnie grew tired of talking about the effect Sam had in shaping his future. A *Texas Monthly* reporter wrote, " ...Taylor quickly grows impatient talking about him [Cooke] today."[15]

CHAPTER 23

DEVIL'S DISCO

J.T. began touring and promoting his latest effort, *Super Taylor*. He continued his workman-like ethic, meeting fans, performing and selling his talent. This part of the job, he had always managed effectively. One such stop was his old stomping grounds in Chicago where he played two performances at the Soul Bowl. Elsewhere, two thousand miles away on the West Coast, Columbia/CBS Records was finally introduced to the soul and R&B world. They snatched up former Stax artists who were searching for a replacement label. Columbia picked up wayward performers such as The Emotions, The Soul Children, and their most notable signing–Johnnie Taylor. At first, J.T. went through an adjustment joining a corporate titan like Columbia/CBS. There was a learning curve Johnnie had to negotiate and with the help of producer Don Davis, who was also hired by Columbia, Johnnie got down to business and worked on new material.

Davis' production contract with Stax expired in May of 1973. He had decided to leave the company after many successful years producing a slew of hit records. He and Stax leader Al Bell had an acrimonious parting which led to litigation. The controversy began when The Dramatics' LP, *The Devil Is Dope* was in the can and Davis had yet to deliver the masters to the company. This led to Stax suing Davis for alleged over-advances and demanding that he pay back the amounts owed and return The Dramatics' masters. They eventually settled out of court, and the masters were returned with one stipulation: that Davis could continue to produce Johnnie.[1] He and Taylor reconnected at Columbia around the same time that a dramatic shift was occurring in the music world. The advent of disco music was sweeping the country, and the craze took the listeners into uncharted territory. Caught up in the torrent were soul and R&B artists who looked for ways to capitalize on the rage and sell records. Disco was ignited from music of the Bee Gees and John Travolta's *Saturday Night Fever*. Along with the music, new, fresh dance styles surfaced, followed by videos, new fashion statements and disco clubs. Dance fever took the country by storm. R&B acts such as Earth Wind and Fire, The O'Jays, Donna Summer, Chic, Sister Sledge and others bolstered the movement within the Black listening community. Johnnie studied the dynamic landscape and did what he had done time and time again and capitalized on an opportunity.

Harvey Scales, was another native Arkansan who spent time as a producer, singer, and songwriter in Milwaukee. Scales made a name for himself in the R&B arena, and was a contributor with Don Davis in what would become a life-changing event. Scales and Davis had worked together before and Scales knew Davis was always seeking new material. Harvey brought a composition to him entitled, "Disco Baby" to get his opinion. Davis liked the song, although he changed the lyrics. Davis drew his inspiration from observing an audience captivated by an African dancer's moves at a club in Spain. Afterwards he heard The Impressions' song, "Gypsy Woman," then came up with a catchy tagline to integrate with his disco-themed song. "Disco Lady" was the result. "Disco Lady" was Johnnie's first single at Columbia and his team wanted to produce something special so he could get off to an impressive start. Johnnie knew his work was cut out for him at Columbia and mentioned in retrospect, "When I was with Columbia, they had 300 other artists. If you didn't make any noise right off the bat, they forgot about you."[2]

An excited Davis approached Johnnie, "I got you a smash," and Taylor countered, "You tell me that all the time."[3] But Johnnie was savvy enough to give Davis a listen. Harvey Scales had a clear recollection of talking with Johnnie about "Disco Lady." He said, "When I first wrote the song, it was called 'Shake it up, Shake it down.' When Johnnie heard it he replied, yeah … it's alright, but I don't know about that 'Shake it up' and 'Shake it down' stuff man. Give me something to sing."[4] L.C. Cooke recalled Johnnie's reaction to first hearing the tune. "I think that was one of Johnnie's best songs. But you know what, he didn't like the song, he didn't like the song–period."[5] His producer brought in bassist, Bootsy Collins and other members of George Clinton's group Parliament-Funkadelic. Also Bernie Worrell was on keys, Glenn Coins on guitar with vocalists Thelma Hopkins (formerly of Tony Orlando and Dawn) and studio singers from the group Brandy. David Van DePitte arranged the horns, and the album was recorded at Davis' preferred studio, United Sound Studios in Detroit. Taylor turned out to be the perfect artist to carry out the dialogue of the song, which was funky, danceable and had an element of not-so-subliminal sexual innuendos. As mentioned by L.C., Johnnie didn't like the song at first; he didn't feel it was him. Taylor told Davis, "my voice is too low, the record doesn't suit me, and I think we need to go with something else." Later Johnnie expressed his concerns again with the producer, "It's a terrible mix. I can't imagine why you want to release it."[6] Don Davis was the ultimate devil's advocate, to provide ideas and opportunities that may otherwise be overlooked. He was someone who could see the big picture, latch onto developing trends, and objectively explore material that could produce a hit record. The Davis, Scales and Vance "Disco Lady" became the hit of a lifetime for Johnnie. "Disco Lady" was recorded in part at the Sundance Studios in Dallas. As it turns out parts of the song were recorded in studios all over the country and the tapes were sent to Taylor in Dallas so he could add his vocals to it."[7]

"A year earlier, Donna Summer's erotic 'Love to Love You, Baby' pushed disco to the center of America's pop culture. In 1976, Diana Ross entered the disco fray with her 'Love Hangover,' a decided hit. Other sixties artists, like Johnnie Taylor, jumped on the bandwagon. Taylor's smoldering 'Disco Lady,' for example, is one of the great tracks in all rhythm and blues."[8]

An interesting sidebar about "Disco Lady" was shared by David Washington, radio host and music critic: "Columbia actually released "Disco Lady" prematurely. They didn't intend to get it out to the market when it did, but didn't stop it in time."[9] Everyone connected with the "Disco Lady" creation assumed the song would be a success, but no one had any idea of the magnitude of its impact. Disco music had only been an item for a year, and Johnnie was able to capitalize on its momentum.

"Disco Lady" generated more excitement around the movement. Taylor's single was to become the first Hot 100 chart-topper with the word "disco" in its title. "Disco Lady" was soon to become a megaton hit both on Pop and R&B charts. The song held for four weeks at number 1 on the Hot 100 and six weeks at the top of the R&B charts.[10] For music connoisseurs, it became obvious Johnnie's disco song had appealed to White listeners' in equal proportion to African American soul and R&B followers. This broadened his audience. The Record Industry Association of America (RIAA) grants awards for singles and albums of distinction when certain sales thresholds are met. To qualify as a gold record, sales must surpass 500,000. The industry had never experienced sales any greater than this number, so when sales of "Disco Lady" surpassed the unprecedented one-million mark, the Association's brain trust was forced to create a higher level of achievement. The result was to establish a category for record sales of more than a million records. The new classification would be called a platinum record. Johnnie Taylor's "Disco Lady" went platinum and crushed all historical sales records. This forced the RIAA to contend with his revolutionary accomplishment. After the sales volume was tallied, "Disco Lady" would be crowned double platinum, selling over two million copies. The song was also the best-selling record in Columbia's history.[11] As a soul and R&B performer, Taylor was somewhat embarrassed being associated with the disco movement. He didn't want to be seen as a sell-out, portraying the image of a hostage to the almighty dollar. "A lot of people thought it was disco," Taylor quipped. "But it was not a disco tune. We were just talking about disco."[12] True, it really wasn't a disco song, but if it looked like disco, sounded like disco and felt like disco, then it was disco. Johnnie would have been the first to admit he didn't care how it was categorized. If it was bringing in that kind of sales revenue, it could be called whatever the critics desired. An image materializes of Columbia executives sitting around the conference room table, giddy, patting themselves on the back, taking credit for bringing over Johnnie from Stax. They would gush about how R&B and disco would be the label's future and how Johnnie Taylor was their new-found prodigy. Furthermore, when a band or artist is successful selling music, they're congratulated by management, but the next words that usually followed are, "can you do it again?" Johnnie had this to say about the success of "Disco Lady," "I've been recording for 20-some years. You build up quite a following after so long, and I think when you get a 'Disco Lady,' it just kind of pushes you over the top. Now a guy who comes along with his only hit record–you never hear of him before and you never hear of him afterwards–that's kind of a different ballgame. I think." Taylor continued, "You've got to have more than just a record going for you. The public's kind of fickle, and with the number of records released in one day, you can get lost–especially if you don't establish yourself in the first place. And one record doesn't establish you. I don't care how big it is."[13] The song carried with it plenty of sexual implications. About this, Johnnie responded casually, "I never thought about the sex overtones until someone mentioned them. And this is when it dawned on me that people were really looking at the sexual aspects of it. And I'm glad I didn't think about it when I was cutting the record because I would probably have overdone it by trying to add the sex in it. But by not being aware of it, there was just enough sex in it to get people interested."[14] All respect to Johnnie, but it's hard to believe he wasn't aware of the provocative lyrics when he recorded the song.

About the recording of "Disco Lady," Johnnie recalled, "'Disco Lady' was sent to my producer, who is Don Davis out in San Francisco. I thought the tune had great possibilities, but we did the tune twelve times at the session, and at first, I didn't like it too much. And they can always tell when I have a hit if I don't think too much of the song. Any song I don't like is a hit. If I like it, it's mediocre. But if I don't like it, everybody knows it's a smash. I didn't like 'I Believe in You' and that sold a million and a half copies." He went on to explain, "I overdub all my songs," he noted, "We'll cut the tracks at Muscle Shoals. We might put the strings on in Detroit and we might put the horns on in Memphis. See you might have a good rhythm section in Muscle Shoals, but the horns might not be too hot. You might have a heck of a horn section in Memphis, but the strings might be better in Detroit. So we just pick the best of the lot. And because you might not be able to get the sound you want in one place, we take the tapes to all the different studios."[15] The runaway hit "Disco Lady" was honored with a Grammy nomination for Best Male R&B Vocal Performance at the 19th annual awards. Taylor's fellow musician, Bobby Rush remarked, "We were labelmates and good friends and entertainers that shared the stage many, many times, in many, many places. I think Johnnie Taylor is an image that we all like to have because he came through in a big way through the disco thing. He came up with a song called "Disco Lady" when entertainers, blues acts, or R&B acts weren't doing very well or doing very much."[16] After "Disco Lady" had begun its ascension and broke sales records "it was reported that Columbia executive Bruce Lundvall sent crates of Dom Perignon to Taylor, who drank some and took a bath in what was left."[17] "Disco Lady" was also popular enough to become a number 6 hit in New Zealand, a number 14 hit in Canada, and a number 42 hit in Australia."[18]

The iconic song made a huge impact on Johnnie's future as explained by Gregg A. Smith, "That kept him working where a lot of other artists couldn't work, so he became part of the discotheque movement."[19] Rodgers Redding saw it the same way. "He was blessed because most steady soul singers, most of them just faded away, you know, after disco came in."[20]

"Disco Lady" would be a blessing and a curse as the future would reveal. The song helped Johnnie achieve the pinnacle of success he had been searching for all his life. However, Alan Walden, familiar with the 'what-have-you-done-for-me-lately' world of the record business, observed. "When you bring in a monstrous hit like that the record company gets to where they expect you to do it again, again and again."[21] For a time, Johnnie Taylor had arrived in the major leagues and had hit one out of the ballpark. However, not all fans were happy about Johnnie's success with "Disco Lady," "I don't see how God can get any praise out of anybody singing 'Disco Lady,'" grumbled Helen Gibbs, a salesclerk who was asked about her feelings regarding "Disco Lady." "That's mockery to God, doing these songs and makin' these kinds of songs and you know what they're saying. Even Al Green needs to hang it up. He's a reverend, but he goes out and sings and does all this stuff, and I don't go along with that. They have dancers and stuff in his church, and that's the work of the devil. I would be scared."[22] Helen proved the point made earlier about how gospel listeners felt about R&B, disco, or for that matter, any other secular music. Johnnie responded to similar comments made by churchgoers, "If a guy drives a truck, nobody asks him if he believes in God because he runs a red light. My belief in God, I don't think has anything to do with what I do for a living."[23] After the success of "Disco Lady," Johnnie commented on the massive hit, "Having a good record is nice, but I would hate to base my career on how big my last record was. I'm seasoned enough to know 'Disco Ladies' don't come every day, Taylor admitted. "I'd like to continue recording good music. I would like to strive for another 'Disco Lady.' But I'm a realist. I know to cut another 'Disco Lady' back-to-back would be phenomenal." He went on, "I'm concentrating on the day when I don't have to be as big as my last record. I'm concentrating on becoming a personality. It's great to have a record, but you have to work year-round and it's not guaranteed that you're always going to have a hit record. So, you need to think in terms of becoming the type showman that, whether you have a record or not, you have a built-in audience that's going to support what you do."[24]

The "Disco Lady" 45 was released into the market as a coming attraction for his new album *Eargasm*. On the back cover of the album, Johnnie defined "eargasm" to mean "an astonishing unexpected aural response." Many of the numbers on the album were up tempo, reflecting the effect disco had on what Johnnie recorded. Strings were added to most of the songs which gave them a touch of sophistication, but other times it watered down Taylor's familiar coarseness. Now that Johnnie was on the high profile Columbia/CBS label, it was as if he and his producers felt it necessary to spruce up his material. The album unveiled dual personalities. Some of the tunes soared on disco wings and others were traditional soul tracks and borderline blues. After the original recording of "Disco Lady" kicked off the LP, seven songs were sandwiched between the monster hit and the seven minute extended version of "Disco Lady" at the end. "Running Out of Lies" written by Perry Jordan was one of Johnnie's better efforts. The recording was a cross-pollination of snazzy blues and synthetic soul. It featured timely keyboard interludes employed to add zest to the tune. Don Davis threw in everything but the kitchen sink, strings, horns, and background singers supporting Johnnie's forlorn vocals. "I'm Gonna Keep on Loving You," is the most dramatic song on the album, with its subdued instrumentation, pop-in synthesizer, and Johnnie's slowly intensifying intonation. When the song hits a groove, it ensnares the listener and begs the question why Taylor couldn't do more of those tunes. The disc ends with an instrumental version of "Somebody's Gettin It," a repeat of the first version found earlier on the disc. Outside of "Disco Lady," the album didn't quite live up to its *Eargasm* description. Notwithstanding the mediocre tracks accompanying "Disco Lady," the album was certified gold and eventually became platinum. "Johnnie Taylor and Don Davis may have seemed like a match made in heaven, but there was much friction behind the scenes. "Musically we were very close, but socially we were two different people," Davis explained. "Johnnie like to drink. Johnnie like to get high. That wasn't my thing, so we didn't have very much to socialize with. All of my encounters with him were in a studio or in a hotel room learning songs. Most of my contact with him was when I'd go down to Dallas. We'd get in the studio and rehearse the stuff, and he'd get on it. I always thought he never gave a hundred percent. Maybe sixty five percent. He actually did not feel the music that I was trying to put him into. When 'Disco Lady' came out, he told me, 'You got a bad mix on that record.' I said, 'I think you better check your sales.'"[25]

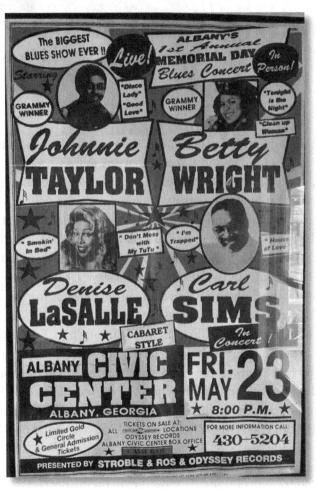

PHOTO COURTESY OF RODGERS REDDING

CHAPTER 24

PAY DIRT

Back in Dallas, Johnnie had become a local hero after "Disco Lady" broke. He was in constant demand across the city as well as Texas, performing in clubs, dancehalls, and ballrooms. One of his favorite venues was the Longhorn Ballroom, just outside downtown Dallas which featured a wide-open dance floor and seated over 2,000 patrons. Many of the blues, soul and country western greats had played the Longhorn which was briefly owned by Jack Ruby. There Johnnie established his headquarters and played periodically to raucous, sold out shows. J.T. was also involved in charity work. He became a prominent member of the Big Brothers nonprofit organization in Dallas. "Members of the group play 'big brother' to boys, thus providing the youth friendship and a meaningful male image."[1] In what little time he had to spare Johnnie became a Freemason and achieved the thirty-third degree which exemplified his outstanding service and contributions.[2] Pat Arnold, wife of Johnnie's son Anthony remarked, "In Dallas Johnnie was always generous. He would take can goods to the needy and help advise young people trying to make it in life.[3]

Joe Jackson, Ida Mae's husband and Johnnie's stepfather, passed away in 1976. Taylor made his way to Kansas City for the funeral service. This gave his son, T.J., who was fourteen at the time, an opportunity to finally spend some quality time with his dad. The family congregated over at his Aunt Queenie's and Uncle Willie's house where T.J. and Johnnie had one of their few father-son conversations. T.J. asked him why he was never around for his birthdays or the holidays and Johnnie's reply was that he was out making a future for all of the family and busy with his career. He went on to tell T.J. that he would have to make his own way in life and counseled him about the danger of using drugs. Johnnie also quizzed T.J. on what he wanted to do with his life, how he felt about girls and if he ever thought he would get married. The priceless time T.J. was able to share with Johnnie inspired him to pursue a career in music. Those moments together, although brief, formed a long-needed connection between T.J. and his father.[4]

On his tours across Texas, Johnnie played at JBs Entertainment Center in Houston and the Eastwood Country Club dancehall in San Antonio. Johnnie soon found himself in big demand after his charting success, "Disco Lady" and his publicity was skyrocketing. He was invited to perform his hit on *American Bandstand* and afterward conducted an interview with host Dick Clark. Johnnie was also a frequent guest of Don Cornelius on *Soul Train*, rockin' the house with his soul laden renditions while trendy dancers moved past the camera. He also

JOHNNIE–DOWNTOWN DALLAS
PHOTO COURTESY OF CRYSTAL WRIGHT

appeared in the Playboy's Playmate Party movie, the Midnight Special TV series, the Merv Griffin Show and the Rosey Grier Show. On one of his scheduled appearances, Taylor was to be a guest on a TV program, but whatever reason, wouldn't come out of the dressing room. He stood up the host. This didn't go over well and damaged his professional reputation. From that point forward, he got very few invites to do interviews or perform on TV shows. He was blackballed from public appearances.[5]

CHAPTER 25

HIT PARADE

In 1977, Johnnie appeared in the movie *Disco 9000*, the second of two movies directed by D'Urville Martin, an actor in the movie. The action-thriller also known as *Fass Black* is about a hotshot who ran a record label and a Sunset Strip dance club on the top of a high rise in L.A. The plotline established Fass Black, as the struggling Black entrepreneur who went to war with White mobsters when he refused to surrender to their bullying to play their records at his disco club.[1] Johnnie had a minor part in the film and played an in-house music producer named Gene Edwards. He had several lines of dialogue and seemed to fit the part perfectly. Although it was a B movie, Johnnie benefited from the exposure both on the screen and on the radio. Johnnie would never admit he was swept up in disco mania craze, but his role in *Disco 9000* settled any argument on the subject. Taylor was now officially a subject of the disco movement, belying his blue-collar soul image. Besides the primary *Disco 9000* album, J.T. also recorded the album's soundtrack that represented his eleventh album. The first *9000* disc predictably included "Disco Lady" which launched the ten-song collection. The LP rehashed a previously published song, "Somebody's Gettin' It," along with "Ever Ready," and "Your Love is Rated X." Both of these tunes would be released later, but were added to the *Disco 9000* long play, to fill the open real estate. The title track, "Disco 9000" was serviceable, but felt like a lightweight compared to earlier Taylor efforts. Columbia/CBS was obviously exploiting the disco obsession and forced Johnnie's talents into a sound that was a foreign concept.

The World Premier of *Disco 9000* movie was held at the Chicago Theatre in July 1977. They had featured several showings throughout the day advertised as "The First Disco Movie." The *Chicago Tribune* movie ad promoted Johnnie Taylor's live appearance along with the *Disco 9000* Dancers sharing the stage with actors from the show. The quarter page ad boasted "Funky Sound, Slick Chicks and lots of room to slide around." The announcement also promoted Johnnie's original motion picture soundtrack.[2] For a home-town boy, this must have been a proud moment, showing everyone in Chi-town he was now a star on the silver screen. Also during this period, Taylor performed in Washington D.C. at a benefit concert sponsored by CBS Records. The corporate giant arranged the show as a fundraiser for the Black Caucus of the United States Congress. Over 10,000 attended and 2,500 dined at the $100-a-plate banquet. Johnnie performed alongside other music notables The Jackson Five and B.T. Express.[3] What went through Johnnie's mind during this period of finding himself in the limelight? Fresh off his *Disco 9000* movie role he was dining with Rosalyn Carter, Claretta Scott King, and Walter Mondale in Washington. It had been a startling rise to fame after riding the rails for so many years on the Chitlin' Circuit.

But 1977 offered Taylor's most prolific moments recording music. The Dallas soul and R&B singer posted four albums in a single twelve-month period. Beyond the *Disco 9000* album, he released the *Disco 9000 Soundtrack*, and new-material albums: *Rated X-traordinaire* and *Reflections*. The *9000* soundtrack was similar to making gravy without flour. Diluted and lumpy, the disc featured the pedestrian "Disco 9000" title track for a second time, as well as two instrumentals. The song, "Right Now" was an over-produced melody that qualified neither as disco or soul. It resembled a number that Johnnie might be singing in his tenth year at a Vegas resort. Allmusic.com rated the album only two-stars. The *Disco 9000 Soundtrack* turned out to be baggage CBS flung onto the break-away disco train. Following the two disco releases, Johnnie completed his *Rated X-traordinaire* album that utilized yet another sexual reference in its title. Inside, the songs reveal the album title wasn't a lost leader. Taylor fills his twelfth album with tracks about making love, chasing women and booty calls. At times, it comes across as if Johnnie is preoccupied with the topic or he may have felt this was what his listeners wanted to hear. Regardless, *X-traordinaire* is a good album and has several high quality compositions. Producers re-released "Your Love Is Rated X," which they had included on *Disco 9000*. It probably should have been saved for the *X-traordinaire* album. The song draws on Taylor's earlier competencies at Stax and takes listeners back in time. Johnnie toyed with the concept of X-rated love, but ran it through a sanitizer for commercial airplay. J.T.'s son, Jonathan noted, "I don't think dad ever wanted to get too explicit, but 'Your Love is Rated X' that means you're extra special girl. So we give you the double entendre, which you know what we're telling you, but we're not telling you."[4] The songs, "Did He Make Love to You?," and "And I Panicked," with its Barry-White-style introduction, were cut from the same cloth as "Your Love is Rated X." "Love Is Better in the A.M." is an outstanding number whose climatic introduction builds into a funk-driven locomotive, bolstered by a sultry backbeat. A duet of trumpets introduces "I'm Just a Shoulder to Cry On," exhibiting Johnnie's masterful vocal elasticity, Sam Cooke runs and superlative vibrato. Overall, *X-Traordinaire* qualifies as one of Johnnie's best works, although the album marked a sales decline. Marcus Chapman provided insight about where Johnnie was headed: "'Your Love Is Rated X' started to kind of bring about the downward spiral. Because the late seventies were about selling albums in particular. He wasn't really able to do that with those songs, so Columbia began to lose interest because he was not reaching the pop audience."[5]

Reflections is an abbreviated, eight-song effort, which absorbed the appealing characteristics of *Rated X-traordinaire*. Taylor and his producers were amassing material in the months leading up to 1977 and these two LPs were vintage quality. *Reflections* deviates from earlier recordings in that all eight tracks are slow burners and featured Johnnie's soul-drenched vocals. Taylor may have grown weary of Columbia's disco product, so he shrugged off the trend and got down to serious business. Coincidentally, the album was recorded at RCA Records, which poses other questions about his relationship with Columbia. Suffice it to say Taylor went back to his roots, complimented by a mature, seasoned approach, dispensing lessons learned from his many years singing gospel, soul, and blues. Songs of note are, "Never My Love," a cover of the Association's 1967 hit, although with added verve, and "Forgive and

Forget." The latter is the only funk driven cut on the album constructed once again from a strong bass underpinning, riding just below the down-tempo construction. Most every song on *Reflections* is a keeper and the LP showed a more sedate side of Johnnie unseen to this point.

CHAPTER 26

TAG TIME

As a young singer, Taylor had run-ins with club owners and promoters who stiffed him after a performance. Ernie Johnson, a long-time gospel singer and bluesman, said there were many times, especially on the Chitlin' Circuit, where the owner of an establishment would hurriedly leave before the show was over to avoid paying the performer. Other times, the entertainer would be given a lesser sum than agreed or shortchanged in some way.[1] Johnnie himself was burned a few times and it didn't take long for him to remedy the situation by demanding payment in advance. No pay, no play was his calling card. When given his pay for the night, he'd count the money in front of the owner until he was satisfied the cash was all there. This carried over to his time after signing with Columbia/CBS. "CBS was no more accustomed to the workings of the soul circuit than Johnnie was to the corporate record world, and there was a period of adjustment for both parties. Bruce Lundvall, who had become president of CBS Records, was at a company convention. Johnnie's band was onstage vamping. However, star attraction Johnnie Tayor was nowhere in sight. Rushing backstage, Lundvall was told that Johnnie wasn't performing until he got paid. "I ran upstairs," explained Lundvall and "I said, Johnnie, get on stage willya! He said, 'I don't go on until I get paid'".[2] After much haggling, he was finally convinced to play, but not without significant wrangling. Singer and songwriter Deanie Parker had a great respect for J.T.'s business sense. "Johnnie was no fool. He may have acted like one sometimes, but he really wasn't. I think Johnnie was very clever–clever like a fox. He became a very shrewd business person. He was very independent. He handled his own stuff. He did a lot of things right, apparently, because in the end, he didn't miss a beat. He kept stepping. I can count the others on both hands who just were not practical, but Johnnie was in a lot of ways."[3]

Johnnie was a stickler when it came to his performances. He didn't mess around. Once his band hit the stage he expected perfection and would let the musicians know if they screwed up. Manager Alan Walden elaborated in his dialogue heard on *Unsung 818:* "His temper could be bad. He'd fire a band in a minute. And I used to keep a band on stand-by, because, I

JOHNNIE TAYLOR
PHOTO COURTESY OF RODGERS REDDING

mean, he'd pull over and put the guys out on the curb." Walden went on, "He demanded respect from his band, and he didn't ask for it, he demanded it."[4] Songwriter Bettye Crutcher added, "He wanted it to be where he wanted it. He made sure that everybody did their part 'cause he was gonna do his."[5] Taylor had a low tolerance for miscues and wouldn't even allow the band to leave the hotel the day of a show to make sure they were on point once onstage.[6]

Johnnie was cautious with his money. "Al Bell recalled hearing stories about him appearing as an opening act at concerts starring established Motown artists. When they sometimes attempted to belittle him by boasting of having bigger hits than he had, J.T. would counter with a brilliant stroke of one-upmanship: 'You may be number one, Pete, but I've got ten thousand dollars in my pocket," he'd say, pulling out a fat bankroll, 'How much you got in your pocket?'"[7] Because of the mistrust of influential professionals around him, Johnnie slowly became an independent man, and wanted to handle his own affairs. He formed his own company in Oak Cliff called TAG Enterprises, which employed several workers and was located on the southbound service road of South R.L.Thornton Freeway. Taylor was a trendsetter as one of the first entertainers who had his own label and publishing company. "In the early years nobody wanted to do it because there was no money in it. So I started making deals and doing it myself. When I worked it up to a point where there was money, I thought, 'What the hell. I might as well keep doing it.'" Johnnie recalled.[8] The company name TAG, according to sources, stood for 'Taylor and God'. This is where he formed his business headquarters. Ernie Johnson shed light on his financial savvy: "Johnnie knew how to handle his business, he was a good businessman. Cause, you know, they take advantage of you when you don't know the business like that."[9] Daughter LaTasha added, "My dad would, you know, go to the office and leave with his briefcase. I'm like, you're a singer, what's in that briefcase? I think that was heavy weight to carry, but I guess you're skipping all the people who could potentially be setting you back because of their shadiness, by doing it yourself."[10] Son, Jonathan added, "I think it gave him sanctuary; it gave him a place to do his business. I think it was a home away from home for him. I mean, you know, he had managers off and on and things like that but he was running his own show."[11] As president of TAG Enterprises, Taylor became a successful entrepreneur running a talent management agency, a record label, a music publishing firm, an advisory service, and a part-time booking agency.[12] Johnnie liked the finer things in life and practiced a very simple spending guideline: bring 50 percent of the earnings back home for living expenses and the other 50 percent he could blow on cars, drugs, wardrobe, bling or entertainment.[13] TAG was the place Johnnie would invite close friends to hear music, sing together, record, drink cocktails or just get away from it all. TAG was also where Taylor displayed his gold and platinum records. Johnson, who visited Johnnie often at TAG, remembered how they would sit for hours, sipping Courvoisier VSOP Cognac or drinking Heineken. J.T. bought himself a black and red tour bus for $37,000 because he preferred not to fly. After Otis Redding's tragic airplane accident Johnnie was mindful of the perceived risks of flying, plus he liked being on the road. Since he grew up riding the circuit, his traveling miles of pavement on trips from town to town became a common practice. Taylor was in his element when he was with the band and friends on the road, going from city to city. Passersby could look over at the TAG offices and tell when Johnnie was in town if they could see the tour bus parked nearby. He fittingly called the tour bus "Disco Lady."[14] On a few occasions he'd pack up LaTasha and Jon and they'd head out on the road together when he was on tour. After the school year was out, daughter Sabrina would come for the summer and stay with stepmom Geri and "Daddy Taylor" in their Dallas home.[15] Taylor was an intermittent family man, and when in town, he'd shower his kids with luxuries. His son Johnnie Jr. who lived in Chicago recalled when he turned 14, that his father rented a two-room motel suite for a birthday party. It was soon jammed with more than fifty youngsters, all eating gallons of ice cream, a huge cake and drinking gallons of punch.[16]

There are hundreds of adjectives that describe Johnnie. His personal qualities, appearance, talent, and abilities have all been celebrated by friends, critics, admirers, and fans over the many years he was a performer. The following was compiled from personal interviews, on-line sites, newspapers, magazines, and books that chronicled his life.

His live shows featured an entertainer who had good moves on stage, always understated and classy. The slight rock of his head back and forth was his signature motion, attractive, as much as it was cool. Johnnie was said to have a gut-bending voice and rhythmic dexterity, and charismatic, bejeweled vocals. He had the suave of the big city and the authenticity of a dirt farmer. Taylor had a certain raspy urgency to his delivery that was sexually charged. J.T. was flamboyant, yet gritty, a compelling balladeer, passionate, and deeply soulful with a free spirit. Johnnie was known to have the voice of a minister, and when he hit the high notes, it was like finding yourself in church. He showed a mix of polish and grit, was stylistically flexible with industrial-strength vocalization that could be salacious and suggestive. Taylor had that special something that one is born with. It can't be developed. He had the star quality many performers searched for their entire career. Johnnie was impossibly cool and considered the high priest of blues. He could conquer any type of music, easily crossed musical boundaries, and adapted to the times. Taylor spanned multiple genres and generations connecting history and heritage. He only got better with age and remained relevant over a half century with unparalleled style and class. Best of all, he was a regular person, and never seemed uppity. The *Dallas Observer* wrote that Johnnie was "a guy that sang with a leer behind his eyes, the man recounted back-door love affairs through the deep, luxuriant voice of a minister delivering a sermon against such things. He was Al Green without the high notes, Otis without the smile, Sam and Dave in the body of one man."[17]

Taylor's prolific record output continued into 1978 with the release of *Ever Ready*. The volume of product CBS was sending to market seemed as if they were milking Johnnie dry. Unsurprisingly, the relationship between Johnnie and CBS had begun to deteriorate over philosophical differences. Johnnie felt he was being pigeonholed into the disco genre and was being strongly encouraged to produce more music like "Disco Lady." Taylor didn't mind reaping the benefits of the monstrous single and album sales and was never one to look a gift horse in the mouth. But as time went on, he realized disco was not what he was all about. He had been a gospel singer, a bluesman and enjoyed singing soul music when the advent of disco came along. Johnnie thought CBS's marching orders were marching him right off the cliff. Thus, his waning enthusiasm was becoming more apparent to CBS leadership. After *Disco Lady*, new record sales began to drop, and Taylor's standing with the company had become more and more tenuous. *Ever Ready*, showed indications of peril in the waters ahead. The eight songs were a collection of various sounds and auras, much of which showed little imagination and were nomadic, at best. Don Davis' production was tight, but it was as if he was searching for various options to make the LP work without stepping on a landmine. The title track, "Ever Ready," and "Give Me My Baby" were the two songs that stood above the rest, but at such a low clearance, proved less than impressive.

CHAPTER 27

RUN-INS AND SHOW-OUTS

Johnnie made a name for himself in the Dallas-Fort Worth Metroplex, but not always the kind of name he would want. Taylor didn't have a spotless record. *Jet Magazine* wrote in 1980, "Attorneys for Johnnie Taylor asked a Dallas court to drop drug and gun charges levied against the singer. They argue that Dallas police illegally searched his car last January in making the arrest. Taylor, already on probation for cocaine possession, was arrested January 15 on Dallas' North Central Expressway and charged with driving while intoxicated, possession of a prohibited weapon and possession of cocaine. Police Sgt. Gary Barnes testified that he stopped Taylor on a speeding violation. He explained the pistol was in open view and that he found the cocaine in one of Taylor's pockets during a search before Taylor was placed in jail. Attorneys Phil Burleson and Lanell Cofer argued that the cocaine and pistol possession charges should be dismissed because Barnes had no legal authority to stop Taylor in the first place."[1] The year before, Johnnie was arrested in Dallas, also for possession of cocaine and received five-years probation. These weren't his only run-ins with the law. Years earlier, in 1974, Taylor was charged with a DWI, and according to the Dallas Police Department, by 1990, he had a total of five DWIs, one of which was a felony. He also had a theft of under $20 which the court dismissed. Johnnie was like Teflon; he always seemed to escape serious trouble. Partly responsible were the expensive attorneys he hired to bail him out, like Burleson.[2]

"Dallas state District Judge Don Metcalfe gave singer Johnnie Taylor, known for his song Disco Lady, a 2-year prison term for his March 7 possession-of-cocaine offense. Just before his arrest, Taylor was driving down Central Expressway in his Stutz Bearcat."[3] Johnnie's sentence was shortened most likely due to turn-around time spent in the county jail to offset or eliminate his punishment. He never served time in the big house.[4] Johnnie's appetite for cocaine was well known although he was viewed by local police as a user, not a dealer. He had, in fact, been obsessive with cocaine but according to friends, he wasn't what one would consider an addict. Taylor knew his limits and probably used the drug for recreational purposes and self-medicated himself to deal with guilt, stress and anxiety. His son, T.J. Hooker rationalized his father's use of alcohol and drugs as a coping mechanism. "He still missing things in his life; there was a void by the children that he left behind. I believe that, to this day, haunted him. He knew what he was doing but he was so caught up, far up in it that he couldn't get out of it." T.J. continued, "And it was easy to hide things by doing drugs. You know, you stay high enough; you know, you're not worried about anything."[5] Daughter Fonda Bryant added her thoughts. " ...and I think that was part of the problem. That he knew he messed up in a lot of ways and drinking and doing the drugs kinda helped him forget about everything."[6] Taylor's former manager, Alan Walden observed, "Johnnie loved to smoke, he loved to drink and he enjoyed a little snort here and there as well."[7] L.C. Cooke, Sam's brother, tried to counsel Johnnie, "I said, Johnnie you don't need all that to get high. No coke, none of that. I said marijuana get you high enough. [Johnnie replied], 'Ah well, I like this and I like that.'"[8] Although he was a regular user, he never promoted his habit or tried to influence others. For the most part, he kept it to himself. Rodgers Redding confirmed this and observed, "Now he never did drugs around me, I mean; and I respect him for that, but the drugs affected him." When hearing about Johnnie's brush with the law, Rodgers recalls "Well you know what Johnnie told me, he said it's for the sake of publicity; it's alright. So that's the way Johnnie felt about it, whether it was good or bad. He was in the news, he said my name out there, so they know who I am."[9] Friend Mae Young warned Johnnie, "And I just told him you have to slow up. You know you just can't do everything; you can't try to party, do your shows and think that nothing's gonna happen to you."[10] In a foreboding reply, Johnnie would tell his friends and wife Gerlean as they constantly voiced their concerns, ""Well you gotta die of something.' It just didn't matter to him".[11] "No one ever had control of Johnnie Taylor, but Johnnie Taylor."[12]

On the music front in 1979, Johnnie released, in gatling-gun fashion, another LP, called *She's Killin' Me*. Unfortunately, Johnnie lost his crack producer Don Davis, who guided him through his formative days at Stax, and the corporate maze at Columbia. Davis had been Johnnie's right hand, and Taylor would suffer from the loss. Johnnie expressed his respect and admiration for Davis when they worked together and explained how they collaborated, "My producer, Don Davis, brings the songs to me. He is indispensable. He is very good at selecting song material. In our years together, I can't recall one time when we have had a disagreement about a tune. He brings the song to me, and, of course, I make final approval. Basically, we hear the same things, musically. We'll take a [instrumental] track and listen to it over and over again. Then I will take the story [lyrics] and try to fit it into the soundtrack, for we have already settled on a basic beat. And then, that's it. We used to have a lot of people in the studio when we were trying to do this," but when many people are involved, "a conversation starts, and the next thing you know, you are not as serious about doing what you ought to be serious about doing. And the whole thing can turn into a party. We've cut that out. Now, we have only closed sessions–myself, Don and maybe the engineer. I can concentrate better that way." He goes on, "My experiences certainly have a lot to do with how I hear and select a tune. I've lived a lot, paid the dues."[13]

Don Davis left CBS to pursue personal and professional interests, which included managing his own label called Groovesville. He also became a commercial banker and took over the struggling First Independent Bank of Detroit. He was quite successful with FIB, which he grew to become the twelfth largest African American owned bank in the US. Brad Shapiro replaced Don Davis as Johnnie's producer at Columbia, but for Johnnie, things would never be the same. The *She's Killin' Me* LP had some quality songs, however Shapiro seemed to dump everything and the kitchen sink into the disc's production. Included was a little disco, a few bland soul numbers, and a couple of keepers that spotlit Johnnie's smoky vocals. CBS and Shapiro were still trying to integrate disco into Taylor's music, but their efforts fell flat, and the music sounded redundant. The only songs worth mentioning are "Baby Lay Down," reminding listeners of the J.T. of yesteryear, featuring his ashen and resplendent vocals. The opening melody from the piano transports listeners into a dark, smoke-filled room, at an out-of-the-way club in nowheresville. "Play Something Pretty" had an interesting line in the lyrics where Johnnie sang that he doesn't want to see any more disco. This could have been a not-so-subtle message to CBS management. "Love Account" is another song worth listening to with its unhurried approach and soulful flavor. Unlike Johnnie's typical MO, in "Love Account," he sang disparagingly about material items like homes and fine cars, and how they won't make you happy. One could wonder whether he was speaking from a personal perspective. The new producer's over-exuberance in his use of strings, horns, and background vocals choked out Johnnie's delivery. The rest of the LP, for the most part presented forgettable tracks and confused the listener with the dizzy mix of music.

CHAPTER 28

MUSIC MADE THE MAN

Not all of Taylor's live shows were memorable. It's virtually impossible for a performer to have top flight performances night in and night out. There's sure to be evenings where things are just off. One such occasion was at the Starwood Theatre in Hollywood. Fans left the theater lukewarm after the show, saying "'He was okay," they complained, 'but not really much more.'"[1] It seemed the cause for disappointment was what was described as Taylor's 'punchless backup unit.' The show got off to a dreadful start when the crowd had to wait ninety minutes between acts; and, when the band finally appeared, they nonchalantly milled about the stage in seemingly no particular hurry. Another thirty minutes passed, and the audience was growing more and more irritated. After the MC took the stage and was forced to page a few missing band members, they were finally assembled and Johnnie made his appearance. Although Taylor's show included some of his current hits which thrilled the audience, the performance was lackluster. "Although he did engage in some limited stage-side patter with the audience, he seemed unexplainably distant from them. He was not reserved, just distant. The distance manifested itself in his performance, and several times, it was as if he was just doing another show, and just going through the same old routines."[2] With the hundreds upon thousands of shows Johnnie performed, there would be nights like that. Artists can be exhausted from the travel, jaded from the rigorous schedule, not feeling well or maybe too high to be effective. This particular instance was the exception rather than the rule as Johnnie most always took the crowd to memorable heights at his live shows.

Taylor caught the attention of other mainstream artists and in a *Rolling Stone* interview in 1983, Elvis Costello was asked "What new artists have excited you?" He replied, "Recently Johnnie Taylor and Lamont Dozier have gotten their courage back to make great soul records and not conform to the less imaginative end of the disco market."[3]

Johnnie continually sang at the Longhorn Ballroom in Dallas. The venue provided everything at Taylor's disposal to make his shows unique: a larger-than-life stage, tables and chairs for a few thousand fans, room to dance and great acoustics. It had a playhouse atmosphere. Playing at the Longhorn, Johnnie developed good friendships with other local artists like Ernie Johnson, Bobby Patterson, Z.Z. Hill, Little Milton and Gregg A. Smith. Some of the entertainers would open for Johnnie or they'd appear for one another's show sitting in. When the Soul Stirrers came to Dallas, Johnnie would join the group and add his unique tenor vocals to the sound. Taylor, who had been a touring war-horse, over time, began to tap the brakes on his travel schedule. Earlier, a normal week might include being on the the road performing five to six nights a week. As Johnnie found himself in his mid-to-late forties, he had to slow the pace. He purposely cut back to four nights a week so he could recuperate and spend more time at home with his Geri and his kids. Taylor also suffered a personal misfortune when his Oak Cliff house caught fire. "His fourteen-room [four bedroom] $75,000 home was partially destroyed recently by a fire that started in the heating system. Taylor is in the process of salvaging that while living in an apartment. He has cut his live performing appearances."[4]

His handle was "'Johnnie Taylor, The Blues Wailer", which had become his trademark ID

FRIENDS BOBBY PATTERSON AND JOHNNIE
PHOTO COURTESY OF BOBBY PATTERSON

when he joined KKDA-AM Soul 73 Radio in Dallas. As a DJ, he joined other celebrities such as Millie Jackson and Bobbi Humphrey on Big D's radio waves. Here on the local soul station, he played listener favorites and added his dusky intonation to the airwaves. Johnnie was a fan's sweetheart, especially since he was a known resident of Dallas. Taylor could be seen cruising around town in his Rolls or his Excalibur convertible, dressed in sunglasses, a full-length fur coat and, matching fur hat. He drew stares from those unaccustomed to seeing a Black man dressed like he was in such an expensive ride. Taylor drove through tough parts of Oak Cliff and South Dallas and was never accosted or bothered; people knew who he was. Johnnie was revered, not envied, and was always left alone. It was as if the middle-age singer had a get-out-of-trouble passport each time he took to the streets. He was a man of the people and a friend to the common man. Johnnie never forgot where he came from and honored his past by portraying a man who understood life and understood the everyday-person's problems. He'd been where they were. Now that he had made it, Johnnie was willing to share his knowledge and spent time giving advice to up-and-comers in the music business and guided them through the maze of uncertainty. He was generous with his time and his wisdom; when he spoke, people listened. He had that way about him. One of Taylor's favorite pastimes was playing cards. Gambling was common in the back rooms of clubs and bars where friends and performers would cuss, drink, smoke cigars and cavort. Johnnie often played at his TAG offices and was a shrewd card man whose street smarts framed his poker face.

It was in this comfortable, welcoming setting of Dallas that Johnnie had his first heart attack. Taylor was attending a social event at the familiar Longhorn Ballroom when the attack occurred. " …he was swiftly taken to St. Paul Hospital and remained in intensive care until physicians stabilized his condition," *Jet Magazine* reported on the frightful incident. Johnnie commented to *Jet* that he suddenly started sweating in the ballroom. ""I took off my coat,' he explained, 'and my shirt was soaking wet.'" According to the article, Johnnie knew something was wrong when he couldn't stop sweating so he was rushed to the hospital. Now convalescing at home, Taylor says he has begun an exercise program outlined by his physician and hopes that he will soon be able to resume recording an album. 'I've got to change my diet,' he acknowledged. 'No spice, no salt and no beef or red meat,' he added, 'The doctors are now running tests to see if heredity had anything to do with my heart attack,' he went on, 'but the only illness in my family was my mother who was diabetic.'" *Jet* stated that Johnnie, " ...will be allowed to work thirty hours a week when he begins recording again. He reported that the doctors will allow such a schedule because recording is not as strenuous as touring and concert dates."[5]

Johnnie's lifestyle had been typical of a touring musician, smoking, drinking, drugs, late night soirees, catch-it-while-you-can meals, unfamiliar surroundings, exhausting hours on the bus and the pressure of constantly being in demand. This had been his way of life. The stress of performing for thousands of fans and trying to meet their demands had eventually taken a toll on his health. When combined, these lethal ingredients finally caught up to Johnnie. CBS only made his condition worse. The oppressive label that attempted to dictate his musical direction into a category of dance-laden pop-disco, was slowly beating him down. His heart and mind were somewhere else and his efforts had become more and more indifferent. Images of a wild beast being trapped in a cage may best describe Johnnie's plight during that time. Sales plummeted amid the loss of his producer Don Davis and the corporate red-tape and politics only alienated Taylor further. Johnnie recorded one last record for CBS called, *New Day*. It became obvious Johnnie was trying to end the pain with CBS and wanted to get one last recording out before his departure. The nine-track disc included three songs released on the previous album, *She's Killin' Me*, and were obviously used for filler. The other songs ranged from mediocre to lackluster with "Baby Don't Hesitate," being the best of the worst. Johnnie's voice was starting to age and although it lacked the crispness of the younger version, his fermentation added a layer of authenticity many other performers lacked at the time. The album had also become a sign of the times with the advent of synthetic keyboard play, cowbells, and string-thumping plucks on the bass. Unfortunately, the incessant disco sound continued to invade some of the songs. Inevitably Johnnie was dropped from the label after the *New Day* LP. He was relieved and anxious to return to releasing genuine Johnnie Taylor songs as opposed to putting out fabricated facsimiles. The Columbia/CBS era had ultimately come to an end and was most likely the longest five years of Taylor's life. Johnnie was finally free, free at last.

CHAPTER 29

SINGING Z.Z. HOME

Taylor took a couple of years off before recording more music. He signed with Beverly Glen Records run by Otis Smith, another California label that had signed similar artists such as Bobby Womack and Anita Baker. Bobby and Johnnie were tried and tested, long-time friends and both partook in the snowy, white drug of choice on many occasions. Bobby married Sam Cooke's widow Barbara, only months after Cooke's death; and Bobby and Barbara, together, weathered the horror of Sam's murder. Womack and Taylor sang together on the gospel circuit before they both wound up with Sam and SAR Records. After SAR's demise, Bobby became a catalyst for Johnnie joining Beverly Glen. J.T.'s new album *Just Ain't Good Enough* was only a six-track effort, although Taylor extended the duration of his songs from three-to-four minutes to five-to-six minutes. In essence, the buyer still got their money's worth. The LP was decent work, given the new work environment and transition. The results could also be attributed to Johnnie's two years off, which allowed him to breathe and return with fresh, new ideas, apart from the inflexible atmosphere at CBS. A couple of numbers stood out: "I Need a Freak" and "I'm So Proud," both of which dared the most bashful to stay off the dance floor with its driving funk-busting rhythm. The cut was similar to bump-classics "Brick House" by Rick James and songs by KC and the Sunshine Band. "I'm So Proud," written by Curtis Mayfield and Cecil Womack (Bobby's brother), is reminiscent of some of Johnnie's Stax classics and transports listeners back to the good ole days. Taylor also takes a political swipe at the newly elected president Ronald Reagan as the album concludes with "Reaganomics," which turned out to be a legitimate mover and shaker.

Unfortunately Beverly Glen was a cluster, a company that didn't really know the recording business. Not long after its release, Johnnie became dissatisfied with the label's ineffectiveness in promoting his material. Other clients of BG, namely Anita Baker were also disenchanted. Anita left the label after being recruited by Warner Records without officially being released from her contract. The disagreement escalated into a lawsuit, and Beverly Glen sued Baker to prevent her from signing with Warner. At its conclusion, Beverly Glen lost the litigation when the court ruled in Baker's favor and that Beverly Glen couldn't deprive Ms. Baker of her livelihood. Johnnie left Beverly Glen not long after he joined the label. His departure landed Taylor back on the streets without a recording deal. Johnnie's historical record sales had been good over the preceding decades and held up despite all the changes, but were not enough for the singer to receive the measure of stardom he once enjoyed. Taylor took a few more years off, but continued touring, playing major houses around the country including the Apollo in Harlem, the Howard in D.C. and in the Midwest at the annual Thanksgiving Breakfast Dance in Kansas City. Taylor was always the opening act at the KC morning event where folks dressed in their finest attire and enjoyed the holiday spread in the laid-back, peaceful environment.

Z.Z. Hill was a successful Oak Cliff bluesman known for his famous song "Down Home Blues," which remained on the Billboard charts for over two years.[1] Hill had been recording on the small Jackson, Mississippi label known as Malaco Records and issued the single, which sold a surprising 500,000 copies. The sales resurrected the specialty label that had been struggling. However, Z.Z. was involved in a serious auto accident in 1984, which led to complications. After recovering from the accident, he performed at the popular Longhorn Ballroom. A few weeks later a blood clot formed in his leg causing Z.Z. to die suddenly at his home in Dallas. He was only forty-eight. Johnnie was a friend of Z.Z.'s and attended his funeral held in Hughes Springs in East Texas. Taylor felt honored by being asked to sing at Z.Z.'s service. Tommy Couch Sr. and others from the Malaco label attended the funeral in honor of Hill and were impressed when they heard Johnnie sing in celebration of Z.Z.'s life. Taylor delivered an impassioned vocal tribute to his fallen colleague, singing "Love of God." Before his death, Z.Z. had been booked to play with Teddy Power on a northeastern tour. His passing left Power in a quandary without Z.Z. to open the show. Rodgers Redding, working as Johnnie's promoter, called Taylor and asked if he could help Teddy finish out the tour, which he did.[2]

CHAPTER 30

Malaco Records of Jackson, Mississippi, was established in the early '60s by White college students Tommy Couch and brother-in-law Mitchell Malouf, who began booking bands for fraternity parties. The Malaco name was derived from the combined, shortened name of each. Wolf Stephenson joined the company soon after. They segued into promoting concerts, some recognizable to popular music fans like Herman's Hermits, The Who and The Animals. In 1967, the company expanded upon opening a recording studio; and once underway, worked with the

Pointer Sisters, Rufus Thomas and Paul Simon. Over time, Malaco had its ups and downs, closely skirting bankruptcy on a couple of occasions before being rescued by Dorothy Moore with the release of her popular "Misty Blue" record in 1973. After Moore's success, the company branched out, working with gospel musicians and slowly built an impressive gospel stable. Z.Z. Hill's "Down Home Blues" set the stage for the label to become a significant player in the blues genre and attracted other performers like Denise LaSalle, Little Milton, Bobby Bland and Benny Latimore. Famed Black music promoter Dave Clark introduced Couch to Johnnie at Z.Z.'s funeral and served as a key influence for Taylor signing with Malaco. Clark was formerly with Stax and had worked with J.T. before, promoting his music back in the label's prime. During Clark's time at Malaco, he became well-known for attracting talent, including Johnnie, to join the team.[1] Malaco management had followed Johnnie's rise to fame and knew his work long before they met. After Z.Z.'s funeral, Tommy Couch invited Johnnie to sign with the label in hopes of landing a new flagship artist. Taylor had been languishing without a record deal and was receptive, based on Malaco's reputation in the blues and gospel field, and his relationship with Clark. "Malaco was really kinda the premier down-home southern label at that time in the '80s for artists who were not necessarily considered mainstream anymore. So Johnnie was able to go to Malaco and create some songs that got him back on track."[2]

Musical tastes began transitioning once again in the early eighties. J.T. and his fellow soulmates had been "consigned to the industry margins" when selling 100,000 units was the best they could muster. This, far from his bigger hits that sold 500,000 or more during his heyday. "Soul was reclassified as blues because of an aging demographic. To most radio programmers, older Black people listened to the blues. So when Johnnie Taylor's fans grew older he had become a 'blues artist.' The music hadn't changed, but the way it was understood, marketed and consumed had shifted significantly."[3] In his piece, *The Story of Malaco Records*, Bob Mehr provided this perspective relating to author Rob Bowman's book *The Last Soul Company*. "All those soul-blues artists Malaco signed–Little Milton, Bobby 'Blue' Bland, Johnnie Taylor–they were all anachronisms at that point. The only reason they signed with this small company in

Jackson, Mississippi, is because none of them could get a deal anywhere else."[4]

Malaco was in need of a prominent headliner to join the label, while Johnnie needed a place to call home. The union was a perfect match. Johnnie felt like he was coming home, back in the South where he grew up and away from the glitz and glamor of stuffy L.A. Malaco was similar to Stax, that was at one time headquartered just up the road on I-55, less than three hours away. After signing, Taylor didn't waste any time returning to the studio. He was anxious to resume his career and make it known he was alive and well after he turned fifty. Having suffered through a two year hiatus, J.T. was able to bring an uncluttered mind and renewed enthusiasm to a team of eager and spirited music professionals at Malaco. Johnnie commented on what drew him to Malaco: "A couple of ol' boys running the company, and brothers doing all the music."[5] "Malaco reminds me of the early days of Stax, I feel like I'm part of a building process. Everybody works hard and pulls together. Malaco is into selling albums, Stax was into selling singles. We did albums there [at Stax] but usually they had a couple of good songs and the rest were fillers."[6] According to Tommy Couch Sr., Taylor was very easy to work with in the studio. Since he wasn't a songwriter, the Malaco team was typically in total control of the entire process. Couch explained that other artists who wrote their own music were much more difficult to deal with and wanted more input into the arrangements. Conversely, Taylor would come into the Malaco sound studio, do his thing, and, once finished, leave, and get back out on the road. Couch felt this recipe was the primary reason why Johnnie's relationship with Malaco endured for over a decade and a half. Asked if J.T. always gave 100 percent during his recording sessions, Couch replied, "when you've got a great voice like Johnnie's, it's hard to tell if they're giving 100 percent or not".[7]

Johnnie's next album was called *This Is Your Night* released in 1984. The ten-song effort was an obvious departure from earlier LPs which focused on the hunt for women and bedroom trysts. A more mature and seasoned Taylor now sang songs about his contentment and love for his woman–that was all that mattered. In the past, listeners gravitated to Johnnie's records to hear about his exploits with the opposite sex and being a bad boy like Jody. His fans enjoyed hearing the stories about failed relationships, infidelity, and looking for love. It seemed Johnnie spoke from a place of experience. He had worldliness that men could relate to. These features were missing in *This Is Your Night*. The new Johnnie wasn't necessarily a bad thing, but simply a retreat from his hedonistic croonings and was now focused on fulfillment, dedication and gratification. The title track establishes the shifting tides as if he was talking directly to his wife Geri in a slow and sweet cadence. Several other songs are noteworthy including a ponderous blues number, "Drown In My Own Tears." This cut shows Johnnie's capacity to get down and- dirty with gospel-like intonation. "A Love to Call My Own" is an easy-going soul piece that talks about commitment and devotion to his lady at home. "Still Called the Blues," written by Earl Forest, George Jackson and R.A. Miller, represents an authentic, funk tune that begs the listener to dance while no one's looking. "She's Cheating on Me" featured lyrics that mention Taylor's constant running around, and how he's changed his ways, which could serve as a signature theme for the album. Perhaps the best cut on the LP is "Lady, My Whole World Is You." The slow, soulful tune reveals the many incomparable qualities Johnnie has as a vocalist and could serve as the entertainer's tribute song. As a body of work, *This Is Your Night* soars above the mundane refuse that CBS released. The Malaco production team toned down the horns and strings, and moved them out of the way of Johnnie's enduring voice. They then used the instrumentation in a complimentary fashion rather than a focus. Malaco let Johnnie be Johnnie. The LP is down-to-earth, meaningful, and polished.

Malaco's house band was a premier ensemble of talented musicians. The fraternity included Carson Whitsett on keyboards, Larry Addison also on keys, James Robertson on drums, Ray Griffin on bass and Dino Zimmerman on guitar. The Malaco label had been soul music's best kept secret, featuring a treasure trove of songwriters: George Jackson, Larry Addison, Rich Cason, and Jimmy Lewis. The entire Malaco team gave the artists freedom to explore their comfort zone–which made a major difference in the final product. It was obvious Johnnie's new home was where he belonged. Two years would pass before Johnnie would release any new material, and when he did, it resulted in two albums, *Lover Boy* and *Wall to Wall*. The first, *Lover Boy* was a good sequel to the previous album *This Is Your Night. Lover Boy* was produced by Wolf Stephenson and Tommy Couch Sr. and contained some fine Southern soul numbers starting with the opening track, "Don't Make Me Late." Also noteworthy, the song "Nothing Like a Lady," written by Addison. Malaco captured Taylor's precise enunciation and vocalization perfectly. "Happy Time" has a catchy rhythm reminiscent of the old Stax days with a Sam-and-Dave sound. "Girl of My Dreams" stands out from the rest, with the dense backbeat of the four-string guitar that lays down an honest groove. Noticeable was the absence of the string accompaniments that dominated the CBS records and was replaced by more contemporary guitar work and keyboards. The second LP of '86, *Wall to Wall* proved to be lackluster overall. The first half of the record consists of quality soul numbers, particularly "Just Because" and "I'm Changing," where Johnnie talks about neglecting his home, and being in the wrong places he didn't belong. The song was an obvious message to his loved ones on the home front. The title track "Wall to Wall" had an interesting origin. Writer George Jackson penned the song especially for James Brown. Before Brown heard the tune, "Wilson Pickett expressed interest in cutting it. Believing in the song to the end; and before Pickett got into the studio, Jackson played the song for Johnnie at his hotel while Johnnie was in Memphis playing a gig. Taylor didn't have to hear it twice before declaring 'I'm cutting it.'"[8] Most of the other buoyant cuts failed to provide a hook and were somewhat unimaginative. Since arriving at Malaco, Taylor had produced a lot of material, but the efforts didn't register high enough for distinction. In the end, Johnnie sold records to his long-time fans, but not so much to the younger listeners moving into the evolving marketplace.

CHAPTER 31

TIME WAITS FOR NOBODY

Johnnie's latest recordings made it clear he was aging. The many years of smoking and drinking had lowered his voice and coated his throat and nasal cavities with chalky, gutural layers. His voice, although different, was still beguiling and compelling. What was absent, however, was fresh, imaginative material and the disinterested buyers kept their money in their wallets. It could very well have been the lack of sexual innuendos, stories of cheating or being with someone else's woman that was missing from his new material. Additionally Johnnie was selling primarily to Black blues fans and hardcore soul aficionados in a declining market. The audience had become older and were consuming less. It became obvious these genres had entered into an extended decline from their reign many years before. This led Malaco to expand into new areas. The label built its stable of gospel acts like the Jackson Southernaires and Johnnie's old outfit, The Soul Stirrers. The company then acquired the catalogs of Savoy and Apollo Records, two of the most prominent gospel labels known worldwide. The small Mississippi company had also cornered the market on Southern blues and soul with the signing of Bobby Bland, Johnnie, Shirley Brown, Bobby Rush, and Artie "Blues Boy" White–all adding to the formidable line-up.

Taylor still toured, but not like before when he reached out to see his fans in out-of-the-way places along the road. He did continue to utilize the "Disco Lady" tour bus, on occasion, traveling across state lines to navigate his personal soul-circuit built over the years. As Johnnie began to travel less, the tours he did make were brief. Tommy Couch Sr. spoke of an intense moment involving a show Johnnie had agreed to play in the deep South. It was scheduled just after casinos began operating, and Johnnie was booked for a show in Philadelphia, Mississippi. Couch was headed west on I-20 leaving Jackson toward Vicksburg when he saw Johnnie's tour bus going the opposite direction on its way to Philadelphia. Couch was aware Johnnie had a show that night and looked at his watch. He knew Taylor would never make it on time for the 8:00 p.m. scheduled start. Couch was right; Johnnie was an hour late. When the tour bus coasted into the gambling-house parking lot at 9:00 p.m. the casino manager made his way outside and met Taylor before they parked. He told Johnnie and his driver to "get off my parking lot" and to leave the premises. Management wouldn't allow Johnnie to play that night if he couldn't make it on time. Johnnie was accustomed to arriving late when touring the soul circuit where he was able to get by with his all-familiar tardiness. Johnnie learned that night that casinos took their commitments more seriously and were rarely in the mood to joke around. Since it was standard practice for Johnnie to be paid in part or in full before a show, if he had already been paid, Taylor likely would have to return any advances he received for the performance.[1]

Johnnie had a number of good friends who were entertainers in Dallas and orbited the metroplex playing at various bars, nightspots and clubs. Three of his closest friends were Ernie Johnson, Gregg A. Smith, and Bobby Patterson. Well-known celebrities in their own rights, each had a local and national following with numerous devoted fans scattered around Dallas. Taylor shared the stage with his buddies and many times they'd play on the same bill with Johnnie featured as the main attraction. Besides hanging out with friends and his musical contemporaries, Taylor loved his cars. He was a man who cherished the opportunity to cruise around town for everyone to see, driving his high-tone pricey rides. It was his way of showing off a little while touring the city, revealing his accomplishments as a successful Black entertainer. Johnnie certainly earned the rights to his celebrity, and this was evident when riding around with the Excalibur's top down. He looked like a star. In 1968, Chevrolet produced forty-four of the unique Excalibur models, one of which Johnnie owned. It was called the Excalibur SSK (Super Sport Kurtz) Roadster. The long sleek design was patterned after the Mercedes

Benz SSK, made in Germany, and the Excalibur was described as a "lithe, ferocious performer." Passersby would crane their necks to take a second look at Johnnie as he zoomed by in his sports car with French-made freestanding headlamps, side-mounted, cord-esque exhaust pipes and the spare tire riding below a small luggage rack on the trunk. He also owned a classic 1958 Ford Royal-Coach. This classic model featured inset headlights and ten-inch tailfins that punctuated the obnoxiously long body. Johnnie's fabled ownership of the Ford would later mark the official name of the model. But since 1963, after a prestigious car magazine featuring an article about the Ford misspelled Johnnie's name, the Ford became and is now known as the "Johnny" Taylor Ford. J.T. also owned a 1975 Stutz Bearcat. Stutz Motor Company was an American auto manufacturer that produced ultra-luxury cars, one of which Johnnie purchased. The brown and cream-colored, two-toned hardtop was a sight to be seen, especially on his frequent drives through the ghettos of South Dallas and Oak Cliff.

Johnnie also drove his flamboyant vehicles in other parts of Dallas. He visited upper-crust neighborhoods that didn't necessarily appreciate Johnnie flaunting his flashy rides. During the eighties, Dallas was still bristling from contentious segregation and ongoing racism. White folks didn't take kindly to a Black man galavanting around town in a glitzy sports car. The Dallas Police didn't either. Since Johnnie had a criminal record, it wasn't unusual for the men in blue to shake him down from time to time. One such case was when Taylor was on his way to the Longhorn Ballroom on Corinth. Johnnie's friend, Bobby Patterson told the story of the day he was to meet him at the club. When he was driving up to the Longhorn, Bobby noticed a police car had pulled a man over. As he neared, Patterson recognized it was Johnnie's Stutz Bearcat parked in front of the squad car. Bobby observed the sparkle of J.T.'s diamond rings reflecting in the sun while the officer had Johnnie turn to face the car with his hands up. Taylor was then asked to place his hands on top of the Stutz. Patterson slowly approached in his vehicle, taking in the development. From the corner of his eye, Johnnie noticed Bobby drawing near. They made eye contact. Taylor silently signaled Bobby to stop and give him some support. Patterson didn't want any part of the ordeal, so he kept driving. The next day, Johnnie called Bobby and asked him why he didn't stop to help. Bobby responded, trying to make light of the situation, and told Johnnie, "Better for you to go to jail than both of us."[2]

Johnnie's next new album was *In Control* released in 1988. The two years between releases produced a genuine classic LP and Taylor's best collective effort in some time. A bottomless bass kicked off the groove on the title track, and showed a fresh departure from previous string arrangements and horns. In contrast, the song thrived on its simplicity, utilizing conventional guitars, drums and keys. The cut-and-dry number was successful in its bare-skinned approach and set the tone for the tracks that followed. The storyline of the album spoke of relationship troubles, hurt and disappointment. "Now That You Cheated," "Got to Leave This Woman" and "It Don't Hurt Me Like It Used To" showed a pattern of love misfortunes Johnnie may have experienced in the past. When a person undergoes hard luck from relationships gone wrong, the sadness and grief seem to produce the most genuine song material. For the listener, *In Control* becomes

FAMED DALLAS BLUESMAN
BOBBY PATTERSON
PHOTO COURTESY OF BART
KUDLICKI AND BOBBY PATTERSON

understandable and relatable. Johnnie was able to impart those feelings in song because he lived through the situations. Taylor sang the blues without actually sounding like the blues. The music felt more like authentic soul. Other notable cuts are "Got to Leave," "Everything's Out in the Open," and "That's the Way It Is." Observing the merits of the LP, Johnnie and his team created a fresh approach with an earthy, unwilted sound that avoids over-production and concentrates on catchy rhythms and forlorn lyrics. Taylor's songs were often recorded in different locations. The rhythm, horns, background singers, and, finally, his vocals were assembled to complete the final work. Johnnie's vocals would typically be recorded by his friend at Butch Bonner's Butchie Boy Studios in far South Oak Cliff. Butch "Butchie Boy" Bonner was a guitarist in Johnnie's band playing on stage and toured with Taylor on the road. His studio was near Johnnie's home on Red Bird Lane where they spent many hours recording, overdubbing and laying tracks for Taylor's albums. Butchie reflected on their relationship, "We were good friends. In the studio he was no nonsense, but easy to work with. Johnnie was very particular in maintaining the Johnnie Taylor sound and always liked to get things right."[3] Bonner was well regarded in the music business having played guitar for Freddie King and Zoom in addition to his many years with Johnnie.

CHAPTER 32

HEYDAY

As the decade began to close, Johnnie and Gerlean contemplated a move from their Oak Cliff home on Red Bird Lane. Taylor's fame and fortune had grown to the extent he felt the need to place himself among the Dallas elite and to live in a wealthy, upscale neighborhood. Johnnie was always keen for the bright and shiny, the lavish, the posh, and extravagant, so he set his sights on a dream home on the north side of town. His Oak Cliff neighborhood was starting to age and didn't offer the comfort it once did. The transitional area became unsettled which convinced the couple it was time to make a change. The Taylor kids, Jonathan and LaTasha, were now attending Greenhill, a private school in Addison, quietly nestled in swanky North Dallas. The move made sense in that the family home would be closer to the teenagers' school; and the move would bring them into the realm of the rich surrounded by the affluent. Johnnie and Geri's close friend Viola Ross was their real estate agent who assisted in selling the Oak Cliff home and helped the couple purchase their new place at 5937 Gladeside Court, in the prestigious Preston Trails-Bent Tree neighborhood.[1] The house was situated on nearly an acre of land in the heart of some of the most expensive real estate in town. Only a few hundred yards away, golfers played the exclusive Preston Trail Golf Club, and half a mile away was the upscale Bent Tree Country Club. Johnnie had moved into high cotton. Living nearby was Dallas Cowboys' Hall of Fame running back, Tony Dorsett. The five bedroom, four-and-a-half bath, 7,000 square-foot house was a showplace among the neighboring residences. It was surrounded by a knee-high wrought-iron fence with ornate designs, and the entry featured an extensive circle driveway that led to the front door. The large estate was perfect for accommodating his collection of treasured sportscars. The home was chic, snazzy, and imposing, and reflected Taylor's persona. When he moved into the neighborhood, the flamboyant performer didn't go unnoticed. Curious eyes from pretentious White neighbors looked disparagingly at the Black man moving into their ritzy, cozy confines. Racism was obviously still alive and well in North Dallas. Johnnie's friend Ernie Johnson told a story about the day Taylor was in the front yard mowing his lawn at the Gladeside mansion. A luxurious car drove up and motioned for Johnnie to come over. Taylor left the mower running and walked over to their vehicle. The passengers asked Johnnie if he would be interested in mowing their lawn after he was finished, thinking he was a lawn caretaker. In typical J.T. fashion, he was able to politely put them in their place. He said, "Well as soon as I finish mowing *my* yard, I'll come mow yours." They drove away sufficiently embarrassed and mildly insulted.[2] Johnnie's next-door neighbor wasn't thrilled about him and Gerlean moving in either. The Taylors had parties, probably loud ones bringing lots of traffic in and out of the neighborhood. Living next door to Johnnie's property, one of the neighbors wanted to block out the new resident and distance himself from whatever was going on at the Taylors. Thus, Johnnie's neighbor submitted plans to the city for a permit to build a fence that would separate the two properties. The city took exception to the request because of the unusual height he wanted to build the structure. After wrangling with the city's building code administrators, he finally got approval and constructed an immense barrier successfully shutting out Johnnie and Gerlean. Such was life for a Black man in North Dallas during the late eighties, especially when surrounded by suspicious, nosy White neighbors.[3]

The move had no effect on Johnnie's recording. He released a new effort in 1989 called *Crazy 'Bout You*. The new LP continued Taylor's validity in, and dedication to, the soul genre after his previous effort, *In Control*. The disc featured a number of quality compositions including the title track which questioned Taylor's relationship with his companion. It made one wonder about the condition of Johnnie's lovelife given the number of sad melancholy songs he sang for the album. "Money's

Running Funny," had a vigorous intro, accentuated by Johnnie's dialog and background chatter from accompanists which turned out to be one of the best tracks. "For Your Precious Love," underscores the virtues and character of Johnnie's voice, never sounding better than on this classic tune. A humorous ingredient added to the LP was "Airtight Alibi," which is self-explanatory and portrays Johnnie asking male listeners to provide him a unique alibi to use–rather than another unconvincing line to try with his lady. Taylor added dialogue to a few songs on the album which brought him closer to the listener as if he was offering up a personal relationship. Overall a good effort, but still lacking that one megahit that would reignite his acclaim.

In July of 1989, Johnnie and his fellow Malaco musicians took a trip across the pond to play at the Montreux Jazz Festival in Switzerland. The picturesque landscape framed the fifteen-day musical pageantry played on the eastern banks of Lake Geneva featuring music from all genres. Viewers glimpsed the Rhone Plains spreading northward far below the towering Swiss Alps looming in the distance. Never a more perfect place to perform could be found. This Malaco European Tour of '89 brought its top performers scheduled to play Thursday, July 13, on a day described

JOHNNIE'S GLADESIDE MANSION IN NORTH DALLAS

as, "Formidable Rhythm N' Blues." Malaco presented Bobby "Blue" Bland, B.B. King, Johnnie Taylor, Denise La Salle, Little Milton, Moseley and Johnson in addition to Luther Atkinson and Roy Rogers. Accompanying the performers were the Muscle Shoals Rhythm Section and the Muscle Shoals Horns to provide a formidable musical foundation. Johnnie played four songs, beginning with an approximate ten-minute version of "Who's Making Love" transitioning into a medley of "Little Bluebird" to finish off his opener. He then played his hits: "Cheaper to Keep Her," "I Believe in You," and "I Found a Love." The audience gave him a resounding reception, leading to Johnnie's increased popularity and broadening his listener base internationally. Taylor typically traveled from show to show by bus, forgoing air travel. When asked to trek 5,000 miles by air to Europe, he was outside of his comfort zone. According to friend and entertainer, Ernie Johnson, Johnnie made this one trip to Europe for the purpose of increasing his popularity and international fan base. But since he felt more comfortable in the states, after Montreux, he rarely ventured outside the country again. Even with only one performance, Johnnie had attracted a new fanbase as Europeans had begun to appreciate the American R&B scene and sought to hear more. Conversely, Ernie Johnson made several more trips overseas resulting in the growth of his European fan base which rivaled his American followers.[4]

Johnnie took another two years off before issuing his next new-material album. Between times, a record was released entitled *Little Bluebird*, a compilation of previous tracks recorded by Stax plucked from three of his early discs. Six songs came from his first album–*Wanted: One Soul Singer*, three were from *Rare Stamps*, and two were previously released on *One Step Beyond*. "In June 1977, a year-and-a-half after Stax went bankrupt, the company's masters were purchased by Fantasy, Inc., which revived the Stax, Volt, and other subsidiary logos for new records, in addition to reissuing older material."[5] Fantasy Records dug these songs out of the vault, packaged them, and released the material hoping Johnnie's days at Stax would generate some interest from older fans. However, the results proved lackluster.

By the time Johnnie released his twenty-fourth album, he was fifty-seven years old. He had gained some weight, lost some hair and his boyish features had been erased by the unyielding hands of time. His voice had taken on a dusky resonance, a far cry from the crisp tenor of his youth. Justin Davidson wrote an article that studied the aging voice and included a short quote from Dr. Steven Zeitels. Zeitels is a Harvard and Massachusetts General Hospital Voice Center laryngeal surgeon and throat doctor who has operated on renowned singers: Stephen Tyler of Aerosmith, Roger Daltry of the Who, and Adele. His perspective about vocal challenges is simple, "It's not senescence (deterioration with age);

it's use. Just as athletes can reach middle age hobbled by arthritis and concussions, so singers often hasten the end of their careers by abusing their gifts. Singers are constantly trying to find a balance between training their muscles and blowing them out. When your instrument is housed deep within the body, health and habit can separate singers who flame out early from those whose voices will last."[6] Regardless of how Johnnie took precaution to protect his vocal prowess, he continually abused his gifts by succumbing to poor health habits. Years of smoking had inflicted its damage. This unhealthy practice was captured in an image from his new album, picturing Johnnie holding a pipe, representing a vice of smoking tobacco from the bowl of a handheld briar.

The *I Know It's Wrong ... But I Just Can't Do Right* album release in 1991 featured songs written by George Jackson, Johnny Barranco and Robert A. Johnson. Johnnie's work on the new LP continued to exhibit respectable performances even after thirty years of recording. Despite his disregard for essential health measures to ensure his longevity, Taylor continued to defy the odds and pushed his way forward, maintaining consistency and musical integrity. The ten-track record wasn't overflowing with hit songs, but had flashes of his old self in cuts like the title track, "I Know It's Wrong." The funk-driven composition begins with a foot-stomping drum pedal and leads into a strapping bass line and well-woven keyboards. Johnnie's self-admission of not doing right is on display with his rich tenor slipping in and out of baritone registers. An ebullient saxophone ties together the two ends of the song to form a tight, satisfying rendition. Taylor uses a Sam Cooke melisma on "I Want Your Love," stretching "my, my, my" and "whoa, whoa, whoa" over several beats and creating his own signature sound. The other tracks range from mediocre to unremarkable, but remain unswerving from Johnnie's well-oiled production of soul deliveries.

CHAPTER 33

MALACO MUSCLE

Alabama's Muscle Shoals Sound Studios had long been the crown jewel of southern rock and blues recording. The company was located just south of the Tennessee River, halfway between the towns of Sheffield and Muscle Shoals. The studio was established in 1969 by four session musicians, Jimmy Johnson, David Hood, Barry Beckett, and Roger Hawkins who felt they could make more money assisting other entertainers than performing themselves. With this in mind, the four purchased an existing recording studio owned by Fred Bevis, music director of Sherrod Avenue Church of Christ in Florence. Bevis had converted an old coffin factory into a recording studio two years earlier. He eventually sold out to the four musicians who had aspirations of growing the company into something dynamic. Not long after, the young men developed a fruitful relationship with Jerry Wexler and Atlantic Records that supercharged their ability to attract big name musicians. The first performer to record at Muscle Shoals was singing sensation, Cher Bono. After initiating a relationship with the management of Stax Records, Muscle Shoals would grow and thrive. The succeeding years brought a string of famous bands and singers to the studios who went on to become international celebrities. Muscle Shoals produced rock music by the Rolling Stones, Joe Cocker, Leon Russell, Lynyrd Skynyrd, Steve Winwood and Traffic, Bob Seger and Rod Stewart. The company also featured soul artists like Percy Sledge, Aretha Franklin, The Staple Singers, Clarence Carter, Sam and Dave, Wilson Pickett, Bobby Womack, Johnnie Taylor, Millie Jackson, Candi Staton and a host of others. The Osmonds, Cat Stevens, Paul

Simon, Linda Ronstadt, Herbie Mann, Ry Cooder and J.J. Cale were also luminaries who utilized the studio for their recordings. What attracted these famous names to Muscle Shoals was the high-quality production and expertise of the engineers, soundmen and session musicians. This, along with what felt like a close-knit family atmosphere, enhanced the appeal of the company; plus the downhome feel of the quiet, laid-back setting contributed to its charm.

Malaco Records purchased the Muscle Shoals Sound Studio in 1985 along with their label and its publishing company. With the acquisition came the well-regarded rhythm players, the four original owners, who joined forces with Tommy Couch, Wolf Stephenson, and Stewart Madison at Malaco. Johnnie's time with Malaco and Muscle Shoals reaped the benefits of the high quality workmanship, camaraderie and southern hospitality to create his own brand of blues and soul. "Recording officials here [Muscle Shoals] believe they turn out more hit records on a percentage basis than the more glamorous, highly publicized recording centers of Los Angeles and Nashville."[1] Keyboardist Barry Beckett, commented on the Alabama vibe, "We're just good ol' Southern Alabama boys. We don't like the L.A. jive. We're straightforward. We don't pull punches. It would be impossible to communicate with those people in L.A. on a day-in-day-out basis." Rick Hall, an employee of Muscle Shoals, added, "The main factor for people coming here is not because they want to see the cotton fields or the town or eat the hamburgers. They know that there are hit records coming out of Muscle Shoals. And that's the only thing the people in the music business are concerned about."[2] Johnnie would go on to develop a long, mutually successful relationship with Malaco and the Muscle Shoals recording studio that would endure over many years to come.

Muscle Shoals Studio–Muscle Shoals Alabama

Studio Inside Muscle Shoals

CHAPTER 34

ON THE ROAD, UP ON STAGE

Three years passed between records before Johnnie released *Real Love* in 1994. The time off didn't seem to improve the offering, as his LP fell short of expectations with less quality music than his previous few efforts. He sang two covers, "The Lady in Red," once a hit for British singer-songwriter Chris DeBurgh; and, although satisfactory, the song didn't quite achieve its potential. The other was a gem which helped make The Staple Singers famous, "Respect Yourself," written by Luther Ingram. Johnnie's version is very good and may be the best of the rest. "Sexy Dancer," brought with it compelling percussion as the song unfolds, then lured the bass tracks into the fray setting the stage for a catchy rhythm. The song, however, seems to be play-acting as a "Disco Lady" replica, but ultimately pales in comparison. A few tunes fade into a gray area posing as blues: "Poor Boy Blues," and "Hurtin' Just Ain't No More Fun," but their real genre was something else. As a complete work, *Real Love* didn't stimulate the cash register as intended.

Johnnie continued his touring although on a scaled-back basis. One such tour was a southern, regional junket. Taylor needed to replace his guitar player, so he asked seventeen-year-old ax phenom, Lance Lopez to fill in for the shows. "We were on what they call the Chitlin' Circuit," Mr. Lopez said, his voice an easy drawl. "I'm the only person on that tour that looked how I look. It was kind of a trip, going through all these places like Little Rock, Columbus, Ga., Jackson, Miss., West Memphis." As for learning on the fly, he commented, "The first time I got hired, I had to learn a 20-something song catalog within a day," he says. "I'd never heard any Johnnie Taylor songs before. I had to learn them on the bus to Atlanta."[1] J.T. would also make the rounds to churches accepting invitations to preach and sing whenever in town. One such occasion was when Rev. Cleophus Robinson, the famed gospel singer and minister at Bethlehem Missionary Baptist Church in St. Louis, asked Johnnie to make an appearance at an upcoming service. Johnnie accepted the invite and roused the congregation with his passionate sermon, then sang the roof off the sanctuary. As customary, Black churches pass the hat for the visiting preacher as a way to show their appreciation. Whatever was received in the plate would be donated to the touring minister as compensation for his efforts. Johnnie's offerings were so generous that day, Rev. Robinson went to the mic and needled the congregation to slow down and not to forget the church needed tithes too.[2]

One of the cornerstones of Johnnie's abbreviated touring circuit was performing in Chicago. He made a name for himself growing up in the Windy City, singing with the Highway Q.C.'s, and then the Soul Stirrers, which led to a strong local following. He had many friends in Chicago and enjoyed returning to the city where he cut his teeth in the business. Since native son Sam Cooke had passed years earlier and Johnnie maintained his longevity, his continual presence held him in high esteem with the fans. Chicagoans had come to admire his accomplishments and would turn out in large numbers whenever he came to town. In 1993, the *Chicago Tribune* described one of his performances and how he held the audience captive. "Slowly, seductively and inexorably, soul crooner Johnnie Taylor brought the house to a near-frenzy in a 45 minute set. Backed by a rhythm section that knows how to hold back the beat and a horn section that punctuated every phrase, Taylor initially sang at almost a whisper. With each number, though, he raised the temperature a few degrees, his warm, crying tenor eventually exhorting his listeners to identify with his romantic yearnings. By the time he reached the full-throttled climax of the show, his horn section was braying in the background, his words were ringing out as if at a church service, his audience was echoing his sentiments with cheers, screams and applause in classic call-and-response fashion."[3] His show preceded Patti Labelle, the headliner that night, and the *Tribune* emphasized Johnnie's repeated standing ovations prior to Labelle taking the stage. Johnnie was a hard act to to follow and apparently stole the show. The year after, July 16, 1994, Taylor played at the second annual Blues Bowl at The Pavillion in Chicago on Racine and Harrison. He headlined the all-day blues-o-rama that also featured Clarence Carter, Bobby Rush, Otis Clay, Denise LaSalle, Bennie Latimore, Buddy Ace, Vernon Garrett, Artie White, Roy C, Lee Shot Williams, Buster Benton, David D, Tyrone Davis and Cicero Blake, among others.[4]

Take This Heart of Mine was the next recording Johnnie released, this time on Fania Records. Fania was known for its Salsa music and Latin performers. How Johnnie ended up on this label is unknown, or how his contractual relationship with Malaco allowed it to happen. None of the songs could be found on-line, so J.T.'s experimentation with Fania must have failed. *Brand New* was the next album from Malaco released in 1996. As in the case with *Take This Heart of Mine*, very little could be found on the songs that made it on the record. For many, Johnnie was considered a blues artist, which was not entirely accurate. He could sing the blues, but his trademark was the gut-wrenching soul that attracted so many followers. Johnnie shrugged off the tag, "I want people to stop categorizing me. Sure, I can sing the blues, but that's not all I do. I've got nothing against the blues. But, it is time that people realize that Johnnie Taylor doesn't just sing blues. Most of the hits I had were not blues."[5]

The club scene for Black performers in Dallas, especially bluesmen, was electric. Clusters of bars, nightclubs and dance halls turned up along the predominantly Black neighborhoods. Some of the venues were located at Fair Park in South Dallas, also in Deep Ellum, Oak Cliff, Hall and Thomas and the West Lovers Lane area. At the outset, Johnnie played at virtually every club in town, especially when he was trying to make a name for himself in Dallas. Blues performer, writer and promo man, Bobby Patterson shared this about his first meeting with Johnnie. They met in a dark hotel bar. Bobby knew of Johnnie's work from his past association with Sam Cooke, his success at Stax, and playing gigs around town. But Patterson had never had the opportunity to sit and talk, one-on-one. Little Johnny Taylor happened to be in Dallas and was scheduled to play at the Waikiki Beachcomber's Club. Little Johnny had a serious drinking problem which created a tendency to be a no-show at his own performances. Bobby had a bad feeling about Little Johnny's commitment that night and felt there was a risk of him missing the Beachcomber gig. Patterson's reputation as a crack promoter was on the line. So, Bobby arranged a sit-down with Johnnie. Coincidentally it was about this time J.T. was covering "Part Time Love," Little Johnny's smash hit. Patterson was confident J.T. could perform the song and felt he'd be able to pull it off as if he were Little Johnny himself.[6] The two men shook hands and J.T. agreed to sing at the Beachcomber for $200, and pretend he was Little Johnny. Johnnie was spot-on with his impersonation of the other singer, word for word, note for note. Since there were no internet images or photos available during that period, it was anyone's guess as to who was on stage that night. The room was dark, and Taylor didn't miss a note impersonating Little Johnny, so no one in the crowd knew any better. The arrangement the two men agreed to that night began a close personal relationship that spanned over thirty years.

Johnnie and Bobby, along with other notables Ernie Johnson, Little Milton, Millie Jackson, and Gregg A. Smith played all over town at various nightclubs. Other nightspots on the Dallas blues highway were the Blackout Club next to the Beachcomber's, the Empire Ballroom later known as the Ascot Club and the Sunshine Bar at the San Jose Hotel in the Hall and Thomas neighborhood. He appeared at the Hill-Smith Hotel, the American Woodman Hall, and the Forest Theater, where he performed with friend Bobby Womack. The Arandas Club in South Dallas owned by Booker McGill, (described as an airplane hangar for dwarves) was also a favorite venue. Located in Fair Park, there were three or four clubs next to each other. This included Sonny Gibson's club, R.L. Griffin's Blues Palace, and Mr. Magruder's Bar and Club. Patterson recalled that performers congregated at these establishments to have drinks, smoke, gamble, carry on, with some even taking the stage for a show if the mood hit them right. Patrons would wander from one establishment to the next, checking out the action, then mosey over to see what was going on at the next place. Black venues in those days were not cut-throat competitors like in today's dog-eat-dog world. The nightclub owners looked out for one another and would even help each other financially if one fell behind on its obligations.[7] J.T. also played at some of the predominantly White hotels such as the Fairmont or the Statler Hilton's Empire Room.

Other hot spots included The Central Forest Club, The Place Across the Street, the Flying Fox and the Plush Pup.[8] Other popular hangouts were the Diamond Club in far Southwest Oak Cliff on Camp Wisdom Road, in close proximity to the Odyssey Club both near Red Bird Mall. Every Monday night, they'd have jam sessions where Patterson and other local artists would come to showcase their talent. Johnnie would show up and support Bobby at gigs, leading to increased traffic at the club. If J.T. sang, he never charged a fee, he was there only to lend a helping hand to his good friend. Taylor not only supported Bobby, but he was a champion for any new performer trying to gain a foothold in the challenging entertainment business. He and his band appeared at a well-known club in Oak Cliff on Loop 12 and I-35 and performed with Patterson, Willie Mitchell and others–to the delight of a few hundred club goers. Again, he sang for free.[9] Bobi Bush was a well-known blues singer in South Dallas, who sang at various clubs around town including the Gold Rush Club in Oak Cliff. Johnnie and Bobi became friends, and he made unannounced appearances at her shows to provide support and to hear her Center Stage Band. "He would always sit at the same table or at the bar and would usually come alone. He never allowed anyone to pay for drinks, he was always generous and picked up the tab," Bobi remembered. "Johnnie was just a 'regular guy'. He didn't act famous and was very approachable." Bobi added that Johnnie never turned anyone away when they were seeking autographs or stopped to say hello. Bush also recalled a particular hat she saw Johnnie wear from time to time. It was made of felt and he could ball it up and put it away in his pocket. When leaving, Johnnie would pull out the fedora, slip it on and be on his way.

Johnnie's devotion to his friends was remarkable. He and Gregg Smith had just finished a show in Houston and were on their way back to Dallas. They discussed Smith's career and how Gregg had sent Malaco some demo tapes hoping to be signed by the label. Smith was disappointed he hadn't heard any reply from Malaco. As they approached the Dallas city limits, Johnnie yelled to Arthur, who drove the Disco Lady tour bus, to take I-20 and go east. J.T. barked, "We're going to Jackson." Malaco's offices were in Jackson, Mississippi and Johnnie wanted to pay them a visit to ask why Smith hadn't received a response. So all the passengers, band included, made an unexpected, five-hour trek to Jackson. Once they arrived, Johnnie and Smith tracked down Tommy Couch Sr., one of the owners. They had him listen to Gregg's tapes on the spot. Couch and his team were impressed with Smith's demo and recognized his talent. Johnnie also showed compassion to his friends when in need. After Smith's father passed away, Johnnie picked him up in a limo to take him to the funeral and stayed with him "every step of the way." Taylor spent the entire day with his friend and even stood by him graveside. To his close friends, he was always available without fail, offering support. Johnnie attended every one of Smith's birthday parties and would always sing a number or two for the special occasion.[11]

Johnnie and Gregg A. Smith were on tour together and had a show at the 20 Grand in Detroit. The owner was Charles Riggins who had Taylor booked for two nights, both sellouts. Prior to their arrival, Riggins didn't know Smith was opening for Johnnie's shows. The bus pulled up to the club and Riggins was excited to see Johnnie. The club owner's enthusiasm soared from the robust ticket sales and the recently renovated dressing room that was constructed especially for Johnnie. Riggins reserved the dressing area for J.T. only and refused to let any other

PHOTO COURTESY OF
RODGERS REDDING

performers use it. After some small talk, Johnnie introduced Smith and told Riggins that Gregg would open the show. The owner went ballistic and told him "No, no, no. He's not getting on that stage. I paid you to perform and the crowd is here to see you, not him. I paid you already and no one's gettin' up there but you." Johnnie replied firmly, "It's my show and he's gonna open." Riggins was incensed and demanded Johnnie get off the bus. Johnnie refused and shut the door. Flabbergasted, the owner stormed away. Taylor looked over to Smith and quipped, "He'll be back in a minute." Sure enough, Riggins came back in a huff and for a second time unsuccessfully tried to persuade Johnnie to get off the bus. After the owner left, Johnnie told his band to go inside. When they got on stage, they were told to play Gregg's song and his co-star would jump up and sing before Riggins could do anything about it. Before Riggins was able to intervene, Smith had taken the stage, and broke into his first song. Riggins fumed at the back of the club watching the events unfold. Once Smith came on it was too late to stop the show. When the crowd cheered Smith's performance, Riggins calmed down. After the ecstatic reception from the crowd for both Smith and Taylor, Riggins sheepishly approached Johnnie and agreed Smith could play the other performance.[12]

In 1995, Johnnie's son T.J. Hooker was scheduled to perform at the American Legion Post in Kansas City. He was on stage during the middle of his show when he got a dreadful feeling about his mother Mary (former girlfriend of Johnnie's) who was infirmed at a local hospital in ICU. Mary had been suffering from lung cancer caused by many years of smoking and had been admitted in serious condition days before. After the show, acting on his intuition, he went straight to the hospital and found his mother had passed away. Mary's funeral was scheduled a few weeks afterward. A day before the funeral, T.J. was to open a show for Johnnie who was in town to perform at the Midland Theatre. T.J. spoke with Johnnie to make sure he was planning to be at Mary's funeral. Johnnie surprisingly balked and told T.J. he had already booked a show in Denver the following day. Justifying himself, Johnnie told T.J. he had been paid in advance and he had to honor his obligation. T.J. was angry at Johnnie's lack of compassion for his mother, especially since Mary had never uttered a bad word about J.T. and over the years, had never asked anything of Taylor. Johnnie tried to comfort T.J. and told him that if he ever needed anything to let him know, and that he'd always be there for T.J. This didn't satisfy T.J. When Johnnie boarded the tour bus to leave for Denver, T.J. drew a pistol and threatened to shoot the vehicle to prevent Johnnie from leaving. In the confusion, a friend of T.J.'s asked for the gun so he could shoot Johnnie, but T.J. waved him off saying he didn't want to shoot his dad, just the bus. About this time, T.J.'s older brother Anthony intervened and was able to calm down T.J. "Yeah we know he really done nothing for none of us but he's not worth it, don't do it, don't do it, don't do it." Cooler heads prevailed and T.J. put the gun away as

Johnnie sped down the highway en route to Denver. Afterwards, Johnnie couldn't help but be burdened with guilt. For three months afterwards, he called T.J. to check in and told him if there was anything he could do for his career, to let him know. He even offered to help him book shows and get a record contract, but neither of these promises were fulfilled.[13]

Occasionally, when the mood struck him, Johnnie would skate through his show in an abbreviated set, sandbagging the club he was performing. Word got around that owners should be mindful of Johnnie's periodic shortcuts to assure themselves Johnnie would be performing a 'full-show.' On one occasion, Taylor was playing in Detroit for a nightclub run by gangsters. Aware of the rumors, the club's manager met with Johnnie beforehand, looked at him sternly and asked if they were going to see the "full show." Not to tempt fate with the mob, Johnnie meekly replied, "Yes sir," and proceeded to play a full set.[14] It was not uncommon for traveling R&B artists to manipulate their pay for performances. Even if their fee for a show was previously agreed on, the entertainer might demand more if there was a big turnout. In essence, they'd hold the club owners hostage until a more lucrative amount could be negotiated. Taylor used this scheme, especially after his 1996 hit, "Good Love." At one particular show, Johnnie arrived at the venue and found a sellout crowd packing the arena. He approached management and said he wanted more money. After all, he'd say, "I've got a hit record, 'Good Love' and they're all coming out to see me." Johnnie was successful in prying more money out of the hands of ownership, but ended up not even playing "Good Love." The owners were furious and demanded to know why he didn't play the song. Taylor responded that "Good Love" had just come out, and the band hadn't had time to practice it yet. Johnnie got away with the ruse on that occasion, but word got around about Johnnie's shiftiness, which earned him a reputation as someone who should be dealt with carefully.[15] Taylor was well known for calling people "Pete." He typically used the name affectionately to certain family members and friends as a way to express his love. There were also times when he'd use "Pete" in the same manner that the British use the expression "mate." "If J.T. didn't know your name, whether or not you were a man or a woman, he'd would call you "Pete" to get your attention or call you over."[16]

CHAPTER 35

Johnnie released three LPs in 1996. The obscure *Brand New* mentioned before, *Good Love*, and *Stop Half-Loving These Women*, which rounded out the busy year. *Good Love* contained two of Taylor's most revered tracks, the title song, "Good Love," and "Last Two Dollars." "Good Love" kicks off the album, setting the tone for an assortment of quality sounds. The song begins with intrigue and anticipation tracking its funk-laden rhythm that calls for heads to nod and feet to move. One of Taylor's most popular tunes followed, that of "Last Two Dollars." With the unmistakable bass barreling down the tracks, Johnnie hits his stride with a groove that's difficult to describe in words. The downtrodden story about the song's character and his last two dollars to use for bus fare, sounds eerily similar to Johnnie's own personal experience. It was reminiscent of forty years prior when Johnnie borrowed bus fare from Mary Hooker to reach L.A. in 1960. There are several other quality tracks that raise the bar from earlier albums. Johnnie closed out the twelve-cut LP with a Leon Russell tune, "The Masquerade," where the instrumentation supports the song respectably; however the vocals revealed how Taylor's voice was slowly fading.

The third disc released in 1996 was *Stop Half-Loving These Women*, a compilation of previously released numbers from a handful of albums, including the title track. It stops short of being what one would call "Greatest Hits" since few are Johnnie's top-shelf material. A decent collection, but as retreads go, it runs middle-of-the-road. That same year (1996), Johnnie received a distinguished honor from the Rhythm and

Blues Foundation for his legendary work over the years. He was awarded the prestigious Pioneer Award.[1] Since its inception, the award has been given to only 150 artists and groups whose achievements contributed to the development of Rhythm and Blues. Taylor's next album to hit the market was entitled *Disco Lady*, pressed in 1997. The album re-released ten Columbia/CBS songs including the heavyweight, "Disco Lady," along with a "Disco 9000" track. Other tunes were taken from *Ever Ready*, *Eargasm*, and *Rated X-traordinaire* LPs. Columbia must have opened their vaults and allowed Malaco to crate-dig through Johnnie's material. Outside of the obvious standout, "Disco Lady," the other cuts are standard issue.

Dallas' Longhorn Ballroom has been around for over seventy years, christened in 1950. The club was built by O.L. Nelms as a music venue for country western legend Bob Wills and the Texas Playboys. Initially it was called Bob Wills' Ranch House. Wills and the Playboys played there regularly in the heyday of the Western Swing era. Dewey Groom joined the company to manage the operation, then bought the nightspot from the owners in 1968. He renamed it the Longhorn Ballroom. Although the dancehall and ballroom targeted country western patrons, over time the club began to lease the venue to R&B, blues and soul performers. Many of the big-name Black musicians and vocalists played the Longhorn, including, B.B. King, Nat King Cole, Al Green, Otis Redding, Ray Charles, and James Brown.[2]

THE LONGHORN BALLROOM–DALLAS
PHOTO COURTESY OF GREGORY M. HASTY

The Longhorn became the number one club in Dallas to see celebrated Black artists and hear favorite tunes and new material. The ownership changed a few times over the years but many of the big names continued to grace the stage. One of the VIP performers was Johnnie Taylor. The

Ballroom reserved Monday nights for R&B and Soul artists and Taylor was one of their regular performers on show night each Monday evening. He always drew a lively Dallas crowd and built a loyal following that packed the house for his shows. If Johnnie and contemporaries weren't playing at the Longhorn, they were in Oak Cliff playing at the Diamond Club or in South Dallas on Grand Street. Johnnie had many pilgrimages back and forth from Kansas City, and he'd always return to play the Longhorn. Later, Johnnie began hosting his annual birthday celebration at the Longhorn. Each May the club held the annual event, building a tradition for Taylor, his band and all his faithful fans. The ballroom was located in close proximity to Black neighborhoods, both in South Dallas and Oak Cliff, making it convenient for fans in the area to attend. Over the years, Black citizens in Dallas adopted the showplace as their own, filling the seats each Monday night. The beloved Longhorn Ballroom had not only been Johnnie's principal hangout, but the club would soon play a pivotal role in Johnnie's future.

Johnnie's next album was *Cheaper to Keep Her*, released the same year as *Disco Lady* in 1997. This disc represented the third consecutive compilation effort with the title track being borrowed from the *Taylored in Silk* album. The lack of fresh music might indicate the shortage of material, loss of interest or the absence of creative juices. It also could have been Johnnie's reluctance to return to the Muscle Shoals studios in Mississippi. Whatever the case, the listening public hadn't been treated to any of Johnnie's original music for quite some time. As Taylor entered his sixties, his time at home and working at a comfortable pace may have taken priority. His forty years recording music was obviously taking its toll. The album's release featured a repeat performance of "Cheaper to Keep Her," which would become an anthem for men who were thinking of wandering from their woman. The lyrics could have been written from Johnnie's own experiences in an attempt to save male listeners the pain and agony of divorce or separation. Taylor asked his audience to weigh the consequences of alimony, doing time, or choosing to weather the storm at home. The song features sage advice mixed with witty common sense, enveloped in a memorable cadence, causing listeners to hum the tune long after hearing the song. The album was cut in Memphis. Rob Bowman, author of *Soulsville U.S.A., The Story of STAX*, provided a backdrop, "Taylor wanted to be more involved in his sessions, so Davis returned to Memphis, figuring Taylor would be more at home there than in Muscle Shoals. The jazzified "Cheaper to Keep Her" was a bit of a novelty for Stax, Davis, and Taylor. The groove was based around a Jazz Messengers' record called "Killer Joe." Davis elaborated, "I really liked what [songwriter] Mack Rice had, but I hated the groove [on the demo]. I thought we had enough going with Johnnie to stretch his base and do a 'Killer Joe' jazz thing. So we took 'Killer Joe' and we put 'Cheaper to Keep Her' on top of it. It was something that was really fresh and it worked. The message was right on. It hit the community dead where it needed to hit it." "Cheaper to Keep Her" successfully charted at number 2 on the R&B listings and 15 on the pop charts.[3]

CHAPTER 36

GOODNESS OF THE MAN

Over the years Johnnie consistently made the rounds across Texas and the nation. Touring was a philosophy he was committed to. He believed that in order to secure fan loyalty he had to meet the masses. He hit festivals, fairgrounds, domed stadiums, amphitheaters, clubs, churches or wherever he could attract an audience. In 1976, Johnnie played at the Dallas Convention Center, one of the largest venues in Dallas, with Tyrone Davis, Dorothy Moore and The Manhattans. Again in 1987, he played for a New Year's Eve celebration, sharing the bill with his friends, Bobby "Blue" Bland, Millie Jackson, and The O'Jays. In 1977 and 1981 Johnnie was one of the headliners at the Kool Jazz Festival at the Astrodome, sharing the stage with names like Natalie Cole, Gladys Knight and the Pips, The Dramatics, The Pointer Sisters, Albert King, The Isley Brothers, Jimmy Cliff and special guest James Brown. J.T. also performed in Dallas at the Benson and Hedges Blues Festival in 1989. The show was a week-long celebration for Juneteenth, affectionately called–Juneteenth Salute-Rhythm Meets the Blues. The event was held at the Starplex within Dallas' Fair Park. Johnnie was one of several headliners along with B.B. King, Etta James, Bobby Womack, and John Lee Hooker. In 1984, J.T. was a featured performer in The Memphis Sound Reunion celebrating former Stax performers, because he led record sales while at the label. The event was held at the Midsouth Coliseum in Memphis and featured a black-tie dinner with performances from Johnnie, the Bar-Kays, Rufus Thomas, Carla Thomas, Eddie Floyd,

William Bell, Shirley Brown, and Albert King. Johnnie also played one year at the East Texas fairgrounds in Tyler.

Taylored to Please, finally brought some much-needed lifeblood to Johnnie's fans. The new album included eleven yet-to-be-released songs of high quality with vintage J.T. "You Couldn't Break Me" written by George Jackson was a definite highlight with its beat-heavy rhythmic pattern and rigorous bass fortification. Timely horns accompanied the message Johnnie conveyed, especially when he mentioned that someone was always after his possessions. "I'm Not the Man You Need," is a deliberate, slow-moving ballad accompanied by strings and piano. The heartfelt tune made use of Johnnie's overly refined vocals and led the listener to ponder thoughts about their own relationship. The unique vibe of "Kickin' Back, Chillin' Out," with its new age, upbeat melody is also a winner, even though it lacked a hook or melodic change of pace within the framework. Johnnie also shined on "Can't Live With You," which opened with a comfortable pulse, making its way across the grooves in classic Taylor fashion. Two other tracks were reserved for more helplings of the song "Disco 9000." This is a head-

CHICAGO BLUES FESTIVAL

scratcher since the album did just fine without including these throwaway tunes. "Throw Your Hands in the Air," injected some interesting hip-hop backchat by Prophet of Pain, Red Dogg and Shampon that established nice progressions for Johnnie's vocals. This song should be played in the car at a volume of ten with bass blasting through the windows. Overall, the record wasn't a masterpiece, but for his aging career, Johnnie didn't disappoint.

Many weren't aware of Johnnie Taylor's generosity and community involvement. He not only donated time and money to charitable causes, he led movements and influenced others to join the campaigns. In 1972, the now defunct, ABA Dallas Chaparrals' basketball team had a sickle-cell anemia night at Moody Coliseum. Johnnie participated in a post-game concert with Little Milton to raise awareness for the illness that afflicts so many Black citizens. In 1991, he led a line-up of national celebrities to participate in the *Light The Way for a Better America* television special. The mini-telethon was presented live from Dallas, Las Vegas and New York with a goal to "bring serious thoughts to education in America." The all-star billing included Robert Goulet, Anne Murray, Johnnie, Billy Paul, and O.C. Smith broadcast live on KDFW in Dallas. Johnnie also supported his many friends in time of need. Bobby Patterson's mother, who lived in a nursing home, was surprised one day when Johnnie appeared to play for her and fellow residents. It was not something he was asked to do. He volunteered to help support his friend. He made frequent visits to various VFW sites and nursing homes around Dallas and delighted tenants with his sweet soul serenades. He never asked for any compensation for his efforts. Not many performers of Johnnie's stature would take the time to help make lives better as he did and continually look for ways to give back to the community. Johnnie also loved the Christmas season. Around the holidays, he'd visit those in need of uplifting. Johnnie offered his services using his God-given talents to take their minds off troubles and to brighten their holidays. He did all of these things for free and never asked for anything in return. As Bobby Patterson related, "He was outgoing and a giving person; when he did positive work, you could see God in him."[1] Johnnie was a member of Good Street Baptist Church in Oak Cliff, and, while not a regular attendee, he called the church home. He was sure to make an appearance when Baptist minister and political activist Jesse Jackson was in town to preach at Good Street. Jackson and the Reverend C.A.W. Clark would ask Johnnie to come to the podium and sing to the congregation. On one particular Sunday, church member Rhonda Grimes recalled that, "he sang 'Swing Low Sweet Chariot,' which she thought was a peculiar selection and she was slightly disappointed he chose such an old classic. Other times he would sing as if he were on stage at the Longhorn. Rhonda's young daughter, Valencia was always at her side Sunday mornings at Good Street and Johnnie began to recognize the young lady from earlier visits. He'd always say hi and shower Valencia with attention. She became fond of his music, hearing songs her mom played at home, and Valencia began to idolize the talented singer. When they ran into each other at church, Johnnie would always address her as his "littlest fan."[2]

Johnnie was a man of the people. Many individuals were interviewed for *I Believe in You*. Each person, without exception, said he never forgot where he came from. He gravitated towards the everyday person, individuals he could relate to; and he could talk on their terms. Bobby Patterson observed that Johnnie never took himself as seriously as other celebrities. Bobby knew he wasn't concerned with image or reputation, and "he didn't succumb to the world."[3] Once you got to know him, it was obvious fame didn't change who Johnnie Taylor was; he was the same person as when he first started in the business. Emmitt Hill was a family friend who frequently helped his mother, Viola Ross babysit the Taylor kids. Viola was Jon's and Tasha's godmother so she and Emmitt saw the Taylors often. In his teen years, Emmitt befriended Johnnie, saying he "was like a big brother." Emmitt was impressed by Johnnie's dedication to his family. Emmitt shared his insight–regardless of what happened on the road, when Taylor returned home he was a committed parent and husband. Jon and Tasha grew up in a secure and functional household with much love from their parents.[4]

J.T. also had a unique gift of being able to talk to anyone in any situation. He'd share his wisdom and experience and could deal with people who were courteous as easily as he could with those who were disrespectful and impolite. In a few words, he could put a brash person in their place, and in the end, they'd respect him for it. He talked in a language they could understand. Johnnie was exceptional in that regard. Taylor often frequented South Dallas clubs, and was able to deal with the constant push and pull of his celebrity, where everyone wanted a piece of him. Rather than avoid the situations, as some might, he knew how to handle each. And when he drove his fancy car into the poorer sections of Dallas with flashy jewelry and sometimes a fur coat, no one accosted him. Taylor was so well-respected and revered as an artist and entertainer that he was held in the highest esteem. People always knew who he was, there was no mistaking Johnnie Taylor for someone else. It was one afternoon during this period when Johnnie was introduced to a young teacher at a local Dallas nightclub who would later become his hush-hush girlfriend. They saw each other consistently over the next several years at shows and events, but kept their relationship inconspicuous to protect his marriage. As it turned out, the affair wasn't that much of a well-kept secret, as many knew of their courtship, but honored Johnnie's wishes to keep the romance under wraps.[5]

CHAPTER 37

NEVER FOUND THE GROOVE

Johnnie recorded his last album in 1999, *Gotta Get the Groove Back*. The LP title makes one wonder if Johnnie felt he had lost the groove and was searching for acceptance as an aging entertainer. The twelve cuts scattered across the disc were all blue-ribbon works. The album's first effort, "Big Head Hundreds," had Johnnie sounding as crisp and convincing as ever. Authentic vocals were backed by attractive, low-toned accompaniment, and a reverberant cadence that created a silky, smooth number. "Juke Joint," was of the same vein, a keeper along with "One in a Million," constructed in fine melodic form. "Too Close for Comfort," was a velvety-smooth rendition featuring a healthy and vibrant bass marking time. The disc's final song is one of Johnnie's all-time signature works, "Soul Heaven." Surprisingly Johnnie never liked the song. It was penned by Rich Cason who had provided him with other tunes in the past. Taylor felt it sounded morbid and wondered why Rich would send him a song mentioning all the people who had died. He brought his friend Gregg Smith to the TAG offices to listen to the cassette and Smith liked it, but Johnnie wasn't sure. Taylor was finally talked into moving forward by Wolf Stephenson at Malaco, and the song was recorded even though J.T. never really felt right about it. Perhaps he had some premonitions about his future. "'Soul Heaven' scared him," [Wolf] Stephenson recalled. "He had a fear about death and leaving this world. He was not very receptive about that tune."[1] Regardless of how Johnnie felt about the song, "Soul Heaven" turned out to be one of his fan's most cherished recordings.[2]

The album proved a point that Johnnie, who had turned sixty-five in

1999, was still a relevant authority in America's R&B scene. Over a half-century of touring, performing, and recording would prove to solidify Taylor's impact on the annals of music history. His staying power was unprecedented, no matter the genre or time period. Johnnie's impact on modern music would be heralded by all of his successors, going forward. Johnnie marked his sixty-sixth birthday on May 5, 2000. The country had just crossed the threshold into the twenty-first century, and all the apprehension about losing data and the world crashing into itself had been alleviated without incident. What would be a more appropriate place to celebrate Johnnie's birthday than the Longhorn Ballroom. May 5th happened to fall on a Friday night, and the Longhorn planned a spectacular, festive affair with Johnnie headlining a line-up with his Dallas friends and musical colleagues. Bluesmen Ernie Johnson, Gregg A. Smith and Bobby Patterson were all on tap for the special gathering. The event featured the four celebratory vocalists and was a tremendous success on a night many will long remember.

JOHNNIE'S BIRTHDAY CELEBRATION SHOW–
LONGHORN BALLROOM MAY 5, 2000
PHOTO COURTESY OF ERNIE JOHNSON

Some three weeks later on May 31ˢᵗ, Johnnie called Ernie Johnson to come by the TAG offices and have a drink. Johnson thought Taylor was calling to arrange payment and make good on what he owed Ernie for his performance at the Longhorn a few weeks earlier. But Johnnie didn't have the cash and would need to pay him the following day. Confused, Ernie asked him, "well if I'm coming over tomorrow why do I need to come over now?" Johnnie replied, "I want to see you," which sounded strange to Johnson. So Ernie made his way over to the converted-home, refurbished to serve as the TAG Enterprises operations. There he met with his friend and they shared some moments over drinks. Johnson voiced his concern over Johnnie's health, as he often did. J.T. responded, "Stop worrying about me Pete, you think I'd leave without tellin' you goodbye?" Ernie thought the conversation was unusual, but left TAG and went to work at KKDA for his radio shift which started at 10 p.m. that night. He arrived around 9:00 p.m. and thirty-minutes later, he received a call from a friend who told him that Johnnie had passed away. Ernie refused to believe the caller and told him it was impossible. "I just saw him a couple of hours ago, he's not dead." Johnson immediately checked news sources and found that the caller's information was unfortunately accurate. Johnnie Harrison Taylor had passed away that night.[3]

Ernie was stunned. As he tried to clear his head, it dawned on Ernie that Johnnie had in fact, told him goodbye. The meet-up at his office was to honor his long-standing commitment not to leave without saying so. During the meeting, Johnson had no idea Johnnie was fulfilling his obligation to orchestrate a proper send-off and farewell.[4] Gregg Smith, who had seen him the day before said they were scheduled to have drinks at their favorite hangout, Coaches Corner in far southwest Dallas. Smith arrived and was talking to owner Frank

Ernie Johnson & Johnnie Taylor
1989

FRIENDS FOR LIFE–ERNIE
JOHNSON AND JOHNNIE
PHOTO COURTESY OF ERNIE JOHNSON

Jones when he got a page from Bobby Patterson. When Smith reached Bobby he was asked if he'd heard anything about Johnnie; there was word that he had died. Smith discounted the notion as a mere rumor having heard other erroneous reports in the past about Johnnie's demise. Not long after, Smith then received a call from Ernie who had been with Johnnie at Charlton Methodist Hospital. He confirmed Johnnie had passed away.[5]

Strangely enough, a few weeks earlier, on May 10, 2000, a divorce decree was finally approved by the courts for Johnnie and his wife Gerlean. They had been together since 1970, however J.T. and his wife had been separated for the last few years pending the divorce.[6] It was uncanny how the timing of their breakup happened just before his death.

JOE "POONANNY" BURNS AND JOHNNIE AT HIS LAST MOTHER'S DAY SHOW HELD IN LAUREL, MISSISSIPPI, MAY 14, 2000
PHOTO COURTESY OF T.J. HOOKER

Irma Parker, his former Dallas girlfriend in the sixties, saw Johnnie occasionally to have drinks either at the Arandas Club or the piano bar at the Hyatt. False rumors of Johnnie's death circulated through Dallas gossip channels even while he was still living. Irma recalled the time she had been shocked after hearing gossip about Taylor's death. She was persuaded to go with her cousin to the Longhorn Ballroom to hear some music. When she sat down, Irma was shocked to see Johnnie sitting two tables over, very much alive and well. J.T. was aware of the false rumors floating around, and when he saw Irma that evening, he shook his head side-to-side indicating he was okay. The last time Irma spoke to Johnnie was a few months before his death. She encouraged him to do a Christmas album. He told her it was a good idea and to remind him in July. Regrettably, the month of July never came for Johnnie.[7]

On the fateful night of his death, Taylor went to see his girlfriend at her place on Shannon Drive in Duncanville, a southern suburb of Dallas. She lived on the same street as Bobby Patterson. Apparently Johnnie had a heart attack while on the driveway in front of her house. Alarmed, she called 911 and EMS hurried over to find Johnnie unresponsive. The EMTs put Johnnie in a mobile medical unit, tried to revive him on the drive while rushing him to Charlton Methodist Medical Center, only minutes away. Sadly, Johnnie Taylor was declared dead soon after his arrival.[8]

CHAPTER 38

AFTERMATH

The music world was devastated. Johnnie's passing stunned friends, fans, music associates and industry professionals across the country and beyond. Johnnie Taylor, the legendary gospel, blues and soul singer who had serenaded fans for nearly sixty years, had departed. Once the grieving city accepted his loss, folks went about the mournful task of preparing for Johnnie's funeral. Since 1971, he had been a member of Good Street Baptist Church in Oak Cliff, so J.T.'s church would be the logical place for his ceremony to be held. Attendees arrived from all over the country and his son Jon flew in from London where he had been on tour.[1] June 8th, the day of his service, mourners began arriving early that morning. Expecting a large crowd, the Sandra Clark Funeral Home had begun to make preparations to control the anticipated throngs of well-wishers. Barbara Kennedy was Johnnie's niece who worked at Good Street and shared, "When we opened the doors, between 8:15 and 8:30 [a.m.], there was already a mile of people." Ms. Kennedy went on to say, "We did everything we could to get everybody seated. It was the place where he'd have wanted this to be."[2] One of Johnnie's public fans, Millie Brown made sure to get there early so she could honor the fallen singer. "I got here at nine o'clock," Millie asserted, "We couldn't even get in. They should've organized things better; this is such a mess."[3]

Johnnie's friend Ernie Johnson, one of the last to see him alive, called the Dallas Police the day before the service and notified the department about the staggering numbers expected to attend Johnnie's funeral. Responding, the city blocked off Bonnie View Road in both directions just before the crowds started to arrive.[4] This allowed for easier access to the church by the teeming foot traffic. The service started at 1:00 p.m. As many as 3,500 people crowded into the church sanctuary which was only designed to hold around one-thousand people. A few thousand other mourners who couldn't make it into the church milled around outside, "either standing by the velvet-roped front walk or under a large tent next door, where two TV monitors broadcast the service. Cars lined the streets for blocks." Another thousand watched the proceedings from a television, set up in an adjoining chapel and many others stood outside the church to pay their respects.[5] The televisions under the tent were difficult to see or hear given the enormous crowds. The noise from the hubbub muffled the ceremonial activities. What was intended to be a celebration of life, at times evolved into more of a party atmosphere and threatened to overshadow the solemn nature of the gathering. The service was conducted by Good Street's renowned pastor, the Rev. C.A.W. Clark who, on a few occasions, had to remind the congregation that they were attending a memorial not an exhibition. During the glory days of blues and soul, record label producers showed up at Black ceremonies like Johnnie's to hear vocalists in hopes of finding a potential new artist to sign. There were plenty in the audience aware of their presence, so there was no shortage of folks who jockeyed about to take the stage. The program featured various speakers, vocalists, entertainers and dignitaries who were Johnnie's friends, family and business colleagues. Johnnie's wife Gerlean sat on the front row of the sanctuary while Johnnie's girlfriend at the time, Dorothy Costanzo, came into the sanctuary late. After Dorothy and her large party arrived, those seated on the back row were asked to move so Dorothy, her family and friends could be seated.[6] Recognizable blues and soul royalty were in attendance; Bobby Patterson, Ernie Johnson, Gregg A. Smith, Tyrone Davis, Al Green, Mel Waiters, Bobby Rush, Millage Gilbert, Bobby Womack, Little Milton Campbell, Millie Jackson, and others who came to say farewell to Johnnie. After she heard the news, Aretha Franklin was too distraught and couldn't bear to attend so she sent one of her representatives.

In Johnnie's obituary distributed at the service, there was a beautiful reading that echoed Taylor's song, "Soul Heaven." "Once more, I close my eyes and see a soul on the wings of an angel. I hear a heavenly choir with voices of angels singing 'Blessed Assurance,' for there is a final resting place for the soul of a Christian. A place where God is in the midst, in a place called Heaven."[7] The services went on for over three hours allowing thousands to file past the casket and see their beloved brother. Johnnie's honorary pallbearers were his closest friends: Ernie Johnson, Bobby Patterson, Gregg Smith and Howard Branch. The active pallbearers were: Bernard Jenkins, Bennie Deer, Jack Williams, Patrick Wick, Paul Denson, James Butler, Bernard Lee, Don Crenshaw, Crystal Thomas, James Johnson, Andre Diggs, Greg Johns, Ray Jones, Jeffrey Aycock and Michael Franklin.[8] The funeral procession finally left at 4:20 p.m.[9] As the crowd departed, Sandra Clark, owner of the funeral home placed rose petals on the hood of her Mercedes before the procession drove away.[10]

Johnnie Taylor had a second funeral the following day, June 9 at Emmanuel Baptist Church in Kansas City, officiated by Dr. W.H. White Sr., Pastor. Kansas City would be his final resting place.[11] Johnnie was interred in the mausoleum at Kansas City's Forest Hill Calvary Cemetery, in a marble crypt at the front and directly below his mother Ida Mae. Johnnie had her remains placed at Forest Lawn's mausoleum twenty-seven years prior. The inscription on Johnnie's crypt lists his birth year as 1937, with no day or month, which is actually incorrect. Johnnie's true date of birth was May 5, 1934. For many years, Johnnie claimed he was born in 1937, however social security records confirm the year of his birth as 1934.

JOHNNIE'S FUNERAL OBITUARY AT GOOD STREET BAPTIST CHURCH IN OAK CLIFF

JOHNNIE'S CRYPT AT FOREST HILL CALVARY
CEMETERY IN KANSAS CITY
PHOTO COURTESY OF GREGORY M. HASTY

Shock waves gripped R&B fans worldwide. The notion Johnnie was gone didn't seem to compute. He was alive one day and the next had disappeared without a shadow's goodbye or an appropriate send-off. From celebrated stars in L.A. to the streets of South Chicago, the Kansas City blues halls, to the East coast nightspots, his followers were in disbelief. His passing came as a blow to Taylor's extended family in many parts of the US. His former lovers and the children he fathered were in denial. The sad news impacted so many individuals from all walks of life. Once Johnnie's death had finally sunk in, the organic design of his legacy would begin to materialize. A special memorial site was set up by Malaco Records in Mississippi, and messages from around the world were posted celebrating Johnnie's life.[12] In her grief, Aretha Franklin honored Johnnie at her upcoming performances. At one of her shows, this observation was made, "For me, the only moving moment [of her performance] came when she went to the piano to accompany herself on Leon Russell's 'A Song for You,' sung for Johnnie Taylor, the recently deceased R&B titan who she had known since the fifties, when they traveled the same gospel circuit."[13]

CHAPTER 39

REMINISCENCE

The hows, whens, and whys inevitably surfaced regarding his passing. Neither Bobby Patterson nor Ernie Johnson observed any signs of fatigue or struggle at Johnnie's performance three weeks earlier when they co-billed at the Longhorn Ballroom.[1] He successfully pulled off his set as he always did, in full command of the audience. Taylor conversed with the crowd, smiled, crooned, and emanated his iconic image as always. Johnnie Taylor was the consummate entertainer, even to his death. As it were, Taylor was booked at shows across the country and when his performances were canceled, it brought finality to his passing. One such event was J.T.'s show scheduled for the Blues Festival at the Petrillo Music Shell at Grant Park in Chicago that June. The concert was to feature Johnnie's performance, arranged to honor Howlin' Wolf's 90th birthday.[2]

It was common knowledge Johnnie had heart issues. His first heart attack in 1980 was a sobering warning signal. It was apparent Johnnie's decades of smoking, drinking, and drug use had left its indelible mark on his physical health. He was well aware of this condition, and at times seemed remorseful and willing to change his lifestyle. Those close to him tried to rationalize his departure: "Dad had some heart issues throughout his life and it was always scary; but that road and that lifestyle, it's, you know–it's not really conducive to taking care of yourself."[3] According to friends and family, Johnnie had considered a possible heart procedure. "He was supposed to get a transplant, but every time he would go to the hospital, he would test positive for drugs so the doctors got tired of it."[4] His friend Mae Young added, "He said 'I think I'm gonna go up to the

Betty Ford clinic and check myself in because I see that I'm messin' up, you know?' And I said, 'Yeah, well do what you gotta do.' He said 'I am, you know, so just pray for me.' I said, 'I will do that.'"[5] Taylor, was ready to make a change and reach out for help, but failed to grasp the hand stretched out in front of him. "We were sitting in church and he said, 'you know what Candi, I'm gonna do better. I gotta get it together girl.' I said, 'I will be so proud of you if you do. Do it Johnnie. Just do it.' He said 'okay.' So I hugged him and that's the last time I saw him alive."[6] Taylor's son, T.J. shared his belief Johnnie was also battling prostate issues.[7] This ailment combined with his heart condition and neglect of a healthy lifestyle probably made matters worse.

When the subject of abusing his body came up, Johnnie's reply to friends who were concerned was his all too familiar, "Well you gotta die of something." And he did. Family members were always fearful of what would eventually happen, "We were always there for him no matter what. We knew who dad was and nobody was gonna change Johnnie Taylor."[8] L.C. Cooke, Sam's brother reflected, "It was just a sad thing. But I'm sure he don't have no regrets because he did what he wanted to do."[9]

Many people shared their thoughts about Johnnie Taylor's life and body of work.

Johnnie " ...was an impossibly cool and learned high priest of love."[10]

Johnnie's loss was devastating to his kids. T.J. Hooker expressed, "I cried man, you know what I'm saying? Even though a child don't see his dad every day you still feel that loss."[11] Johnnie's youngest daughter, Latasha weighed in, "I'm a daddy's girl, so I think about him every day. I don't fall apart because I know he wouldn't want me to. He'd say, 'You're a Taylor and you're gonna be strong.'"[12]

"I love him because he was Johnnie Taylor. I love him because he was my dad," lamented Sabrina Taylor Lewis.[13]

"Johnnie loved life and women; he lived life to the fullest. Some folks didn't understand him, but to me he was a beautiful man, we were like one down home person to another." - Bobby Patterson.[14]

Rashod D. Ollison mentioned in his *Dallas Morning News* article in 1999, "He's a humble, unpretentious man. Like an older uncle. I can imagine him at a family barbecue, trying to dance, embarrassing the younger people."[15]

"He was one of the real kings of R&B–a sweet, soulful singer who could really reach your heart with his music, and also as a person," declared Dallas bluesman Lucky Peterson. "To African Americans, he was a king–right up there with Sam Cooke and Bobby Bland," says Mr. Peterson. "But he's also known all over the world, from New York City to New Zealand to Africa. Everywhere I've been, you hear them playing Johnnie's stuff."[16]

"He wasn't a songwriter, but he was one of the greatest song interpreters in all of R&B," veteran singer and KKDA-AM (730) disc jockey Bobby Patterson shared, "Johnnie had a real knack for putting the right song together with just the right producer." Mr. Patterson, was a close friend and colleague of Mr. Taylor's since the 1960s. "He'd always have R&B hits going, but every now and then he [released] a pop hit and get a whole new audience. His staying power was amazing."[17]

"The best way to put it," his friend and peer Little Milton Campbell voiced, taking time out from a gig in Las Vegas, "is that there was only one Johnnie Taylor. He was a soul man, and there aren't many left."[18] He went on, "When Johnny would choose his material, it would be lyrics that made people go: 'Yeah I've been there, I've done that.' He sang about everyday life. He maintained the heritage of recording about realism. The man was a hell of a singer."[19]

"Johnny was emblematic of the sound that came out of the church," announced author and musicologist Peter Guralnick. "Mr. Taylor had a combination of gospel fervor and vocal sophistication."[20]

"He was very, very important. He kept the trend going for about three decades," said singer and bandleader R.L. Griffin, "He was one of our leaders."[21]

"He was the last of the great soul men and nobody can replace him." Tommy Couch Sr., co-owner of Malaco Records.[22]

"When you heard a Johnnie Taylor song, you didn't have to say, 'Who's that?'" - Bill Minutagio.[23]

"Music lovers in this state were made better by his beautiful voice," observed Casey Monahan, director of the Texas Music Office, a wing of the governor. "I hope people keep him alive by listening to his music."[24]

"You never know why some performers are more well-known than others," observed Peter Guralnick, author of *Sweet Soul Music: Rhythm and Blues and the Southern Dream of Freedom*, recently reissued by Little, Brown. "It's certainly not a question of who's more talented, because Johnnie Taylor is a talented singer who has transcended various eras."[25]

"Ain't no singer alive with more style and class than Johnnie Taylor. Last time I saw the man, he was sitting in a booth in dusty, now-defunct Naomi's Restaurant, wearing a crisp suit and shiny jewels, and it looked as though he sat beneath his own spotlight. Seldom had a man looked more exquisite, or more out of place–the sun come out at midnight." - Peter Guralnick.[26]

"He always had a smile and a kind word, especially for the young, upcoming artist," Timothy Garner recalled. "He was a God-fearing man. He never worried that friends like B.B. King or Aretha [Franklin] were more successful than him; as far as he was concerned, they had theirs and he had his, and that was enough." Garner played in Johnnie's band in the early nineties.[27]

"He was a very honest, loving, down-earth person to me ..."You always think of celebrities as special, but he drove himself around every day. He helped the hungry like a normal person. The city of Dallas lost someone who not only loved the city but the people in it." Niece, Barbara Kennedy.[28]

"How fitting it is that his upcoming single tells of Johnnie having a dream about a party in 'Soul Heaven' with superstars from the past, performing for one night only. As great as all the performers were, they were missing one thing, the closing act! Johnnie, thanks for the memories and enjoy the rest of the show!" - Steve Huey.[29]

"His fans that were his fans thirty years ago are still his fans today even though he's gone. He's not forgotten. Alan Walden.[30]

A year before Johnnie passed away he reflected, "I attribute my happiness to God Almighty. In a career as long as mine, you're going to have some ups and downs." And about his profession, "If I weren't singing, where would I go to apply for a job? I've been singing for forty years. It used to be a labor. Now it's a labor of love."[31]

Even his international followers and fans took note of his passing, "I have played the full variety of his songs on my radio show here in Ireland, and always receive many requests for his music, so I know he leaves a lot of fans on this small island. Music cannot afford to lose such talents–they are not being replaced." Karl Tsigdinos, host of The River of Soul Radio show in Dublin.[32]

"It's a sad day here in France. J.T. will be in our hearts forever." Radio France, Jean Luc Vabres.[33]

To demonstrate how popular Johnnie was with his fans, and the level of importance bestowed on the performer, Rashod D. Ollison wrote a note in the *Dallas Morning News* on August 4, 1999 about a conversation his mom had with his father at the hospital the day he was born, "So, I'm in the hospital," my mother recalls, "about to give birth to you. And your daddy tells me, 'Dianne, 'I'm about to go.' And I'm like, where? He says that he's on his way to the Johnnie Taylor concert in Little Rock, that he would call my sisters [to help me]. I couldn't believe it." Apparently his dad placed more importance on attending Johnnie's show than the birth of his son. Later, whenever his mom and dad had a spat and he threatened to leave her, Ollison recalled his mother saying, "I'd tell him to go [ahead and leave] sometimes, but not before I put on 'Cheaper to Keep Her' by Johnnie Taylor."[34]

Possibly the most poignant and heartfelt message was that of a Dallas fan who summed up the emotions many held for one of the greatest R&B performers of our era. "When I heard of the passing of legendary blues man Johnnie Taylor on the radio on the way to work, I stopped the car and shed more than a few tears. Johnnie Taylor and his music and the way he sang made you laugh, made you cry and made you think. I never personally met Johnnie Taylor but I felt like I had lost an uncle or close cousin. I know there are millions of his fans all over the world, but Johnnie made us in Dallas feel that he only belonged to us. Rest in Peace, Johnnie." E. Smith Mesquite.[35]

PHOTO COURTESY OF
MARK SARFATI

"I do love music," Johnnie admitted, "because it's always loved me. It gives me a certain kind of feeling. The material I choose isn't Black music or White music. It's just music–real, honest music. But as far as my longevity is concerned, I pray a lot."[36] Johnnie Taylor

CHAPTER 40

FAMILY MATTERS

After Johnnie's death, his family reacted with varying emotions. For the most part they were all struck with disbelief. As the patriarch of the family, Johnnie was bigger than life and seemed like a permanent beacon for the clan. He had risen from obscurity in Crawfordsville to somehow climb the ranks to achieve R&B stardom. But now he had suddenly vanished. For some family members, it was a devastating loss of an icon. He was their father, friend, husband, and lover who blazed the trail to fame. He was revered, if not respected by all. To others, his loss was taken in stride as if they knew it would eventually come to pass as a consequence of his lifestyle. Some family members were ambivalent. Johnnie had thirteen known children. Some were either conceived in marriage or by girlfriends he saw over the many years of touring. The illustration below shows Johnnie's various relationships and their children. It's evident Johnnie's courtships were dispersed across the country.

Johnnie Taylor's Acknowledged & Unacknowledged Children

Relationships				
Ruby Richards *Deceased* Kansas City		Anthony Born 1953 Deceased	Acknowledged Child	
Mildred Singletary *Deceased* Chicago		Floyd Born 1954 Deceased	Acknowledged Child	
Harriet Lewis *Deceased* Chicago	1st Wife	Johnnie Jr. Born 1957 Deceased	Sabrina Born 1960 –	Acknowledged Children
Peggye Edwards .. Gastonia, NC		Fonda Born 1961 –	Unacknowledged Child	Proven with DNA Results*
Mary Hooker *Deceased* Kansas City		T.J. Born 1962 –	Unacknowledged Child	Proven with DNA Results*
Susie Smith Jackson - Los Angeles		Schiffvon Born 1963 Deceased	Unacknowledged Child	Proven with DNA Results*
Gerlean Rockett - Dallas	2nd Wife	Jonathan Born 1972 –	LaTasha Born 1973 –	Acknowledged Children

*DNA results came from Johnnie Taylor's siblings gathered for a Paternity Suit in the year 2000.

JOHNNIE'S RELATIONSHIPS AND CHILDREN
PHOTO COURTESY OF NATALIE R. HASTY

CHAPTER 41

SCRUM

Taylor's passing set in motion a series of events that affected his heirs. Johnnie died intestate, meaning he didn't leave a will. This caused a serious problem. There was no clear roadmap on how to sort out the estate and what to bequeath the beneficiaries. This meant that all of Johnnie's assets would be distributed according to Texas state succession laws, which typically follows very strict guidelines. Settling the estate soon became a free-for-all. Johnnie had six acknowledged children: Floyd, [his mother, Mildred Singletary of Chicago], Johnnie Jr. and Sabrina, from his first wife Harriet in Chicago, Anthony Arnold from Ruby Richards, his girlfriend in Kansas City; and two children in Dallas, Jonathan and LaTasha Taylor from his second wife Gerlean. However, three other children came forward claiming they were also Taylor's kids. They were Schiffvon Taylor Brown, T.J. Hooker and Fonda Bryant. At first, Fonda was hesitant to be embroiled in a legal battle, but was persuaded by her mother Peggye to go through with the process and file a petition for paternity. When Fonda discovered there were other secret children, namely T.J. and Schiffvon, Fonda and her mother arranged a meeting to discuss their situation. This resulted in the two unacknowledged siblings asking Fonda if her attorney could represent them also. It was agreed, so the three children filed a paternity suit in order to substantiate their rightful heirship.[1] They had no legal proof they were Johnnie's children, but were hopeful the court would somehow make that determination based on evidence to be presented. What further complicated matters was when Fonda's attorney found out Johnnie and his wife Gerlean had been divorced just weeks before his death. According to Fonda, Johnnie grew tired of the wrangling with Gerlean after four years of negotiating in an attempt to finalize the divorce. After years of disagreement, Johnnie finally gave in to Gerlean's demands.[2] He had agreed to grant Gerlean 50 percent of his estate, which included the North Dallas mansion, valued at $1.2 million. Gerlean would fare well in the proceedings.

When the court hearing opened, there was confusion and increasing animosity between the factions of siblings and Gerlean. The unacknowledged petitioners, T.J., Schiffvon and Fonda were fighting to be recognized by the courts as Johnnie's children and named legitimate heirs of the estate. The three not only wanted to be acknowledged as Taylor's offspring, but there were also financial issues at stake. The three unacknowledged children had received little financial support from Johnnie over the years while they were growing up. Besides having no father in their lives, they were forced to make do with whatever they could earn on their own. For these reasons, they felt it was only right to be included in the distribution of Johnnie's assets. But, the six acknowledged children objected to Fonda, T.J. and Schiffvon suddenly appearing to make a claim on J.T.'s estate. First, there was no proof they were actually Taylor's children. Secondly, acknowledged children wanted to protect Johnnie's wealth from any additional claimants that might surface. It was obvious, to include the three would dilute their inheritance. Beyond the children's clash, Gerlean argued she was entitled to her half of Johnnie's estate. The courts were tasked to determine if Gerlean was entitled to her half of the estate per the Texas joint tenant statutes. The divorce was less than a month before Johnnie's demise and it further clouded the picture. Next, the court had to untangle the chaos between children, determine the rightful heirs and somehow keep the confrontation from escalating.

The claims by the various parties resulted in a contentious court battle for rightful ownership of Johnnie's holdings. Attorneys were hired on both sides and the fight began. Early on, Gerlean attempted to gain control by petitioning the court to permit her to sell off the home before the estate was settled. However, the court ruled against her request.[3] The court intended to clarify who was entitled to Johnnie's assets, thus DNA tests were ordered for the three unacknowledged children. The decision to order DNA samples led to additional hurdles. Taylor's body had been interred several months prior. To make a comparison, the court considered a recommendation by the three claimants to exhume Johnnie's body to obtain a specimen. This would allow officials to analyze Johnnie's DNA and compare it with the three alleged children. The six acknowledged children strongly objected to the exhumation and blocked any attempts to collect the DNA. The court ultimately decided against exhumation. As an alternative, Sabrina, one of Johnnie's acknowledged daughters, volunteered to provide a sample of her DNA to compare with the three.[4] DNA testing at that time was in its infancy and not as sophisticated as what's available today. Technology had just been developed that could accurately analyze what was called sibling samples. This test compared the DNA of a known child with children who were claiming to be offspring. The judge's order for DNA testing angered the acknowledged children. They felt it was an attempt by the three newcomers to finagle their way into their dad's estate. They were also apprehensive of what the results might disclose. This increased hostilities between the two groups of children. Sabrina refused to recognize T.J. as a legitimate heir as did her brother Floyd. Anthony Arnold testified that Johnnie never acknowledged T.J. as a legitimate son which created angst between the two brothers who had known each other for years. While he was on the road performing, Floyd angrily confronted Fonda who happened to work at the venue of his show held in Charlotte. This led to a shouting match that only increased animosity between parties.[5]

In January of 2001, six months after Johnnie's demise, the DNA results were in. However the tests were inconclusive due to a mutation found in one of the samples. The court refused to disclose the identity of the child with the mutation.[6] This led to speculation that Sabrina's sample may have been incompatible with the three unacknowledged children who presumably had identical DNA. This resulted in the court issuing a ruling for another DNA test. According to interviews in the *Unsung 818* documentary, the DNA mutation and an order for another test implied uncertainty as to Sabrina's status as Taylor's biological child.[7]

Regardless of any questions raised by the results of Sabrina's DNA test, Fonda Bryant explained, " ...even if you're born of the marriage, but you're not that person's child, you're still considered that person's child by law. So, either way, she's still an heir even though she might not be his daughter."[8]

A second DNA specimen was subsequently collected, this time from Jonathan and LaTasha, Johnnie's and Gerlean's children. Their DNA would then be compared to the three unacknowledged children.[9]

The unfortunate discord between Johnnie's children and his wife were brought about by Taylor's failure to produce a will or a trust. The absence of estate documents along with his recent divorce clouded the already murky picture. Three unrecognized children surfaced and now grappled with the six acknowledged kids to gain their status as heirs. The first DNA test was thrown out, and another sampling was ordered by the courts.[10] To this point the only parties benefiting from the fiasco were the attorneys, whose fees continually eroded the estate corpus. Gerlean intervened and became anxious to sell the home that represented the majority of Johnnie's assets. After petitioning the court to carve out the mansion for a sale, Judge DeShazo ruled against the motion. All assets were to remain in the estate until final results of the second DNA test were delivered.[11]

An inquest was scheduled for September 11, 2001 at the Dallas Federal Courthouse in downtown to determine next steps to settle the estate. The second DNA test results were in and family members expected to hear the findings. The entire contingent of children drove or flew into Dallas to attend the final hearing that Judge DeShazo had scheduled in her court. A stream of Johnnie's children filed into the courtroom. However, before the hearing got underway, breaking news circulated about a plane crash in New York City. Calls came in describing the terrorist attack and that the World Trade Center was under siege. Despite the national emergency, each of Johnnie's children and others testifying were called into the courtroom one by one. Whenever the group was fully assembled inside, the bailiff entered the courtroom and informed everyone about the terrorist assault. At this point, the courtroom was locked down to restrict entry and exit.[12] Anthony Arnold recalled that morning, "Every federal building was under heavy guard, the security was very tight, the security people running around everywhere with rifles and pistols almost in the ready position."[13] No one quite knew what was happening and the commotion and confusion was evident.

Judge DeShazo was tasked with the decision to move forward with the hearing in light of the terrorist attacks, or canel. If she canceled, it would cause an undue burden on the children who traveled great distances to make the court appearance. Therefore, DeShazo elected to go forward with the proceedings despite the national tragedy unfolding in New York. To do so, everyone was to remain locked in the courtroom as each witness was given an opportunity to testify. A DNA test was presented by the attorney of the three unacknowledged petitioners and was accepted by DeShazo. Once the DNA results were made available to the court, Judge DeShazo unexpectedly decided not to read the analysis in court.[14] Whether it was the chaotic atmosphere caused by the terrorists or the potential for escalating hostilities between sides, she chose to delay the reading. The judge closed the hearing and advised the parties DNA results would be sent to each person by mail.

Once she made the ruling, both sides became angry having waited nearly two years to settle the case and were now faced with the prospects of the trial dragging on even further. Their fears became reality as the litigation was prolonged and attorney fees continued to accrue. A year later, in an unbelievably lengthy delay, the court announced results of the DNA evidence. On October 9, 2002, two-and-a-half years after Johnnie's death, the children received the DNA test results in the mail. The outcome declared, with 99.9999 percent accuracy, that Schiffvon, T.J. and Fonda were all in fact, Johnnie's biological children.[15] This meant the three children born out of wedlock were added to the six who were already acknowledged, bringing the number of beneficiaries to nine, not counting Gerlean. The three new heirs felt vindicated knowing their father was positively identified as Johnnie Taylor. What they had been claiming all along had been confirmed. Sabrina's DNA test results were never discussed in the proceedings.[16]

Once the heirship was determined by the DNA results, the court granted Gerlean 50 percent ownership of the Taylor's North Dallas mansion. The remainder of the estate would be divided equally among the children and Gerlean. Coincidentally, Gerlean was a licensed real estate professional and appointed herself as listing agent for the Taylor home according to *My Plainview*. This allowed Gerlean to be the sole negotiator of the contract, free to agree on a sales price without the input of the nine children. After the house was sold, she would also receive the customary real estate sales commission.[18] As the estate began liquidation proceedings, it was discovered Johnnie owed a number of creditors including a significant amount to the Internal Revenue Service. The IRS swooped in and placed a levy on Johnnie's bank account to pay delinquent taxes. Afterwards there was not enough cash on hand to pay other debts, so the home would need to be sold to clear these obligations. While waiting for the sale of the home, the first order of business was to liquidate Johnnie's personal assets. Brant Laird Estate Sales was engaged to liquidate his personal effects. On September 19, 2003 an estate sale was held. Proceeds collected from the sale would then be applied to Taylor's debt. The sale was widely publicized, and Laird expected to see thousands of people attend, especially after the overseer "priced the things to sell." Before the public event, a private sale was held to give the family an opportunity to purchase some of Johnnie's effects. According to *My Plainview*, only two children attended, (most likely) those who lived in Dallas.[19] Very little was purchased. Johnnie's son T.J. claimed neither he nor the other unacknowledged children were told about the private sale. Whenever they inquired about certain items, the Laird group claimed it had already been sold or the item was unaccounted for.[20] Included in the sale would be Johnnie's 9.66-carat diamond ring, a Rolex, his Mercedes, a diamond-encrusted gold bracelet, a diamond and emerald ring, gold necklaces, furs, a baby grand piano and a restored 1946 Wurlitzer jukebox filled with records from the 1940s. Among the other personal treasurers of Johnnie's put up for sale were his platinum and gold records.[21]

After the home was sold, the real estate proceeds along with the income generated from the estate sale were applied to the debt Johnnie owed. This included the hefty attorney fees that had accumulated over years of paternity litigation. When the dust settled, and real estate commissions were paid, legal fees from the endless continuances by the court were deducted, and the remaining creditors were paid off. Johnnie owned three acres of land in Hawaii that would be sold later. Once the debts were paid, each of the children received whatever remained of their prorated 50 percent of the estate. According to Fonda, each child netted a paltry sum of only $2,000.[22] The protracted legal battle and Johnnie's financial neglect wiped out the majority of their inheritance. The nine children, who had expended untold hours battling for their share only received a meager pay-out for their years of anxiety and legal squabbles. The battle not only cost the kids hundreds of thousands of dollars, but they lost the opportunity to bond with each other as a family. Even though Johnnie's nine offspring were splintered and angry, T.J., Fonda and Schiffvon had been vindicated as rightful children of Johnnie's, and there was a certain feeling of accomplishment in that. As far as his personal inheritance went, T.J. rationalized. "You can't miss what you never had,"[23] and went on, "All I wanted was to let everyone know that I was Johnnie Taylor's son."[24]

CHAPTER 42

NEVER ENDING MESS

Controversy surrounding Johnnie Taylor's case wasn't over. There was still the matter of Taylor's royalties due from the record labels. Beginning in 2011, Fonda began looking into why no royalties were being received from Sony, the successor of CBS/Columbia Records. For nine years Fonda had been badgering the label to provide accounting information on her dad's royalties. Sony's response to Fonda over the years had been that Johnnie had an unrecouped balance on his account. This meant Johnnie took out advances prior any record sales from various releases. As records are sold, the royalties pay down the debt from the advances. This way the label is able to recoup the loans (advances). According to Sony, Johnnie's account had never been fully recouped. In fact, Taylor's account was reported to still owe $72,000.[1] With hits like "Disco Lady," it seemed logical whatever advances Johnnie received would have been eliminated by the staggering sales of the album. It was noted in the November 21, 2021, *Rolling Stone* article about Taylor's royalties, that Johnnie may have had additional advances that increased the debt owed to the label. The article also stated he allegedly owed the label hundreds of thousands of dollars when Johnnie and CBS ended their relationship in 1980.[2] What seemed like a simple accounting exercise to determine if Johnnie had any remaining debt proved to be convoluted and confusing. In the late 1990s and the early 2000s, accounting records for royalty payments were sketchy and very hard to track. Paper trails showing loans and recouped payments were also confidential and it seemed as if no one really understood how the process worked. Based on the information gathered in the story, this was why record companies were hesitant to provide royalty records from that time period.[3]

According to *Rolling Stone*, Fonda was repeatedly stonewalled when she attempted to obtain information from Sony. This led to her speculation that there was fire where she sensed smoke. Ironically, at the time Fonda continued to ratchet up pressure for the label to share royalty information, Sony made a surprising announcement. The company released a statement saying they would donate $100 million to create a fund to support social justice and anti-racist initiatives around the world. Donations would therefore be immediately distributed to organizations that supported equal rights. Fonda saw this as corporate hypocrisy and wrote to a Sony vice president in August of 2020: "If you guys are supposedly getting involved with social justice, clean up your backyard first."[4] The letter appeared to have an impact. Only a month later, Sony told Fonda her dad's $72,000 balance he owed would be waived and a one-time royalty payment of $97,000 would be distributed, pro-rata to Taylor's ten heirs. The payment was a minor victory but didn't satisfy Bryant who thought there was much more owed to the family. Fonda viewed the payment as a way to convince her and the siblings to go away. After Fonda continued to badger the record label, checks suddenly began to show up in the mailbox. According to her brother T.J., the majority of the royalties were going to Geri and her two children.[5] When Fonda began her investigation it became evident she and the other six siblings weren't listed as beneficiaries. This was quickly rectified, and the record labels began making long overdue royalty payments to each heir.[6] Fonda was like a bulldog she didn't let go once she embarked on a mission. T.J. has great admiration for his sister. "She's just like Johnnie Taylor; she's another Johnnie Taylor reincarnated,"[7] referring to how seriously focused they were about their business. "She's nothing to play with," T.J. continued. This never-quit attitude greatly benefited her siblings.

This was another sad chapter on the death of Johnnie Taylor and the repercussions of his passing. The intra-family disagreements and the absence of a will or an executor made life difficult for all involved. The number of children, whether acknowledged or not, and his untimely divorce further complicated the process and increased the trauma.

CHAPTER 43

OFFSPRING

Johnnie had thirteen children who have been identified and claimed to be his offspring. Six underwent DNA testing. By way of a court order, three unacknowledged children were confirmed as his descendents through DNA analysis. Johnnie had five children during his two marriages, the other eight were born out of wedlock and raised by their mothers or other family members. After Taylor's death, groups of children formed a loose association. Anthony and T.J. were able to resolve their differences following the paternity suit and they remained close. Anthony showed regret for alienating T.J. in his testimony and had second thoughts about his statements in court. They remained on good terms for many

L-R Peggye Bryant, Schiffvon Taylor Brown, Susie Smith Jackson (Schiffvon's mother), Fonda Bryant, Martha Youngblood (Fonda's Aunt) and T.J. Hooker
Photo Courtesy of Fonda Bryant

years until Anthony's passing in 2019 after a battle with cancer. T.J. became the de facto intermediary between the unacknowledged family members, and stayed in periodic touch and maintained good relations with both Fonda and Schiffvon.

Sabrina and Floyd never totally accepted the three unacknowledged children as family members. For the most part they remained estranged. Several of Johnnie's children pursued opportunities in the music business. T.J., Floyd, Johnnie Jr., Jon, and Tasha were all talented vocalists and musicians who took to the stage at one time or another. Anthony could sing too, but didn't pursue the undertaking as seriously because of other interests.

Floyd and T.J . took 'Taylor' as their last names so listeners could make the connection to their famous father. T.J., Jon and Tasha still perform today. Johnnie's sons sought to collaborate on a *Sons of Johnnie Taylor* album. Floyd, who was signed with Malaco Records, was the most recognizable name and T.J., Anthony and Johnnie Jr. would contribute songs. The four were excited to come together and make a family album so they could honor their father. However, Floyd backed out at the last minute and told Malaco he didn't want to record with his siblings. This stunned his three brothers and caused serious friction, from that point forward. T.J. lamented the fact that he and Floyd were like, "oil and water," they just couldn't get along.[1] Later T.J. did make an attempt to restore harmony with Floyd by meeting with promoters to arrange a show for him and Floyd to play in Memphis. However when the date arrived, Floyd refused to let his brother take the stage. This led to T.J.'s angst. A couple of years passed, and both happened to be in Little Rock for a show. Floyd ignored T.J. and acted as if he didn't know him, which led to further bitterness. After Floyd's snub of the *Sons of Johnnie Taylor* album concept, Johnnie Jr. developed animosity for his older brother. They never reconciled. T.J. was sad to see the way Floyd treated his brothers and how the three of them missed an opportunity to unite, celebrate their father's accomplishments and gain recognition by recording the album.[2] After Floyd died in 2014, T.J. collected song material and, despite the failure of the earlier project, a family album was released in 2019. The LP included a collection of songs by T.J., Floyd and Johnnie Jr. The record was entitled, *The Sons of Johnnie Taylor A Tribute to His Legacy*. To this day, T.J. remains puzzled by Floyd's decision to spurn his brothers. "He could have gone solo after the sons' album,"[3] but for reasons only known to Floyd, he elected not to. At the time of this writing, four of the nine identified heirs had passed away: Anthony, Floyd, Johnnie Jr. and Schiffvon.

Anthony Arnold, born 1953, Kansas City. His mother was Ruby Richards. Johnnie met Ruby in Kansas City when she was fifteen, during his tour with the Highway Q.C.'s. Ruby remained unmarried and birthed Anthony when she was a teenager. She later married Leon Arnold, who adopted Anthony when he was a young child. He was the

JOHNNIE TAYLOR'S SONS, BACK ROW JOHNNIE TAYLOR JR. LEFT AND RAHEEM MACKEY FRONT ROW-L-R, T.J. HOOKER, FLOYD SINGLETARY AND ANTHONY ARNOLD PHOTO COURTESY OF RAHEEM MACKEY

oldest of Johnnie's children and was often called "Big Brother" by his siblings. Anthony graduated from high school in Kansas City and attended the University of Kansas for two years. Arnold became involved in the construction business and, as a sidelight became an expert horseman and rodeo aficionado. He was most notably associated with the Twin City Invitational Rodeo. Anthony at one time owned as many as sixteen horses. Arnold met his wife Pat in 1992. Pat grew up on a farm nearby and shared his passion for horses. Not surprisingly they were married at The Rodeo Finals in Las Vegas. He loved to two step, play dominoes, travel and bowl. His annual ritual was to attend the Kentucky Derby, which he did for over twenty years. Like many of his siblings he could sing, although he didn't pursue it professionally, but did participate in the church choir. Anthony and his brothers had a memorable performance when he, Floyd, T.J., and Johnnie Jr. sang together at Kansas City's Thanksgiving Breakfast Dance in 2014. Arnold was an active participant in civic and non-profit organizations such as the American

Royal, a food and agricultural education non-profit. He became the first African American to be selected to the board of directors. He was also involved as vice president of the Twin City Riders Saddle Club, Dismas House, president of the Kansas City Blues Society, and was engaged in the Minority Contractors Association, the Tom Bass Mounted Patrol, the Cole Finch Lodge and the 18th and Vine Redevelopment Corporation. Arnold offered up his home for little brother Johnnie Jr. to live when he needed to straighten out his life, and Johnnie Jr. lived

L-R Pat Arnold, Anthony Arnold and Ruby Richards
Photo Courtesy of Pat Arnold

with Anthony and Pat for four years. After a lengthy battle with cancer, Anthony succumbed and passed away in 2019 at sixty-six–the same age as Johnnie when he died.[4]

Anthony Arnold and Johnnie
Photo Courtesy of Pat Arnold

Floyd Singletary, born 1954, Chicago. His mother was Mildred Singletary, a single mother who had a relationship with Johnnie when the singer was only eighteen. Floyd was Taylor's second son, also born out of wedlock. He and Anthony were born three months apart. Floyd was urged by his mother to sing in the church choir at five years of age. Later at Dusable High School he continued performing as a member of a ten-piece Kool & the Gang cover ensemble, named The Peace Band.[5] After graduating from high school, Floyd pursued a singing career and his first show was at the Regal Theater. Other performances followed on the Chicago club circuit. While moonlighting on stage, Singletary was a hospital employee at the Mercy Hospital and Children's Memorial Hospital.[6] Floyd idolized Johnnie and took every opportunity to showcase his talents which closely resembled his dad's. Floyd toured with Johnnie and on occasion, opened for the shows, or sang back-up vocals sharing the spotlight with his dad. As Floyd's career developed, he became a noteworthy blues singer and was signed to Malaco, the same label that recorded Johnnie for over seventeen years. Floyd was honored to sing at his father's funeral service in 2000, at Good Street Baptist Church. Malaco's Tommy Couch Jr. was in attendance and was impressed, so he signed Floyd to a record contract a short while later.[7] Singletary recorded six albums released in 2002, 2005, 2007, 2010 and two in 2014. Floyd sounded hauntingly like Johnnie and was very comparable in style and intonation. A few of Floyd's records charted, and he was voted Entertainer of the Year in 1998 by the Chicago Blues Society. Tommy Couch

JOHNNIE'S SONS L-R
ANTHONY ARNOLD AND
FLOYD SINGLETARY
PHOTO COURTESY
OF PAT ARNOLD

Jr. of Malaco shared that it was eerie being in the same room with Floyd after working so long with Johnnie. Although a larger man, Couch expressed that Floyd was a carbon copy of Johnnie in looks, mannerisms, and speech. He went on to say, when talking with Floyd it was as if he was actually talking to Johnnie.[8] Floyd also sounded like Johnnie in song. Brother T.J. recalls Floyd coming back to Chicago after spending time in the South at Malaco, and was wearing Johnnie's rings and other jewelry. According to T.J. in his interview, they were purchased on Ebay by Malaco management.[9] Floyd had a massive heart attack at his apartment in Chicago and passed away at the age of sixty.[10] After his passing, the

Town Blues Festival in Merrillville, Indiana was forced to cancel his show that was scheduled in March.[11]

Johnnie Taylor Jr., born 1957, Chicago. Junior was Johnnie's first child with first wife, Harriet Lewis. Johnnie was a musician who played the guitar and had very respectable vocals. He lived fast and hard and his big brother Anthony and wife Pat took him in to provide stability in his life. He lived with his brother for four years and honed his skills as an accomplished cook, working in restaurants around town. Spud was the nickname big brother Anthony gave him. He released two albums, *Doing My Own Thing*, in 2001 and later an LP entitled, *Second Time Around* published by Aviara Music. He loved to sing and would seek opportunities to share vocals with his brothers or

JOHNNIE'S SONS ANTHONY ARNOLD LEFT AND JOHNNIE TAYLOR JR. PHOTO COURTESY OF PAT ARNOLD

play guitar at church. As many entertainers do, Johnnie fell victim to poor life choices and suffered from his excesses. He developed heart problems and diabetes and died June 2020 at age sixty-two.[12] Johnnie Jr.'s son Calvin Arterberry also became an entertainer following his father's and grandfather's paths as a performer. He's known as "Verse" and has released his own hip-hop album, *Mixed Emotions* in 2009.

Sabrina Taylor-Lewis, born 1960, Chicago. Harriet Lewis's second child. Sabrina graduated from William Rainey Harper High School in Chicago and, in 1982 received her degree from Arkansas State University. She became her father's road manager and toured with him and the band. Sabrina and Johnnie remained close throughout his career. She now lives in Dallas and worked for Texas Oncology.[13]

Fonda Bryant, born 1961, Gastonia, North Carolina. Her mother was Peggye Bryant who Johnnie met while touring with the Soul Stirrers. He was introduced to Fonda's mother Peggye at her grandmother Aronna

L-R Johnnie's Son Floyd Singletary and Johnnie Jr.'s son Calvin "Verse" Arterberry Photo Courtesy of T.J. Hooker

Bryant's home when Peggye was only fifteen. Arona was a gospel promoter who hosted traveling musicians who needed a place to stay or have meals. "My grandmother [Arona Phillips Bryant] was a gospel promoter in Gastonia, North Carolina," Fonda commented. "They had gospel singings at the high school, and Sam Cooke The Soul Stirrers, Clouds of Joy, and The Staple Singers, would all come to the house, because they couldn't go to hotels or restaurants in Gastonia." Bryant continued, "She was fifteen at the time and dated him for two years."[14] Peggye vividly recalls her first encounter with Taylor. They strolled over to a quiet spot underneath a huge Mimosa tree and Peggye remembers what both were wearing. Peggye sat in the shade wearing her blue dress, Johnnie's head rested in her lap. She was young and impressionable, and Peggye described Johnnie as "really handsome with pretty teeth." She was fascinated by his travels across the country and the adventures performing with a nationally known gospel outfit. The young teenager became smitten, especially after he sang "I Loves You Porgy," from the opera *Porgy and Bess*. Over the next few years Johnnie continued to make

L-R Fonda, mother Peggye and son Wesley Photo Courtesy of Fonda Bryant

stops in Gastonia, and on one of the visits they had their one and only intimate rendezvous. A few months later Peggye realized she was with child.[15]

Fonda recalled the story when her mom found out she was pregnant. Johnnie was in New York playing at the Apollo and Fonda's aunt, Martha (Peggye's Sister) attended the show. Martha saw Johnnie afterward and informed him that Peggye was pregnant. After hearing the news about Peggye's pregnancy, Johnnie never returned to Gastonia. Neither Peggye nor Fonda ever saw Johnnie again. Much later in life, Fonda was working for a radio station and one of the on-air personalities knew Johnnie. He gave Fonda Johnnie's phone number, and

FONDA BRYANT
PHOTO COURTESY OF FONDA BRYANT

Fonda called in an attempt to develop a long-distance relationship, but it wasn't meant to be. Father and daughter talked occasionally, but the conversations weren't always cordial, and, on one occasion Fonda hung up on Johnnie. In one of their talks, Fonda gave Johnnie her mom's number. He and Peggye talked for over an hour, but they never were to meet again. Peggye and Fonda did try to connect by inviting Johnnie for dinner, but he declined. That was the last time Peggye spoke to Johnnie. She heard the news of his passing on WEAS-FM in Savannah. Over the years, Fonda had written several letters to Johnnie. After his passing, Johnnie's ex-wife Gerlean was cleaning out the TAG offices and came upon Fonda's letters to Johnnie. Johnnie kept Fonda's correspondence all those years, but never chose to meet with his daughter. The sentimental letters were never returned to Fonda.[16]

Fonda would become a mental health administrator in Charlotte. Fonda had this to say about her relationship with her father. "The first time I talked to him, I was twenty-eight years old, living in Savannah

[Georgia] working as a pharmacy technician." His first comments to her were not exactly endearing; he asked if she'd inherited her mother's pretty legs. "He knew I was his daughter, so I'm going to get an attitude, and I asked, 'Why didn't you look for me?'" They tried talking over the years. Sometimes they were good chats; sometimes not. "I would call him up, and we would talk, and he'd be all nice and caring. And other times, I would have to hang up on him." He could be rude and harsh, which she blamed on his lifelong use of drugs. Fonda shared, "My son, my pride and joy, was very smart in school and a good athlete." He is Wesley Taylor Bryant, named after my father, and I told him [Johnnie], 'Look, if you

don't come to your grandson's graduation or his party, I'm done with you, because I'm tired of trying to forge a relationship with you." Taylor died on May 31, 2000, a year before Wesley's graduation.[17] Fonda, still bitter about his absence throughout her childhood and young adulthood and the paternity court battle, reflected about her father: "He's not here to take responsibility for all this mess. Once again he put us through something that could have been avoided had he just been a man and took care of his responsibility."[18] She felt her dad had been a victim of the times during extreme racism and hate. During the 1940s-1960s, Black entertainers

FONDA BRYANT AND JOHNNIE'S
GRANDSON WESLEY BRYANT
PHOTO COURTESY OF
FONDA BRYANT

witnessed extremely troubling circumstances while touring the US, especially in the South. Images of beatings and persecution were remembered along with being prohibited from patronizing restaurants, hotels and clubs. Frequent racial violence was a common occurrence. During this period, singer Ike Turner witnessed his father illegally hanged and others like Emmett Till who were victims of lynchings. The "Godfather of Soul", James Brown and many others of his era were also casualties of physical abuse by parents or family members in what was a common occurrence. These experiences left indelible marks on their psyches. Furthermore, there were no solutions for dealing with mental health problems, PTSD or abuse. As a result, said Fonda, Black citizens internalized the sufferings and took it out on other family members or self-medicated with liquor or drugs.[19] This is the environment Johnnie grew up in. Although Fonda had no knowledge of Johnnie being abused, the separation from his parents and being sent to live with his grandmother at a young age indicate an incident might have occurred during his childhood. Since Ms. Bryant is a mental health professional, she makes a compelling correlation to the environmental challenges in Johnnie's youth and the vices he developed as an adult. She feels events he experienced may have triggered his questionable behavior related to alcohol, drug dependency and promiscuity. Fonda sympathized with Johnnie's plight, "I really wished I could have helped my father. I really understand addiction. Addiction and mental health go hand in hand."[20] Ms. Bryant is an avid proponent of suicide prevention and is a frequent speaker on the subject counseling employees and management on coping mechanisms.

Regarding challenges of dealing with the paternity case, Fonda reflected, "So many times I wanted to give up the court fight, but my mom Peggye, kept me going. She told me, 'You are his child. You will win.'" "It's like a big weight has been lifted off my shoulder," admitted Bryant, a former sales and accounting assistant for a local radio station in Charlotte. "I had to wait forty-one years for the legal aspect to be proven. If it hadn't been for DNA, we wouldn't have won."[21]

JOHNNIE'S SON T.J. HOOKER
PHOTO COURTESY OF T.J. HOOKER

Tyrone, "T.J." Hooker, born 1962, Kansas City. Johnnie met T.J.'s mother Mary Hooker at the Ninth Street Missionary Baptist Church, home of Isaac Hooker's congregation. They developed a relationship while in Kansas City, and Mary became his girlfriend. For a while Mary was a single mom, and had been married at one time to Eugene Pernell. They later divorced. Together Mary and Eugene had three children, Donald, Rhonda and Marlin. Even though T.J. was Johnnie's son, the four children grew up together in their mom's household in a tight-knit family. T.J.'s nickname was "Pookie." T.J. grew up without a true father, but Mary made sure he knew who Johnnie was; and T.J. accepted the fact that he and his dad would be estranged. T.J. has a distinct memory of first meeting his father. He was around five or six and visiting his grandmother Ida Mae. That day, Ida Mae gave T.J.

a red bike told him it was from his dad. Right as T.J. was given the bike, Johnnie walked through the door. "The man I'd been hearing about was right in front of me, couldn't say a word," T.J. recalled. "I didn't know this person they called my dad, but I was glad to have one,"[22]

It was a sad day when T.J.'s paternal grandmother, Ida Mae passed away in 1973. Johnnie returned to Kansas City for the funeral, "When my dad finally came

JOHNNIE AND T.J.
PHOTO COURTESY OF T.J. HOOKER

into town, I could tell he was a different person than what I had met before." T.J. remembered, "After the service though, he was over, so me and my dad and my brother Anthony Arnold were upstairs and we got acquainted at Uncle Willie's house. I remember we stayed up all night and we talked." T.J. continued, "This was a real good bonding time from 10 p.m. to 6 a.m."[23]

Johnnie's absence left a conspicuous void in T.J.'s life. He dreamed of someday being able to sing like his dad and maybe have the opportunity to work with him on stage. Over the years, Johnnie's unavailability disappointed T.J. many times. Trying to engage Johnnie's time and attention was difficult, given the many commitments a celebrity of his stature was obligated to make. Johnnie's celebrity commitments occupied much of the time he could have been spending with his girlfriends and children. T.J. was but one victim of the abandonment. At times T.J. felt lost in a vacuum trying to establish a quality relationship with his dad with very little success. Although T.J. grew up fatherless, his dad's imprint was etched into his psyche. T.J. became a professional singer and toured the country, not only showcasing his own talents, but many times singing tributes to his father. Later in Johnnie's life, T.J. was always excited to occasionally open for his dad's shows. Johnnie's death in 2000 was a huge blow for T.J. He had worked so many years for Johnnie's respect and recognition and never felt he had attained the father-son relationship he sought.

After Johnnie's passing, T.J.shared his thoughts, "I loved my daddy and he shared his music with me. He wasn't perfect, no one is. I had a lot of respect for him. I don't have a lot of bad things to say. I've always had a positive outlook on him."[24] T.J. recorded several albums and Johnnie's influence on the LPs is apparent in the titles. T.J. Hooker was determined to make it clear he was Johnnie's son. T.J.'s first album was released in 2005 and was called *2nd Generation of Johnnie Taylor* on Hooked Up Records. His initial work was followed by *Total Package* also released on Hooked Up in 2007. *Your Babies Need a Daddy* was his next disc released in 2009 on CDS Records followed by *Taylorized* in 2012. T.J. also collaborated with The KC Clouds in producing a gospel album, entitled *Going to Church*. His latest solo effort is *Bloodlines-Son of Johnnie Taylor*. T.J. also self-produced a CD called *Like Father, Like Son*. An additional album was mentioned earlier that included tracks from Floyd and Johnnie Jr. for which T.J. also contributed songs, titled "*Sons of Johnnie Taylor*." For a while T.J. worked at Forest Hill Calvary Cemetery in Kansas City as a caretaker. There, he maintained Johnnie's resting place, along with grandmother Ida Mae and his mom Mary, to assure their gravesties would be looked after properly.[25]

T.J. fought for many years to be recognized as Johnnie's son. He was often spurned by the other Taylor children who were family members of Johnnie's two marriages. It was a constant battle to be acknowledged, especially after he began his career, as the siblings refused to accept him as a true family member. Johnnie's death and the settlement process of his estate finally proved T.J. was Johnnie's legal offspring. The DNA specimen collected during the paternity suit laid the issue to rest–once and for all. His long sought-after vindication, though late in coming, gave him the much needed, absolute confirmation of his heritage. It was a fact that Johnnie Taylor's blood ran through his veins. T.J. is married to wife Beatrice and has five children, Tynesha Hooker, Monay Gonzales, Rhonda Wilkerson, Tyrone Hooker Jr., Tasneed Jones and two step-children, Kashif Rashid-Bey and Sakina Rashid-Bey.

T.J. was solely responsible for coming up with the idea to write *I Believe In You*. T.J. is, as many of us are, confounded by the lack of publicity Johnnie has received after such a long, prestigious career. T.J.'s goal was to make sure his father received the praise and accolades he deserved and felt the best way to do this would be to write his story.

Schiffvon Taylor Brown, born 1963 and lived her early years in Los Angeles. Johnnie met Schiffvon's mother, Susie Smith Jackson when she was young. Schiffvon shared she never had the opportunity to meet her father, "We kept it hush-hush," and elaborated further, "My mother was young at the time. I had birth certificates all my life saying that Johnnie Taylor is my dad. My mother was underage. She was only 17 when she had me. That's why it was so hush-hush. She was scared to say anything, and after I got older, I got up under her wing and I didn't want to say anything either. The first time I saw him was on the

SCHIFFVON TAYLOR BROWN
PHOTO COURTESY OF JOSH BROWN

"Disco Lady" *Eargasm* album cover. My mom brought the album cover out on the porch and said, 'This is what your dad looks like. You look just like your dad.'"[26] Schiffvon lived in Bossier City, Louisiana and her son Josh has kept her memory alive by providing images and background for

I Believe in You. Schiffvon passed away in 2014, only two days after her older brother Floyd, died.

At Dallas County Courthouse L-R Johnnie's Daughter Schiffvon, Son T.J. and Daughter Fonda
Photo Courtesy of T.J. Hooker

Jonathan H. Taylor, born 1972, Dallas. Jon Harrison was the son of Johnnie and his second wife, Gerlean Rockett Taylor. Like his younger sister, he attended Greenhill School in Dallas, then earned his Bachelors from St. Edward's University in Austin. Family friend Emmitt Hill described Jon as quiet but very intelligent.[27] His early years were geared toward acting, and he appeared in television commercials, then musicals, *The Whiz*, *Damn Yankees*, and *Little Shop of Horrors*. He loved music like his dad so Jon embarked on a career in a rock band during his college days.[28] He migrated to L.A. where he became a touring and studio musician with Robin Thicke and a singer, songwriter and producer for Hey Pete Productions. From 2006 to 2008, he was owner and operator of E Company Rockett Records, an on-line record store. Also during this time he received a certificate of filmmaking from the Los Angeles Film School. Jon subsequently worked six years at Reediculous Media Entertainment, an advertising company that specialized in videos, music and television. For a brief time he was a quality control analyst for GDMX/Warners

Brothers and a DAI Operator for NFL Digital Media. After spending time as executive producer for Tiny Apples, he took ownership control of Hey Pete Productions based in New York while maintaining his duties as video editor.[29] Jon also recorded an EP in 2016 and released a handful of singles over the past several years.[30]

LaTasha I. Taylor, born 1973, Dallas. Tasha was the youngest of Johnnie and Gerlean Taylor's children and Johnnie's last known child. She was described as a 'daddy's girl' and adored her father.[31] Tasha went to Greenhill School in North Dallas and was named homecoming queen. After graduation, she attended Boston College to study drama. Her goal was to be an actress after she landed a few roles as a child. As an adult, LaTasha had brief appearances on the *Wayans Bros.*, *Malcolm & Eddie*, *Family Matters*, and *Moesha*. After BU, she had cameos on the TV series *Ugly Betty* and *House M.D.* Like Johnnie, Tasha gravitated towards music and sang with Jack Mack & The Heart Attack and later joined the tour review for John Belushi's and Dan Aykroyd's Blues Brothers. She began recording solo soundtracks for the TV series *Men in Trees* and *Lipstick Jungle* before releasing her first album, *Revival* in 2008. Her second LP was issued a few years later, called *Taylormade*, a partial cover album that paid tribute to Johnnie and his songs. The track "Daddy's Girl," is especially moving. Her third LP and last solo album was released in 2016, called *Honey for Biscuits*. Later, a collaborative live album, *Blues Caravan: Blues Sisters* was released in 2017 that featured the trio of Tasha, Layla Zoe, and Ina Forsman.[32]

CHAPTER 44

MORE?

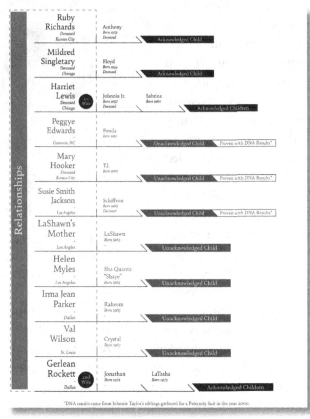

Relationships				
Ruby Richards *Deceased* *Kansas City*	Anthony *Born 1952* *Deceased*		Acknowledged Child	
Mildred Singletary *Deceased* *Chicago*	Floyd *Born 1954* *Deceased*		Acknowledged Child	
Harriet Lewis *Deceased* *Chicago* (1st Wife)	Johnnie Jr. *Born 1957* *Deceased*	Sabrina *Born 1960*	Acknowledged Children	
Peggye Edwards *Gastonia, NC*	Fonda *Born 1961*		Unacknowledged Child	Proven with DNA Results*
Mary Hooker *Deceased* *Kansas City*	T.J. *Born 1962*		Unacknowledged Child	Proven with DNA Results*
Susie Smith Jackson *Los Angeles*	Schiffvon *Born 1963* *Deceased*		Unacknowledged Child	Proven with DNA Results*
LaShawn's Mother *Los Angeles*	LaShawn *Born 1963*		Unacknowledged Child	
Helen Myles *Los Angeles*	Sha Quanta "Shaye" *Born 1965*		Unacknowledged Child	
Irma Jean Parker *Dallas*	Raheem *Born 1965*		Unacknowledged Child	
Val Wilson *St. Louis*	Crystal *Born 1967*		Unacknowledged Child	
Gerlean Rockett *Dallas* (2nd Wife)	Jonathan *Born 1972*	LaTasha *Born 1975*	Acknowledged Children	

*DNA results came from Johnnie Taylor's siblings gathered for a Paternity Suit in the year 2000.

**JOHNNIE TAYLOR'S OFFSPRING INCLUDING
ADDITIONAL CHILDREN
PHOTO COURTESY OF NATALIE R. HASTY**

When Johnnie's six known children were combined with the three newly acknowledged offspring from the paternity case, the collection of nine men and women appeared to close the loop on Taylor's family circle. However, Johnnie's pursuits reached beyond the two marriages and the girlfriends identified in the previous chapter. It was determined Taylor had even more children beyond the nine mentioned above. Three were daughters, Crystal Wright, Shaquanta (Shaye) Myles and La Shawn Webb and an additional son, Raheem Mackey, all who said they were Johnnie's

children. Their biographical profiles are provided below. Each of the children and their families elected not to come forward to claim sibling status. Most stated they were happy with their personal situation and didn't need or want the recognition as Johnnie's heirs. They chose to forego the free-for-all paternity suit and didn't seek validation or monetary gain; they were satisfied with their lives. The children accepted the fact they were collateral damage of Johnnie's philandering during his reckless years as an entertainer. It was apparent when speaking to these children, the absence had profound

JOHNNIE AND HIS DAUGHTER
LA SHAWN WEBB
PHOTO COURTESY OF
LA SHAWN WEBB

effects on their lives. At times they felt abandoned and victimized which damaged their self-esteem. A common theme was that it made them more self-sufficient and independent; each seemed to have pride in their accomplishments without the influence of their father. Obviously none of the four additional children had DNA tests, so the certainty of their biological link to Johnnie could always be questioned. However each of the four mothers assured their children with certainty that Taylor was in fact, their father, and this conviction speaks volumes. His prolific history and reputation for being careless with his affairs and relationships gave considerable credibility to the possibility of additional offspring.

Crystal Wright, born in 1967, St. Louis, still lives in St. Louis. Crystal's mother is Val Wilson. Johnnie was very close to Crystal and took her on many tours when he was on the road. As a teen, she traveled with Johnnie and his band on the Disco Lady bus. One instance that stood out to her was how serious he was with his traveling party. Crystal noted, "He did not play," no one got out of line before the shows, after the shows, on the bus or anywhere else on the road. He ran a tight ship making sure none of the band members tried to see any of the daughters of those on the tour. His band also couldn't

JOHNNIE WITH DAUGHTER
CRYSTAL WRIGHT
PHOTO COURTESY OF
CRYSTAL WRIGHT

miss a beat during a show or the offender would be fined. This way the band was assured to hold up their end of the bargain and most nights performed perfectly in sync. Whenever Johnnie started playing "Disco Lady," it was a cue for everyone who was traveling with the band to start heading toward the bus. He didn't tolerate any delays and expected everyone to be in their seats and ready to go when he and the band finished and boarded the bus.[1] Crystal had fond memories of Taylor calling her "Pete". He told her once, "I meet people all over the world. I can't remember everybody's name." He went on to explain to Crystal that he didn't want people to think he didn't know them or they weren't important so he coined the name 'Pete' for use in those situations. Crystal shared that Johnnie was partial to his daughters and there were higher expectations for his sons. Taylor was old-school in the sense that he expected the men to go out and be productive and make a living on their own. He didn't want the boys riding on his coattails or using his name to further their own careers. He wanted them to "handle their business."

Crystal learned early on not to ask Johnnie for favors or gifts, which he appreciated. Because of this, he often took her shopping and gave to Crystal generously. Taylor was constantly bombarded by fans, friends and family asking for his time, possessions or money–all of which he considered irritants. However, for children like Crystal who simply sought time with their dad, he was overly generous.[2]

Crystal was disappointed when Johnnie didn't attend her debutante ball, but her uncle was able to stand in for him. She claimed Johnnie was there in spirit and "always had his eyes on me."[3] One of the most precious times together she recalled was when she and other members of the family were staying at the Ambassador Hotel in Chicago. Johnnie rented a suite overlooking Lake Michigan. Crystal couldn't sleep and decided to stay up and watch the sunrise. Johnnie arose early and saw Crystal sitting by herself and came over to join his daughter. Taylor asked Crystal what she was doing up so early and she replied, "I wanted to

CRYSTAL WRIGHT
PHOTO COURTESY OF
CRYSTAL WRIGHT

watch the sunrise. I just love the water." Johnnie agreed, "I love the water too." They stared out their hotel window and quietly watched the sun peak over the horizon in a most poignant moment together. Crystal also reflected on first meeting her brother. They were at one of Johnnie's shows, and she was sitting in a chair next to where T.J. was seated. They hadn't met and weren't aware they were siblings. When the guitar player in Johnnie's band saw them sitting next to each other, he walked over and told them they were brother and sister. They were shocked to find out the news and gave each other hugs. That encounter began a relationship that would last for years.[4]

Crystal is a professional boxing judge and has been in the vocation for over thirty years. She travels the country scoring pro bouts and is well respected in the industry. She recalls waiting to board a plane at a Dallas airport departing for Acapulco. She called Johnnie and he told Crystal that whenever she planned her return through Dallas, to stop by so they could spend some time together. On Crystal's third day in Acapulco, she received a call that delivered the dreadful news that Johnnie had passed away. The meeting she and Johnnie were looking forward to never took place. Crystal lost her father and someone that meant the world to her.[5]

L-R PAT ARNOLD, ANTHONY ARNOLD
AND CRYSTAL WRIGHT
PHOTO COURTESY OF PAT ARNOLD

L-R Crystal's Son 'Little Mark', Crystal,
T.J.'s Wife Beatrice Hooker and T.J.
Photo Courtesy of Fonda Bryant

Shaquanta (Shaye) Myles, born in 1963, Los Angeles, now lives in Fort Worth. Shaye's mother is Helen Myles, and as mentioned earlier, Johnnie met Helen in L.A. when her mother sang in a youth choir. Although Johnnie wasn't constantly in Shaye's life, she explained that he wasn't "absent" or neglectful to her or Helen. Taylor would call periodically to talk and always kept in touch with mother and daughter. Shaye was later able to connect with some of her siblings, most notably Floyd, T.J., Raheem and Schiffvon. She and Floyd had been developing a close relationship, and he had arranged a visit to Fort Worth to see her. Before the trip, he called Shaye during a

Shaye Myles
Photo Courtesy of T.J. Hooker

break at one of his performances. Floyd told her what he wanted for dinner when he got to town and said he looked forward to seeing her.

Later that night he texted her. That was the last time she heard from Floyd. The following day, Shaye was shocked to find Floyd had passed

away. She also started talking regularly to Johnnie Jr. and Schiffvon and both passed away just as they were getting to know each other. Shaye was sad the important relationships she was building with her siblings, which were just starting to flourish,

HELEN, SHAYE AND T.J.
PHOTO COURTESY OF T.J. HOOKER

came to an end so quickly. Shaye maintained that she is Johnnie's oldest biological daughter, based on speculation from the court's decision to keep Sabrina's DNA results confidential in the paternity suit. Asked about her decision not to come forward and claim her rights to Johnnie's estate, she replied, "I just wanted to stay out of the way." Shaye said Helen raised her to be a very independent person and she prided herself in always keeping busy. She

was happy with her life and didn't need or want to be known only for being Johnnie Taylor's daughter. Shaye made her own way.[6]

La Shawn Webb, born in 1963, Los Angeles, was a former nurse and now lives in Atlanta. Her mother requested to remain anonymous. Johnnie met La Shawn's mother at a show in L.A. when he noticed her dancing in the crowd and asked to meet her. He was in and out of town, but when in L.A., he would call to take her out. In 1973, La Shawn

L-R RAHEEM MACKEY, SHAYE
MILES AND T.J. HOOKER
PHOTO COURTESY OF T.J. HOOKER

and her mother moved to Ohio. One day, Johnnie visited their home and drove up in a limo. All the neighbors gawked at the sight of Taylor coming down the street. Some of the residents came to the house pretending to need sugar or butter to get a glimpse of the musical megastar. When in town for a performance, Johnnie would pick up La Shawn from school and take her to McDonalds or Burger King for a treat. Taylor was always generous with the family, sending money and gifts to La Shawn's mom. He even bought her grandfather some Stacy Adams shoes. As an adult, La Shawn was able to see her dad perform in Detroit before moving to Georgia. After her move, she was only in touch by phone. About not being able to see more of Johnnie in person, La Shawn was realistic about the situation and understood his time demands. "He was a celebrity doing his thing."[7] The only siblings La Shawn was able to meet were Floyd and T.J. At one of Floyd's shows, she approached him and told Floyd she was Johnnie's daughter. He rolled his eyes and complained, "Well here's somebody else that wants money." This unnerved La Shawn, especially since she was wearing a mink stole and expensive jewelry. She replied, "Why would I want something," showing herself to Floyd. The two had subsequent conversations and over time became friends. It was obvious La Shawn was interested solely in forming a relationship with her brother. She also met T.J. at one of his shows, and they hit it off immediately. A common thread in her relationship with T.J. was that both were Johnnie's unacknowledged children. La Shawn reached out hoping to develop a similar relationship with La Tasha, Johnnie's youngest daughter, but she never responded to La Shawn's calls. When asked about her decision to forego the sibling lawsuit to determine Johnnie's paternity, La Shawn

JOHNNIE'S DAUGHTER
LA SHAWN WEBB
PHOTO COURTESY OF
LA SHAWN WEBB

responded, "I'm okay and he was okay. I'm okay with who I am." After all the gifts Taylor gave her family, she didn't feel obligated to go treasure hunting for more. She was satisfied with how things turned out. La Shawn's favorite song of Johnnie's was "Soul Heaven." She declared that at some point in time, he changed the way he lived and "sang those songs with meaning."[8]

Raheem Mackey, born 1965 in Dallas, now lives in Anna. His mother is Irma-Jean Parker. Raheem knew at an early age he was Johnnie's son. His mother kept it 'hush-hush,' but mentioned it to some people they knew. He loved Johnnie's music and listened to his songs around the house and got to know him, if only through his voice. Mackey disclosed that living without a father figure caused trauma and a feeling of abandonment.

JOHNNIE AND DAUGHTER
LA SHAWN
PHOTO COURTESY OF T.J. HOOKER

Early on, Mackey was compelled to move in with his great-grandfather and great-grandmother. Johnnie's absence left an indelible mark on Raheem. As he entered his teen years, he began to harbor resentment. This was especially true when Raheem got in trouble at age sixteen, and Johnnie arranged to meet him at the house to see how he was doing. Johnnie made an effort to help and offered to take Raheem with him on the road. When Johnnie drove up, Raheem saw him, was frightened, and ran away. Mr. Mackey explained that his resentment toward his father led him to avoid the meeting; he couldn't face him, and just wanted to escape. That's the last time he ever saw his father. Johnnie never followed through on his commitment to take his son on the road. Later on in life, because they both lived in Dallas, Raheem tried to reach Johnnie on several occasions at the TAG offices, hoping to talk. However, he never could catch up with Johnnie, and never got a call back. Raheem had mixed feelings about being Johnnie's son. On one hand, he was proud to be the son of such a famous, venerated entertainer like Taylor, but on the other he was disgruntled about growing up without a father. Raheem never got to see his dad perform; though he would have loved to see him in person. After Johnnie died, Raheem became emotional especially when he found out there were other siblings who had lived out similar circumstances with Johnnie as their absentee father. When Taylor's children came together at the court hearings, Raheem cherished being part of a larger family that he didn't know he had.[9]

JOHNNIE'S SON RAHEEM MACKEY
PHOTO COURTESY OF RAHEEM MACKEY

CHAPTER 45

GIVE THE MAN HIS DUE

Johnnie Taylor goes down as one of the most celebrated soul and R&B artists of all time. His career spanned nearly sixty years, singing from the church-house stage as a child, to The Highway Q.C.'s, The Soul Stirrers, then thirty years as a critically acclaimed solo performer. He not only thrived in the R&B genre, he was a legendary gospel singer who blazed a trail on the Chitlin' Circuit. Taylor released some twenty-seven albums over his career and dropped hundreds of singles. The number of records he produced was not only impressive from a sheer volume standpoint, but the consistent quality found on each is without rival. Very few of his LPs were undistinguished. Taylor had hit, after hit, after hit from the sixties and beyond through the nineties and cultivated a dedicated fanbase for decades. He had two gold records, a platinum single and album, *Eargasm*. Taylor was the first artist who cracked the ceiling, breaking all-time sales records for a single, forcing the RIAA to create a new milestone award, called the platinum record. "Disco Lady" sold over two million copies.[1] No entertainer had ever accomlished this. Johnnie broke all Stax sales records, and, to this day, no artist has sold more Stax records than Johnnie Taylor, including Otis Redding, Wilson Pickett or Sam and Dave. When moving to Columbia/CBS Records, his mega-hit, "Disco Lady" rocked the music world, not only creating a platinum record, but crossing over maintaining one foot in R&B and the other in Pop/Disco. His ability to adapt to the times and reinvent himself over and over, continually solidified Johnnie's relevance, even as music and listener tastes changed. J.T. was a multi-modal performer, becoming successful in gospel, then R&B, making history in pop-disco, all the while maintaining his faithful soul music following. He had fans all over the world and could be heard anywhere you traveled. Indeed, he had become an internationally acclaimed vocalist. Johnnie also released a soundtrack to a movie, *Disco 9000* and even played a minor role in the big screen production. Johnnie Taylor was a trailblazer as one of the first performers to form his own booking, publishing and label company before music artists ever considered this an option. Johnnie Taylor played more shows and traveled more miles than most anyone in his profession. Through these efforts, he created an unparalleled, loyal fanbase that welcomed him like a favorite relative who comes to town. Beyond his personal career, Johnnie also influenced his own children to enter the music field, several of which have become notable artists.

JOHNNIE'S BRASS NOTE TO BE PLACED ON BEALE STREET WALK OF FAME IN MEMPHIS PHOTO COURTESY OF DEAN DEYO AND THE BEALE STREET WALK OF FAME

The scope of Johnnie's work includes the volume of albums he released, the superior quality of his music, the number of hit records, several music awards, his influence on the industry, his impact on other artists, plus his impressive longevity. Johnnie Taylor is a once-in-a-generation talent. Here are some of his achievements:

- Nominated for three Grammys
- 1997 W.C. Handy Blues Award Nominee
- 1998 W.C. Handy Blues Award Nominee
- 2001 W.C. Handy Blues Award Nominee
- Inducted into the Arkansas Black Hall of Fame, 1999

- Recipient of the Rhythm and Blues Foundation, Pioneer Award, 1999
- Inducted into the National Rhythm and Blues Hall of Fame, 2015
- Inducted into the Blues Hall of Fame 2022
- Brass Note placed on the Beale Street Walk of Fame in Memphis, 2024

With all of these honors and accomplishments it staggers the mind why Johnnie Taylor has not been inducted into the Rock and Roll Hall of Fame. A quick glimpse at some of the former inductees who can be compared to Johnnie's impact on the music business show how they pale in comparison. None of the musicians and vocalists listed below achieved the *complete* success Johnnie attained. Many had shorter careers, fewer hits, or less numbers of albums and 45s sold. Some never attained the level of acclaim Johnnie earned, especially the number of gold and platinum records. Very few had more influence on the music industry than Taylor. Compare the list of artists who have been inducted in the Rock and Roll Hall of Fame. It goes without saying that Johnnie Taylor has been passed over.

Sam Cooke, 1986
T-Bone Walker, 1987
Jackie Wilson, 1987
Soul Stirrers, 1989
Ike and Tina Turner, 1991
Bobby Blue Bland, 1992
Al Green, 1995
Little Willie John, 1996
Sex Pistols, 2006
Bobby Womack, 2009
Jimmy Cliff, 2010
Freddie King, 2012
Albert King, 2013
Bill Withers, 2015
Notorious Big, 2016[2]

One can make an argument that Sam Cooke was a bigger name than Johnnie in the R&B field. However, his career in the business was a fraction of what Johnnie accomplished, and Cooke didn't sell anywhere near the volume of records. T-Bone Walker, Jackie Wilson, Al Green, and Little Willie John were talented performers but their accomplishments also paled in comparison to Johnnie's.. Comparing the Sex Pistols to Johnnie Taylor is like comparing apples to oranges. However if one weighs the impact on the industry, record sales, and longevity, the Sex Pistols were a minor blip in the history of modern music whereas Johnnie was a seismic eruption. Johnnie's exclusion remains a mystery, and calls to question who's in charge of the selection and what it takes to earn this status.

Ironically, The Soul Stirrers were the very group Johnnie led and rescued after Sam Cooke went secular. They were inducted, but Johnnie wasn't. Could it be Johnnie's reputation as a womanizer and substance abuser affected his consideration? If this is the case, why then was Sam Cooke, Bobby Womack and others with the same afflictions included? Based on excerpts from *The Triumph of Sam Cooke Dream Boogie* written by Peter Guralnick, it was well-known that Sam had a reputation as a womanizer and philanderer.[3] Johnnie cast a mere shadow of Cooke's self-indulgence.

"It troubled us greatly that, perhaps in his death, Johnnie Taylor's greatness would not be realized, because he never received the recognition he deserved from his peers, the music industry, or the general public. We believe that this lack of recognition served, from time to time, as a source of frustration for him."[4]

Is it possible one needs to know the right people or make the right monetary contributions to be considered for the Rock and Roll Hall of Fame? Hopefully this isn't the case. If it is, the Johnnie Taylor fan base needs to assemble and petition the decision makers at the Hall of Fame. If contributions are a factor, perhaps fans could raise what's needed. If it's who you know that counts, certain introductions could be made. The Rock and Roll Hall of Fame has an obligation to induct the most deserving artists and performers. Johnnie Taylor, is without question, one of these entertainers. The unexplained delay considering this honor can be rectified if Johnnie is once and for all selected as a recipient.

This task may fall to Johnnie's fans to lobby the Hall of Fame. If enough support is mustered perhaps the decision makers will understand the depth and breadth of his popularity. After all it's not what a few chosen people think, the decision should rest with the listening public and his fans. These are the people that count.

Please write to the following address to voice your support for Johnnie's induction.

Rock and Roll Hall of Fame Foundation
Nomination Committee
750 Lexington Avenue
New York, NY 10022-1200

Additionally, you can call the foundation today at 212-484-1754 and help Johnnie get the recognition and notoriety he deserves.

CHAPTER 46

DISCOGRAPHY

Here's a list of Johnnie's albums with their respective record labels. Additional works have been added which are compilations, greatest hits, split tracks, two album combinations or remasters.[1] [2] [3] [4] [5]

1967 Wanted One Soul Singer Rhino
1968 *Who's Making Love* Stax
1969 *The Johnnie Taylor Philosophy Continues* Stax
1969 *The Roots of Johnnie Taylor* Soul City
1969 *Raw Blues* Stax
1970 *Rare Stamps* Stax
1970 *Johnnie Taylor's Greatest Hits* Fantasy
1971 *One Step Beyond* Stax
1972 *The Best of Johnnie Taylor* Stax
1973 *Taylored in Silk* Stax
1974 *Super Taylor* Stax
1974 *The Best of Johnnie Taylor* Malaco
1974 *Chronicle-The Twenty Greatest Hits* Stax
1976 *Eargasm* Columbia
1977 *Disco 9000* Sony
1977 *Disco 9000 Soundtrack* Columbia
1977 *Rated Extraordinaire* Columbia
1977 *Reflections* Fever Dream
1978 *Ever Ready* CBS
1979 *She's Killing Me* CBS

1980 *A New Day* CBS
1981 *The Best of Johnnie Taylor* Atco
1982 *Just Ain't Good Enough* Capitol
1983 *Super Hits* Stax
1984 *This is Your Night* Malaco
1984 *Best of the Old and The New* Beverly Glen
1986 *Lover Boy* Malaco
1986 *Wall to Wall* Malaco
1987 *Best of Johnnie Taylor* Stax
1988 *In Control* Malaco
1989 *Crazy 'Bout You* Malaco
1989 *Somebody's Gettin' It* Charly R&B
1990 *Little Bluebird* Stax
1990 *Great Soul* CBS
1991 *I Know I'm Wrong, But I ... Just Can't Do Right* Malaco
1991 *Greatest Hits Vol. 1* P. Vine
1991 *Blues From the Montreux Jazz Festival* Malaco
1992 *The Best of Johnnie Taylor on Malaco* Malaco
1992 *Raw Blues/Little Bluebird* Stax
1993 *Disco Lady* Soul Music
1993 *Chronicle: The Twenty Greatest Hits* Stax
1994 *Real Love* Malaco
1994 *The Johnnie Taylor Philosophy Continues/One Step Beyond* Stax
1995 *Take This Heart of Mine* Fania
1996 *Brand New* Malaco
1996 *Good Love!* Malaco
1996 *Stop Half-Loving These Women* Paula
1996 *Rated Extraordinaire: The Best of Johnnie Taylor* Columbia
1997 *Disco Lady* EMI-Capital
1997 *Cheaper to Keep Her* Six-O-One
1998 *Taylored to Please* Malaco
1999 *Gotta Get the Groove Back* Malaco

After Johnnie's death, his record labels released several albums to commemorate his many successful recordings.

2000 *Funk Soul Brother* Fuel
2000 *Taylored in Silk & Super Taylor* Stax
2000 *Greatest Hits* Malaco
2000 *Lifetime* Stax
2001 *Rated Extraordinaire-Disco 9000* Westside
2002 *Super Hits* Sony
2003 *There's No Good in Goodbye* Malaco
2006 *Stax Profiles* Stax
2007 *Super Hits* Sony
2007 *Live at the Summit Club* Stax
2012 *Rated Extraordinaire/Ever Ready* Soul Brothers
2013 *Best of the Old & the New (The Complete Beverly Glen Sessions)* Solaris
2014 *She's Killing Me/A New Day* Soul Music

Johnnie didn't often tour England or Europe, yet developed a dedicated fanbase leading to requests for his music to be released overseas.

1969 *Looking for Johnnie Taylor* Atco
1969 *The Roots of Johnnie Taylor* Soul City
1978 *The Johnnie Taylor Chronicles* Stax
2007 *The Very Best of Johnnie Taylor* Concord, Released in Europe
2017 *Stax Classics* Concord, Released in Europe
UNK *Portrait* Stax
UNK *Best of Johnnie Taylor on Malaco* Malaco

Johnnie has scores of videos that can be viewed on Youtube including special moments when he played the Fairmont Hotel in Dallas (1989) and the Longhorn Ballroom (1998). The videos reflect his professionalism, charisma, crowd-pleasing magnetism and his extraordinary vocal talents. Johnnie Taylor was second to none.

CONCLUSION

So ends the story of Johnnie Taylor. The remarkable entertainer goes down in history as one of the all-time colossal musical legends. Rather than allow his memory to fade, I'm hopeful this biography will forever solidify his mark on the annals of soul, blues, and gospel, and his imprint eternally emblazoned on the era of the twentieth century and into the twenty-first century. What has made Johnnie's story so unique is his success, despite being tormented by inner demons for over half a century. Regardless of his faults, he excelled at his craft and positively impacted the lives of hundreds of thousands around the world. He shall always be remembered for his bobbing head, his mischievous smile, his immaculate dress, his sparkling jewelry, and, most importantly, his impassioned crooning. Johnnie interacted with the crowd like no one else; he held the audience spellbound, and made them feel as if he was talking to each one personally. He was a heartthrob, a darling, a serenader, a confidant, a soothsayer, and a wiseman who shared his insight to life's mysteries. Johnnie Taylor carved himself into a lasting legend. He sold tens of millions of records, he performed in hundreds upon hundreds of venues and brought his traveling entertainment to churches, homes, clubs, bars, and concert halls. His soulful evangelism to the masses compares to how politicians might operate on the campaign trail. He was quick-witted, a dedicated friend and companion and could charm with a simple, comforting smile. Though Johnnie's loss will be felt for some time to come, his music still plays on.

CREDITS

Thanks to Ed "The Commish" Gray for making the introduction to T.J. Hooker. In the process of finishing another book, the historical narrative of *Oak Cliff and the Missing Pieces*, my friend Ed and I had a conversation about famous residents of Oak Cliff. Johnnie Taylor's name came up. Even though I had spent many years in Oak Cliff, I didn't recall Johnnie having lived in the city. Of the many biographies featured in *Missing Pieces*, Johnnie became an important addition to the community of notable individuals whose legacy would be etched in the Oak Cliff chronicles. As more research was done on *I Believe in You*, it was discovered Johnnie lived on 1818 Red Bird Lane, three houses down from where I grew up on Bar Harbor Drive. It seemed my involvement with this project was predestined. I never met Johnnie or attended any of his shows, but after conducting research, doing interviews, reading historical accounts and visiting some of the places Johnnie frequented, I feel like we're long lost friends. At least as much as we could be without having the opportunity to meet.

Thanks to Johnnie's companions and partners who willingly shared their moments and memories of when they first met and how they got to know this great entertainer. It was a pleasure hearing their stories and listening to them recall distant memories that helped construct a timeline of his life. I'm sure it brought those exciting, vivid times back to life for each of his friends and girlfriends. Many thanks to Peggye Bryant, Irma Jean Parker, and Helen Myles. Mary Hooker, Harriet Lewis and Ruby Richards are now deceased and could not be interviewed. Pat Arnold, widow of Johnnie's son Anthony Arnold, was extremely helpful in recounting some of Johnnie's days as a celebrated artist. Thank you

Pat. Interviews with Johnnie's unacknowledged children were pivotal in capturing their time growing up without a father and relating how Taylor conducted himself during these periods. Many thanks to Crystal Wright, Fonda Bryant, La Shawn Webb, Shaquanta "Shaye" Myles, Raheem Mackey, and Tyrone "T.J." Hooker who collectively made this book possible. Without the efforts of these unacknowledged children, these words would never have been written. These six children will carry forth the effort to enshrine their father into the Rock and Roll Hall of Fame as well as organizing support for renaming streets in his honor. Even though you lived a life without your father, the dedication you've shown to preserve his legend speaks volumes. I commend you all.

Unfortunately Schiffvon Taylor Brown, Anthony Arnold, Floyd Taylor and Johnnie Taylor Jr. all passed away before *I Believe in You* was written. Due to ongoing acrimony between some of the siblings, we elected to forego interviewing Johnnie's acknowledged descendents. To Johnnie's close friends, I offer my deep gratitude for sharing your stories and celebrating the friendship that was so important to each of you. Thanks go to Ernie Johnson, Bobby Patterson and Gregg A. Smith. Appreciation is also sent to those who contributed information, photos, stories, ideas and inspiration; Rodgers Redding, of Rodgers Redding and Associates entertainment agency, Jeff Kollath, Executive Director of the Stax Museum, Mark Sarfati, Natalie R. Hasty, Tommy Couch Sr. and Tommy Couch Jr. of Malaco Records, Johnnie's grandson, Josh Brown. Also Emmitt Hill, Lamar Brooks, Donna Molden, Bobi Bush, Floyd "Butchie Boy" Bonner, Dolores Elder-Jones, Bart Kudlicki, Donald Payton, of the Dallas African American Genealogy Interest Group; David Washington, WPON-AM Detroit; Kim Sanders, retired Dallas Police Department, and Rhonda Grimes of Good Street Baptist Church in Oak Cliff. You were all blessings to this project.

JOHNNIE TAYLOR

PHOTO COURTESY OF THE STAX MUSEUM
OF AMERICAN SOUL MUSIC

SOURCES

Chapter 1

1   "Crawfordsville". arkansas.com. https://www.arkansas.com/crawfordsville. Accessed May 19, 2023.
2   Hildebrand, Lee. Liner Notes *Johnnie Taylor Lifetime A Retrospective of Soul, Blues, & Gospel 1956-1999*. 2000. Page 17. Quote from Johnnie Taylor.
3   *Unsung 818 Johnnie Taylor*. October 30, 2018. LaTasha Taylor quote. https://vimeopro.com/user15889254/unsung/video/297999415. Accessed April 27, 2023.
4   Ollison, Rashod D. "Dallas' Mr. Soul - Legendary Johnnie Taylor isn't bitter about standing in the shadows". *The Dallas Morning News*. August 4, 1999, Page 1C.
5   Hildebrand, Lee. Liner Notes *Johnnie Taylor Lifetime A Retrospective of Soul, Blues, & Gospel 1956-1999*. 2000. Page 17. Quote from Johnnie Taylor.
6   "Johnnie Tells How His Hits Are Tailored". *Jet Magazine*. March 2, 1972. Pages 58-59.
7   Interview with Bobby Patterson, May 11, 2023.
8   *Unsung 818 Johnnie Taylor*. October 30, 2018. Jonathan Taylor quote. https://vimeopro.com/user15889254/unsung/video/297999415. Accessed April 27, 2023.
9   "Crawfordsville". arkansas.com. https://www.arkansas.com/crawfordsville. Accessed May 19, 2023.

Chapter 2

1   Marovich, Bob. "The Rise Of Chicago's Highway Q.C.s During Gospel's Golden Era (1947-1964)". *Journal of Gospel Music*. https://journalofgospelmusic.com/quartet/rise-chicagos-highway-q-c-s-gospels-golden-era-1947-1964/. Accessed May 1, 2023.

Chapter 3

1   Interview with Pat Arnold. May 3, 2023.
2   Hildebrand, Lee. Liner Notes *Johnnie Taylor Lifetime A Retrospective of Soul, Blues, & Gospel 1956-1999*. 2000. Page 18. Quote from Johnnie Taylor.
3   Marovich, Bob. "The Rise Of Chicago's Highway Q.C.s During Gospel's Golden Era (1947-1964)". *Journal of Gospel Music*. https://journalofgospelmusic. com/quartet/rise-chicagos-highway-q-c-s-gospels-golden-era-1947-1964/. Accessed May 1, 2023.
4   Guralnick, Peter. "The Triumph of Sam Cooke Dream Boogie". New York. Back Bay Books / Little Brown and Company, 2005. Page 119.
5   Marovich, Bob. "The Rise Of Chicago's Highway Q.C.s During Gospel's Golden Era (1947-1964)". *Journal of Gospel Music*. https://journalof gospelmusic.com/quartet/rise-chicagos-highway-q-c-s-gospels-golden-era-1947-1964/. Accessed May 1, 2023.
6   Answers. "Did Johnnie Taylor Have Wife and Kids?". https://qa.answers. com/entertainment/Did_johnnie_Taylor_have_wife_an_kids. Accessed December 24, 2023.
7   Marovich, Bob. "The Rise Of Chicago's Highway Q.C.s During Gospel's Golden Era (1947-1964)". *Journal of Gospel Music*. https://journalofgospelmusic. com/quartet/rise-chicagos-highway-q-c-s-gospels-golden-era-1947-1964/. Accessed May 1, 2023.
8   Guralnick, Peter. "The Triumph of Sam Cooke Dream Boogie". New York. Back Bay Books / Little Brown and Company, 2005. Page 191.
9   Gordon, Robert. "Stax Wanted A Soul Singer, And Johnnie Taylor Delivered". VMP. https://www.vinylmeplease.com/blogs/magazine/johnnie-taylor-liner-notes. Accessed April 15, 2023.
10   Hildebrand, Lee. Liner Notes *Johnnie Taylor Lifetime A Retrospective of Soul, Blues, & Gospel 1956-1999*. 2000. Page 18. Quote from Leroy Crume.

Chapter 4

1   Guralnick, Peter. "The Triumph of Sam Cooke Dream Boogie". New York. Back Bay Books / Little Brown and Company, 2005. Page 158.
2   Guralnick, Peter. "The Triumph of Sam Cooke Dream Boogie". New York. Back Bay Books / Little Brown and Company, 2005. Page 165.
3   Guralnick, Peter. "The Triumph of Sam Cooke Dream Boogie". New York. Back Bay Books / Little Brown and Company, 2005. Page 168.

4   Guralnick, Peter. "The Triumph of Sam Cooke Dream Boogie". New York. Back Bay Books / Little Brown and Company, 2005. Page 177.

5   Guralnick, Peter. "The Triumph of Sam Cooke Dream Boogie". New York. Back Bay Books / Little Brown and Company, 2005. Page 179-180.

6   Guralnick, Peter. "The Triumph of Sam Cooke Dream Boogie". New York. Back Bay Books / Little Brown and Company, 2005. Page 188.

7   Melhem, Hisham. "Blues, the Devil's Music". *Alarabiya News*. https://english.alarabiya.net/views/news/world/2015/05/18/Blues-the-Devil-s-music-. Accessed May 22, 2023.

Chapter 5

1   Guralnick, Peter. "The Triumph of Sam Cooke Dream Boogie". New York. Back Bay Books / Little Brown and Company, 2005. Page 190.

2   Hildebrand, Lee. Liner Notes *Johnnie Taylor Lifetime A Retrospective of Soul, Blues, & Gospel 1956-1999*. 2000. Page 19.

3   Interview with David Washington. April 16, 2023.

4   Interview with Gregg A. Smith. May 12, 2023.

5   Hildebrand, Lee. Liner Notes *Johnnie Taylor Lifetime A Retrospective of Soul, Blues, & Gospel 1956-1999*. 2000. Page 19. Quote from Leroy Crume.

6   Guralnick, Peter. "The Triumph of Sam Cooke Dream Boogie". New York. Back Bay Books / Little Brown and Company, 2005. Page 671.

7   Guralnick, Peter. "The Triumph of Sam Cooke Dream Boogie". New York. Back Bay Books / Little Brown and Company, 2005. Page 671.

8   Guralnick, Peter. "The Triumph of Sam Cooke Dream Boogie". New York. Back Bay Books / Little Brown and Company, 2005. Pages 295-296.

9   Watts, Paul. Liner Notes *The Soul Stirrers The Singles Collection 1950-1961*. 2016. Page 17.

10   Hildebrand, Lee. Liner Notes *Johnnie Taylor Lifetime A Retrospective of Soul, Blues, & Gospel 1956-1999*. 2000. Page 19. Quote from Johnnie Taylor.

11   Hildebrand, Lee. Liner Notes *Johnnie Taylor Lifetime A Retrospective of Soul, Blues, & Gospel 1956-1999*. 2000. Page 14. Quote from Al Bell.

12   Hildebrand, Lee. Liner Notes *Johnnie Taylor Lifetime A Retrospective of Soul, Blues, & Gospel 1956-1999*. 2000. Page 20. Quote from Leroy Crume.

13   Hildebrand, Lee. *Liner Notes Johnnie Taylor Lifetime A Retrospective of Soul, Blues, & Gospel 1956-1999*. 2000. Page 19.

14   Hildebrand, Lee. Liner Notes *Johnnie Taylor Lifetime A Retrospective of Soul, Blues, & Gospel 1956-1999*. 2000. Page 20. Quote from Al Bell.

Chapter 6

1   Guralnick, Peter. "The Triumph of Sam Cooke Dream Boogie". New York. Back Bay Books / Little Brown and Company, 2005. Page 299.

2   Watts, Paul. Liner Notes *The Soul Stirrers The Singles Collection 1950-1961*. 2016. Page 9.

3   Guralnick, Peter. "The Triumph of Sam Cooke Dream Boogie". New York. Back Bay Books / Little Brown and Company, 2005. Pages 265-266.

4   Yarborough, Chuck. "Johnnie Taylor's daughter: Put my dad in the Rock and Roll Hall of Fame." *cleveland.com*. https://www.cleveland.com/entertainment/2016/02/60s_singer_johnnie_taylors_dau.html. Accessed May 15, 2023.

Chapter 7

1   Guralnick, Peter. "The Triumph of Sam Cooke Dream Boogie". New York. Back Bay Books / Little Brown and Company, 2005. Page 340.

2   Guralnick, Peter. "The Triumph of Sam Cooke Dream Boogie". New York. Back Bay Books / Little Brown and Company, 2005. Page 340.

3   Hildebrand, Lee. Liner Notes *Johnnie Taylor Lifetime A Retrospective of Soul, Blues, & Gospel 1956-1999*. 2000. Page 20. Quote from Leroy Crume.

4   Hildebrand, Lee. Liner Notes *Johnnie Taylor Lifetime A Retrospective of Soul, Blues, & Gospel 1956-1999*. 2000. Page 20. Quote from Wolf Stephenson.

5   Edwards, David & Callahan, Mike. "The Specialty Records Story". *bsnpubs. com, newspapers.com*. https://www.bsnpubs.com/specialty/specialtystory.html. Accessed May 29, 2023.

6   Interview with T.J. Hooker, April 11, 2023.

7   Interview with T.J. Hooker, April 11, 2023.

8   Interview with Helen Myles. June 12, 2023.

9   Interview with Helen Myles. June 12, 2023.

10 Interview with Helen Myles. June 12, 2023.

Chapter 8

1   Hildebrand, Lee. Liner Notes *Johnnie Taylor Lifetime A Retrospective of Soul, Blues, & Gospel 1956-1999*. 2000. Page 21-22. Quote from Johnnie Taylor.

2   Ritz, David. "The Life of Aretha Franklin". New York. Little Brown and Company Hachette Book Group. 2014. Pages 68-69.

3   *Unsung 818 Johnnie Taylor.* October 30, 2018. Rodgers Redding quote. https://vimeopro.com/user15889254/unsung/video/297999415. Accessed April 27, 2023.

4   *Unsung 818 Johnnie Taylor.* October 30, 2018. David Washington quote. https://vimeopro.com/user15889254/unsung/video/297999415. Accessed April 27, 2023.

5   Guralnick, Peter. "The Triumph of Sam Cooke Dream Boogie". New York. Back Bay Books / Little Brown and Company, 2005. Page 402.

6   Guralnick, Peter. "The Triumph of Sam Cooke Dream Boogie". New York. Back Bay Books / Little Brown and Company, 2005. Page 374.

7   "A Tribute To Johnnie Taylor". *Living Blues.* September-October 2000, Issue 153 vol. 31 no. 5. Pages 38-39.

8   Hildebrand, Lee. Liner Notes *Johnnie Taylor Lifetime A Retrospective of Soul, Blues, & Gospel 1956-1999.* 2000. Page 17.

9   Hildebrand, Lee. Liner Notes *Johnnie Taylor Lifetime A Retrospective of Soul, Blues, & Gospel 1956-1999.* 2000. Page 17. Quote from Johnnie Taylor.

10   Brown, Geoffrey F. "Johnnie Taylor's Daughter Debuts At Sweet Sixteen:". *Jet Magazine.* July 24, 1975 Page 28.

11   Interview with T.J. Hooker, April 11, 2023.

Chapter 9

1   "Johnnie Taylor". *Concord.com.* https://concord.com/artist/johnnie-taylor/#:~:text=The%20singer%20cut%20six%20singles,by%20Cooke%2C%20were%20regional%20hits. Accessed May 15, 2023.

2   "Part Time Love". *Billboard Database Hot 100.* https://billboard.elpee.jp/single/Part%20Time%20Love/Little%20Johnny%20Taylor/. Accessed May 13, 2023.

3   Rush, Bobby with Powell, Herb. "I Ain't Studdin' Ya My American Blues Story". New York. Hachette Book Group, Inc. Page 35.

4   Guralnick, Peter. "The Triumph of Sam Cooke Dream Boogie". New York. Back Bay Books / Little Brown and Company, 2005. Page 612.

5   Interview with David Washington, April 16, 2023.

6   Interview with Ernie Johnson, April 27, 2023.

7   "A Tribute To Johnnie Taylor". *Living Blues.* September-October 2000, Issue 153 vol. 31 no. 5. Page 39.

8   Guralnick, Peter. "The Triumph of Sam Cooke Dream Boogie". New York. Back Bay Books / Little Brown and Company, 2005. Page 398.

9   Guralnick, Peter. "The Triumph of Sam Cooke Dream Boogie". New York. Back Bay Books / Little Brown and Company, 2005. Page 398.

10 Guralnick, Peter. "The Triumph of Sam Cooke Dream Boogie". New York. Back Bay Books / Little Brown and Company, 2005. Page 398.

11 *Unsung 818 Johnnie Taylor*. October 30, 2018, Marcus Chapman quote. https://vimeopro.com/user15889254/unsung/video/297999415. Accessed April 27, 2023.

12 *Unsung 818 Johnnie Taylor*. October 30, 2018, L.C. Cooke quote. https://vimeopro.com/user15889254/unsung/video/297999415. Accessed April 27, 2023.

13 Interview with Rodgers Redding, August 2, 2023.

14 Interview with Rodgers Redding, August 2, 2023.

15 Interview with Rodgers Redding, August 2, 2023.

16 Guralnick, Peter. "The Triumph of Sam Cooke Dream Boogie". New York. Back Bay Books / Little Brown and Company, 2005. Page 265.

Chapter 10

1   *Unsung 818 Johnnie Taylor*. October 30, 2018. Rodgers Redding quote. https://vimeopro.com/user15889254/unsung/video/297999415. Accessed April 27, 2023.

2   *Unsung 818 Johnnie Taylor*. October 30, 2018. Laura Lee quote. https://vimeopro.com/user15889254/unsung/video/297999415. Accessed April 27, 2023.

3   Interview with Helen Myles, May 11, 2023.

4   Interview with Rodgers Redding, August 2, 2023.

5   Guralnick, Peter. "The Triumph of Sam Cooke Dream Boogie". New York. Back Bay Books / Little Brown and Company, 2005. Page 612.

6   Guralnick, Peter. "The Triumph of Sam Cooke Dream Boogie". New York. Back Bay Books / Little Brown and Company, 2005. Page 686.

7   Guralnick, Peter. "The Triumph of Sam Cooke Dream Boogie". New York. Back Bay Books / Little Brown and Company, 2005. Page 516.

Chapter 11

1   Morthland, John. "Soul Survivor". *Texas Monthly*. Page 54. https://www.texasmonthly.com/articles/soul-survivor/. Accessed May 15, 2023.

2   Oppel, Pete. "Taylored in Dallas". *The Dallas Morning News*. June 26, 1976, Page 1F.

3   Interview with Bobby Patterson, May 24, 2023.

4   Oppel, Pete. "Taylored in Dallas". *The Dallas Morning News*. June 26, 1976, Page 1F.

Chapter 12

1   Guralnick, Peter. "The Triumph of Sam Cooke Dream Boogie". New York. Back Bay Books / Little Brown and Company, 2005. Page 619.

2   Guralnick, Peter. "The Triumph of Sam Cooke Dream Boogie". New York. Back Bay Books / Little Brown and Company, 2005. Pages 643.

3   *The Two Killings of Sam Cooke*. *Netflix*. Director, Kelly Duane de la Vega. Remastered release 2019.

4   *The Two Killings of Sam Cooke*. *Netflix*. Director, Kelly Duane de la Vega. Remastered release 2019.

5   *The Two Killings of Sam Cooke*. *Netflix*. Director, Kelly Duane de la Vega. Remastered release 2019.

6   Guralnick, Peter. "The Triumph of Sam Cooke Dream Boogie". New York. Back Bay Books / Little Brown and Company, 2005. Page 644.

7   Franco, Samantha. "Sam Cooke's Death: Was It Really a Justifiable Homicide?" *The Vintage News*. https://www.thevintagenews.com/2022/09/23/sam-cooke-death/?safari=1&Exc_D_LessThanPoint002_p1=1. Accessed May 24, 2023.

8   Guralnick, Peter. "The Triumph of Sam Cooke Dream Boogie". New York. Back Bay Books / Little Brown and Company, 2005. Page 647.

9   *Unsung 818 Johnnie Taylor*. October 30, 2018. L.C. Cooke quote. https://vimeopro.com/user15889254/unsung/video/297999415. Accessed April 27, 2023.

Chapter 13

1   Guralnick, Peter. "The Triumph of Sam Cooke Dream Boogie". New York. Back Bay Books / Little Brown and Company, 2005. Page 646.

2   Interview with T.J. Hooker, April 11, 2023.

3   Morthland, John. "Soul Survivor". *Texas Monthly*. Page 54. https://www.texasmonthly.com/articles/soul-survivor/. Accessed May 15, 2023.

4   Hildebrand, Lee. Liner Notes *Johnnie Taylor Lifetime A Retrospective of Soul, Blues, & Gospel 1956-1999*. 2000. Page 22. Quote from Johnnie Taylor.

5   Hildebrand, Lee. Liner Notes *Johnnie Taylor Lifetime A Retrospective of Soul, Blues, & Gospel 1956-1999*. 2000. Page 23. Quote from Johnnie Taylor.

6   Hildebrand, Lee. Liner Notes *Johnnie Taylor Lifetime A Retrospective of Soul, Blues, & Gospel 1956-1999*. 2000. Page 23. Quote from Johnnie Taylor.

Chapter 14

1   Interview with Irma Jean Parker, May 24, 2023.

2   Interview with Gregg A. Smith, May 12, 2023.

3   "Stax History". *Stax Record Co*. https://staxrecords.com/history/#:~:text=STAX%20HISTORY&text=Originally%20known%20as%20Satellite%2C%20the,letters%20of%20their%20last%20names. Accessed June 30, 2023.

4   Gordon, Robert. "Respect Yourself Stax Records and the Soul Explosion". New York. Bloomsbury USA, 1972. Pages 73 and 74.

5   *Unsung 818 Johnnie Taylor*. October 30, 2018. Alan Walden quote. https://vimeopro.com/user15889254/unsung/video/297999415. Accessed April 27, 2023.

6   Bowman, Rob. "Soulsville U.S.A. The Story of Stax Records". New York. Schirmer Trade Books, 1997. Page 85.

7   Interview with Rodgers Redding, August 2, 2023.

Chapter 15

1   Bowman, Rob. "Soulsville U.S.A. The Story of Stax Records". New York. Schirmer Trade Books, Page 42.

2   Gordon, Robert. "Stax Wanted A Soul Singer, And Johnnie Taylor Delivered". VMP. https://www.vinylmeplease.com/blogs/magazine/johnnie-taylor-liner-notes. Accessed April 15, 2023.

3   Gordon, Robert. "Stax Wanted A Soul Singer, And Johnnie Taylor Delivered". VMP. https://www.vinylmeplease.com/blogs/magazine/johnnie-taylor-liner-notes. Accessed April 15, 2023.

4   McCann, Ian. "'Who's Making Love': The Johnnie Taylor Classic That Updated Stax In '68". Udiscovermusic.com. https://www.udiscovermusic.com/stories/johnnie-taylor-whos-making-love/. Accessed July 1, 2023.

5   "A Tribute To Johnnie Taylor". *Living Blues*. September-October 2000, Issue 153 vol. 31 no. 5. Pages 40.

6   Hildebrand, Lee. Liner Notes *Johnnie Taylor Lifetime A Retrospective of Soul, Blues, & Gospel 1956-1999*. 2000. Page 46. Quote from Al Bell.

7   Gordon, Robert. "Stax Wanted A Soul Singer, And Johnnie Taylor Delivered". VMP. https://www.vinylmeplease.com/blogs/magazine/johnnie-taylor-liner-notes. Accessed April 15, 2023.

8   Bowman, Rob. "Soulsville U.S.A. The Story of Stax Records". New York. Schirmer Trade Books, 1997. Page 90.

9   Bowman, Rob. "Soulsville U.S.A. The Story of Stax Records". New York. Schirmer Trade Books, 1997. Page 92.

Chapter 16

1   Gordon, Robert. "Respect Yourself Stax Records and the Soul Explosion". New York. Bloomsbury USA, 1972. Pages 165-167.

2   Bowman, Rob. "Soulsville U.S.A. The Story of Stax Records". New York. Schirmer Trade Books, 1997. Page 133.

3   Ritz, David. "The Life of Aretha Franklin". New York. Little Brown and Company Hachette Book Group. 2014. Page 177.

4   *Unsung 818 Johnnie Taylor.* October 30, 2018. Marcus Chapman quote. https://vimeopro.com/user15889254/unsung/video/297999415. Accessed April 27, 2023.

5   Interview with Rodgers Redding, August 2, 2023.

6   "Rodgers Redding - Macon, Georgia." *The Blues Foundation.* https://blues. org/blues_kba_winner/rodgers-redding-macon-georgia/#:~:text=As%20 one%20musician%20has%20said,soul%20and%20soul%20blues%20 musicians. Accessed August 30, 2023.

7   deVries, Pati. "Blues Hall of Fame". *The Blues Foundation.* https://blues. org/2022-blues-hall-of-fame-inductees/#:~:text=—%20The%2012%20 honorees%20of%20The,the%201950s%20through%20the%201990s. Accessed August 15, 2023.

8   "Respect Yourself Stax Records and the Soul Explosion". New York. Bloomsbury USA, 1972. Page 203.

9   "Steve Cropper The Bio". *playitsteve.com.* https://playitsteve.com/?work projects=the-whole-story. Accessed August 15, 2023.

10 *Unsung 818 Johnnie Taylor.* October 30, 2018. Bettye Crutcher quote. https:// vimeopro.com/user15889254/unsung/video/297999415. Accessed April 27, 2023.

11 Bowman, Rob. "Soulsville U.S.A. The Story of Stax Records". New York. Schirmer Trade Books, 1997. Page 163.

12 *Unsung 818 Johnnie Taylor.* October 30, 2018. Bettye Crutcher quote. https:// vimeopro.com/user15889254/unsung/video/297999415. Accessed April 27, 2023.https://vimeopro.com/user15889254/unsung/video/297999415. Accessed April 27, 2023.

13 Bowman, Rob. "Soulsville U.S.A. The Story of Stax Records". New York. Schirmer Trade Books, 1997. Page 164.

14 Gordon, Robert. "Respect Yourself Stax Records and the Soul Explosion". New York. Bloomsbury USA, 1972. Pages 204.

15 Gordon, Robert. "Respect Yourself Stax Records and the Soul Explosion". New York. Bloomsbury USA, 1972. Pages 204.

16 Bowman, Rob. "Soulsville U.S.A. The Story of Stax Records". New York. Schirmer Trade Books, 1997. Page 164.

17 Gordon, Robert. "Respect Yourself Stax Records and the Soul Explosion". New York. Bloomsbury USA, 1972. Page 204.

18 *Unsung 818 Johnnie Taylor*. October 30, 2018. Sabrina Taylor quote. https://vimeopro.com/user15889254/unsung/video/297999415. Accessed April 27, 2023.

19 *Unsung 818 Johnnie Taylor*. October 30, 2018. Bettye Crutcher quote. https://vimeopro.com/user15889254/unsung/video/297999415. Accessed April 27, 2023.

20 *Unsung 818 Johnnie Taylor*. October 30, 2018. Bettye Crutcher quote. https://vimeopro.com/user15889254/unsung/video/297999415. Accessed April 27, 2023.

21 A Tribute To Johnnie Taylor". *Living Blues*. September-October 2000, Issue 153 vol. 31 no. 5. Pages 39.

22 "Johnnie Tells How His Hits Are Tailored". *Jet Magazine*. March 2, 1972, Page 61.

23 *Unsung 818 Johnnie Taylor*. October 30, 2018. Marcus Chapman quote. https://vimeopro.com/user15889254/unsung/video/297999415. Accessed April 27, 2023.

24 McCann, Ian. "'Who's Making Love': The Johnnie Taylor Classic That Updated Stax In '68". Udiscovermusic.com. https://www.udiscovermusic.com/stories/johnnie-taylor-whos-making-love/. Accessed July 1, 2023.

25 *Unsung 818 Johnnie Taylor*. October 30, 2018. Marcus Chapman quote. https://vimeopro.com/user15889254/unsung/video/297999415. Accessed April 27, 2023.

26 *Unsung 818 Johnnie Taylor*. October 30, 2018. L.C. Cooke quote. https://vimeopro.com/user15889254/unsung/video/297999415. Accessed April 27, 2023.

27 Haralambos, Michael. "Soul Music-The Birth of a Sound in Black America." Cambridge, Massachusetts, Da Capo Press, 1974. Page 113.

28 Deming, Mark. "Who's Making Love - Review". *allmusic.com*. https://www.allmusic.com/album/whos-making-love-mw0000317655https://www.

allmusic.com/artist/johnnie-taylor-mn0000198162/biography. Accessed April 8, 2023.

29 "Johnnie Tells How His Hits Are Tailored". *Jet Magazine*. March 2, 1972, Page 59.

30 Bowman, Rob. "Soulsville U.S.A. The Story of Stax Records". New York. Schirmer Trade Books, 1997. Page 161.

31 Interview with Rodgers Redding, August 2, 2023.

32 Interview with T.J. Hooker, April 11, 2023.

Chapter 17

1 Bowman, Rob. "Soulsville U.S.A. The Story of Stax Records". New York. Schirmer Trade Books, 1997. Page 167.

2 George-Warren, Holly. "Janis". New York. Simon & Schuster. 2019. Pages 264-265.

3 Huey, Steve. "Johnnie Taylor Soul Heaven". *vermonthunter.com*. https:// vermonthunter.mystrikingly.com/blog/johnnie-taylor-soul-heaven. Accessed May 15, 2023.

4 Interview with Kim Sanders, retired Dallas Police Department Detective, April 27, 2023.

5 Interview with Kim Sanders, retired Dallas Police Department Detective, April 27, 2023.

6 Interview with David Washinton, April 16, 2023.

7 Bowman, Rob. "Soulsville U.S.A. The Story of Stax Records". New York. Schirmer Trade Books, 1997. Page 172.

8 Bowman, Rob. "Soulsville U.S.A. The Story of Stax Records". New York. Schirmer Trade Books, 1997. Page 177.

Chapter 18

1 *Unsung 818 Johnnie Taylor*. October 30, 2018. Al Bell quote. https:// vimeopro.com/user15889254/unsung/video/297999415. Accessed April 27, 2023.

2 *Unsung 818 Johnnie Taylor*. October 30, 2018. Candi Staton quote. https:// vimeopro.com/user15889254/unsung/video/297999415. Accessed April 27, 2023.

3 *Unsung 818 Johnnie Taylor*. October 30, 2018. David Washington quote. https://vimeopro.com/user15889254/unsung/video/297999415. Accessed April 27, 2023.

4   *Unsung 818 Johnnie Taylor*. October 30, 2018. Gregg A. Smith quote. https:// vimeopro.com/user15889254/unsung/video/297999415. Accessed April 27, 2023.

5   Hildebrand, Lee. Liner Notes *Johnnie Taylor Lifetime A Retrospective of Soul, Blues, & Gospel 1956-1999*. 2000. Page 19. Quote from Don Davis.

6   Interview with Helen Myles, May 11, 2023.

7   "Johnnie Taylor". *Concord.com*. https://concord.com/artist/johnnie-taylor/#:~:text=The%20singer%20cut%20six%20singles,by%20 Cooke%2C%20were%20regional%20hits. Accessed May 15, 2023.

8   Zeiler, Millie. "Top 10 Johnnie Taylor Songs". *classrockhistory.com*. https:// www.classicrockhistory.com/top-10-johnnie-taylor-songs/. Accessed May 15, 2023.

9   *Unsung 818 Johnnie Taylor*. October 30, 2018. Al Bell quote. https:// vimeopro.com/user15889254/unsung/video/297999415. Accessed April 27, 2023.

10   *Unsung 818 Johnnie Taylor*. October 30, 2018. Al Bell quote. https:// vimeopro.com/user15889254/unsung/video/297999415. Accessed April 27, 2023.

11   *Unsung 818 Johnnie Taylor*. October 30, 2018. Ray Jones quote. https:// vimeopro.com/user15889254/unsung/video/297999415. Accessed April 27, 2023.

12   *Unsung 818 Johnnie Taylor*. October 30, 2018. Candi Staton quote. https:// vimeopro.com/user15889254/unsung/video/297999415. Accessed April 27, 2023.

13   *Unsung 818 Johnnie Taylor*. October 30, 2018. Bernard Jenkins quote. https://vimeopro.com/user15889254/unsung/video/297999415. Accessed April 27, 2023.

14   Rush, Bobby with Powell, Herb. "I Ain't Studdin' Ya My American Blues Story". New York. Hachette Book Group, Inc. Page 77.

15   *Unsung 818 Johnnie Taylor*. October 30, 2018. Sabrina Taylor Lewis quote. https://vimeopro.com/user15889254/unsung/video/297999415. Accessed April 27, 2023.

16   *Unsung 818 Johnnie Taylor*. October 30, 2018. T.J. Hooker quote. https:// vimeopro.com/user15889254/unsung/video/297999415. Accessed April 27, 2023.

17   *Unsung 818 Johnnie Taylor*. October 30, 2018. David Washington quote. https://vimeopro.com/user15889254/unsung/video/297999415. Accessed April 27, 2023.

Chapter 19

1   Zeiler, Millie. "Top 10 Johnnie Taylor Songs". *classrockhistory.com*. https://www.classicrockhistory.com/top-10-johnnie-taylor-songs/. Accessed May 15, 2023.

2   Bowman, Rob. "Soulsville U.S.A. The Story of Stax Records". New York. Schirmer Trade Books, 1997. Page 214.

3   "Words'n'Chords, 'Jody's Got Your Girl and Gone'". *Chicago Tribune*. April 25, 1972, Page 136.

4   "Auditorium Theatre". *Chicago Tribune*. January 31, 1971, Page 3.

5   "Who is Jody Anyway?". *Military Cadence*. https://www.army-cadence.com/who-is-jody-anyway/. Accessed August 15, 2023.

6   *Unsung 818 Johnnie Taylor*. October 30, 2018. Harvey Scales quote. https://vimeopro.com/user15889254/unsung/video/297999415. Accessed April 27, 2023.

7   "A Tribute To Johnnie Taylor". *Living Blues*. September-October 2000, Issue 153 vol. 31 no. 5. Page 40.

8   *Unsung 818 Johnnie Taylor*. October 30, 2018. Anthony Arnold quote. https://vimeopro.com/user15889254/unsung/video/297999415. Accessed April 27, 2023.

9   "Other Notable". *Chicago Tribune*. February 25, 1973, Page 140.

Chapter 20

1   McCabe, Allyson. "Wattstax drew 100,000 people–this 1972 concert was about much more than music". *npr.com*. https://www.npr.org/2023/03/02/1158876105/wattstax-drew-100-000-people-this-1972-concert-was-about-much-more-than-music#:~:text=Allyson%20McCabe-,Wattstax%20drew%20100%2C000%20people%20—%20this%201972%20concert,about%20much%20more%20than%20music&text=The%20Bar%2DKays%20at%20Wattstax%20in%201972.,-Courtesy%20of%20Stax&text=On%20August%2020%2C%201972%2C%20Stax,release%20of%20a%201973%20documentary. Accessed April 30, 2023.

2   Gordon, Robert. "Respect Yourself Stax Records and the Soul Explosion". New York. Bloomsbury USA, 1972. Page 298.

3   Gordon, Robert. "Respect Yourself Stax Records and the Soul Explosion". New York. Bloomsbury USA, 1972. Page 301.

4   *Unsung 818 Johnnie Taylor.* October 30, 2018. Rodgers Redding quote. https://vimeopro.com/user15889254/unsung/video/297999415. Accessed April 27, 2023.

5   Gordon, Robert. "Respect Yourself Stax Records and the Soul Explosion". New York. Bloomsbury USA, 1972. Page 404.

6   Bowman, Rob. "Soulsville U.S.A. The Story of Stax Records". New York. Schirmer Trade Books, 1997. Page 272.

7   "The Super Soul Bowl". *Chicago Tribune.* January 28, 1972, Page 47.

8   *Unsung 818 Johnnie Taylor.* October 30, 2018. Sabrina Taylor quote. https://vimeopro.com/user15889254/unsung/video/297999415. Accessed April 27, 2023.

9   "Johnnie Tells How His Hits Are Tailored". *Jet Magazine.* March 2, 1972. Page 62.

10 Bowman, Rob. "Soulsville U.S.A. The Story of Stax Records". New York. Schirmer Trade Books, 1997. Page 298.

11 Zeiler, Millie. "Top 10 Johnnie Taylor Songs". *classrockhistory.com.* https://www.classicrockhistory.com/top-10-johnnie-taylor-songs/. Accessed May 15, 2023.

12 Zeiler, Millie. "Top 10 Johnnie Taylor Songs". *classrockhistory.com.* https://www.classicrockhistory.com/top-10-johnnie-taylor-songs/. Accessed May 15, 2023.

Chapter 21

1   Interview with T.J. Hooker, April 11, 2023.

2   "WFLD Special" *Chicago Tribune.* November 10, 1973, Page 10.

3   Gordon, Robert. "Respect Yourself Stax Records and the Soul Explosion". New York. Bloomsbury USA, 1972. Page 330.

4   Gordon, Robert. "Respect Yourself Stax Records and the Soul Explosion". New York. Bloomsbury USA, 1972. Page 332.

5   Gordon, Robert. "Respect Yourself Stax Records and the Soul Explosion". New York. Bloomsbury USA, 1972. Page 333.

6   Gordon, Robert. "Respect Yourself Stax Records and the Soul Explosion". New York. Bloomsbury USA, 1972. Page 333.

7   Gordon, Robert. "Respect Yourself Stax Records and the Soul Explosion". New York. Bloomsbury USA, 1972. Pages 336-337.

8   Gordon, Robert. "Respect Yourself Stax Records and the Soul Explosion". New York. Bloomsbury USA, 1972. Page 342.

9   Gordon, Robert. "Respect Yourself Stax Records and the Soul Explosion". New York. Bloomsbury USA, 1972. Page 349.

10 Gordon, Robert. "Respect Yourself Stax Records and the Soul Explosion". New York. Bloomsbury USA, 1972. Page 354.

11 Bowman, Rob. "Soulsville U.S.A. The Story of Stax Records". New York. Schirmer Trade Books, 1997. Page 353.

Chapter 22

1   *Unsung 818 Johnnie Taylor.* October 30, 2018. Anthony Arnold quote. https://vimeopro.com/user15889254/unsung/video/297999415. Accessed April 27, 2023.

2   Brown, Geoffrey F. "Johnnie Taylor's Daughter Debuts At Sweet Sixteen. *Jet Magazine.* July 24, 1975, Page 34.

3   Brown, Geoffrey F. "Johnnie Taylor's Daughter Debuts At Sweet Sixteen. *Jet Magazine.* July 24, 1975, Page 34.

4   Brown, Geoffrey F. "Johnnie Taylor's Daughter Debuts At Sweet Sixteen. *Jet Magazine.* July 24, 1975, Page 34.

5   Brown, Geoffrey F. "Johnnie Taylor's Daughter Debuts At Sweet Sixteen. *Jet Magazine.* July 24, 1975, Page 34.

6   "Johnnie Tells How His Hits Are Tailored". *Jet Magazine.* March 2, 1972. Pages 58-59.

7   *Unsung 818 Johnnie Taylor.* October 30, 2018. Gerlean Taylor quote. https://vimeopro.com/user15889254/unsung/video/297999415. Accessed April 27, 2023.

8   *Unsung 818 Johnnie Taylor.* October 30, 2018. Jonathan Taylor quote. https://vimeopro.com/user15889254/unsung/video/297999415. Accessed April 27, 2023.

9   *Unsung 818 Johnnie Taylor.* October 30, 2018. Anthony Arnold quote. https://vimeopro.com/user15889254/unsung/video/297999415. Accessed April 27, 2023.

10 "Paranoid Personality Disorder". *Cleveland Clinic.* https://my.clevelandclinic.org/health/diseases/9784-paranoid-personality-disorder#:~:text=Paranoid%20personality%20disorder%20(PPD)%20is,demean%2C%20harm%20or%20threaten%20them. Accessed May 18, 2023.

11 Minutaglio, Bill. "Remembering Johnnie - Taylor combined fervor and sophistication". *The Dallas Morning News.* June 8, 2000, Page 5C.

12 Ollison, Rashod D. "Dallas' Mr. Soul - Legendary Johnnie Taylor isn't bitter about standing in the shadows". *The Dallas Morning News*. August 4, 1999, Page 1C.

13 Morthland, John. "Soul Survivor". *Texas Monthly*. Page 54. https://www. texasmonthly.com/articles/soul-survivor/. Accessed May 15, 2023.

14 Hildebrand, Lee. Liner Notes "Johnnie Taylor Lifetime A Retrospective of Soul, Blues, & Gospel 1956-1999". 2000. Page 26. Quote from Deanie Parker.

15 Morthland, John. "Soul Survivor". *Texas Monthly*. Page 54. https://www. texasmonthly.com/articles/soul-survivor/. Accessed May 15, 2023.

Chapter 23

1 Bowman, Rob. "Soulsville U.S.A. The Story of Stax Records". New York. Schirmer Trade Books, 1997. Pages 301-302.

2 "A Tribute To Johnnie Taylor". *Living Blues*. September-October 2000, Issue 153 vol. 31 no. 5. Page 40.

3 Dellar, Fred. "Mojo Time Machine: Johnnie Taylor Wins The First Ever Platinum Single". *mojo4music.com*. https://www.mojo4music.com/time-machine/1970s/mojo-time-machine-johnnie-taylor-wins-the-first-ever-platinum-ingle/. Accessed May 5, 2023.

4 *Unsung 818 Johnnie Taylor*. October 30, 2018. Harvey Scales quote. https:// vimeopro.com/user15889254/unsung/video/297999415. Accessed April 27, 2023.

5 *Unsung 818 Johnnie Taylor*. October 30, 2018. L.C. Cooke quote. https:// vimeopro.com/user15889254/unsung/video/297999415. Accessed April 27, 2023.

6 Dellar, Fred. "Mojo Time Machine: Johnnie Taylor Wins The First Ever Platinum Single". *mojo4music.com*. https://www.mojo4music.com/time-machine/1970s/mojo-time-machine-johnnie-taylor-wins-the-first-ever-platinum-single/. Accessed May 5, 2023.

7 Oppel, Pete. "Taylored in Dallas". *The Dallas Morning News*. June 26, 1976, Page 1F.

8 Ritz, David. "The Life of Aretha Franklin". New York. Little Brown and Company Hachette Book Group. 2014. Pages 294.

9 Interview with David Washington, April 16, 2023.

10 "Disco Lady by Johnnie Taylor". *songfacts.com*. https://www.songfacts. com/facts/johnnie-taylor/disco-lady. Accessed April 18, 2023.

11 "1976: Johnnie Taylor "Disco Lady". *Chicago Tribune*. September 17, 1978, Page 252.

12   "Disco Lady by Johnnie Taylor". *songfacts.com*. https://www.songfacts.com/facts/johnnie-taylor/disco-lady. Accessed April 18, 2023.

13   "1976: Johnnie Taylor "Disco Lady". *Chicago Tribune*. September 17, 1978, Page 252.

14   Oppel, Pete. "Taylored in Dallas". *The Dallas Morning News*. June 26, 1976, Page 1F.

15   Oppel, Pete. "Taylored in Dallas". *The Dallas Morning News*. June 26, 1976, Page 1F.

16   Rush, Bobby with Powell, Herb. "I Ain't Studdin' Ya My American Blues Story". New York. Hachette Book Group, Inc. Page 38.

17   Dellar, Fred. "Mojo Time Machine: Johnnie Taylor Wins The First Ever Platinum Single". *mojo4music.com*. https://www.mojo4music.com/time-machine/1970s/mojo-time-machine-johnnie-taylor-wins-the-first-ever-platinum-ingle/. Accessed May 5, 2023.

18   Zeiler, Millie. "Top 10 Johnnie Taylor Songs". *classrockhistory.com*. https://www.classicrockhistory.com/top-10-johnnie-taylor-songs/. Accessed May 15, 2023.

19   *Unsung 818 Johnnie Taylor*. October 30, 2018. Gregg A. Smith quote. https://vimeopro.com/user15889254/unsung/video/297999415. Accessed April 27, 2023.

20   *Unsung 818 Johnnie Taylor*. October 30, 2018. Rodgers Redding quote. https://vimeopro.com/user15889254/unsung/video/297999415. Accessed April 27, 2023.

21   *Unsung 818 Johnnie Taylor*. October 30, 2018. Alan Walden quote. https://vimeopro.com/user15889254/unsung/video/297999415. Accessed April 27, 2023.

22   Pitts, Leonard Jr. "Johnnie Taylor Tries". *Soul*. June 22, 1967, Page 19.

23   Pitts, Leonard Jr. "Johnnie Taylor Tries". *Soul*. June 22, 1967, Page 19.

24   Oppel, Pete. "Taylored in Dallas". *The Dallas Morning News*. June 26, 1976, Page 1F.

25   Hildebrand, Lee. Liner Notes *Johnnie Taylor Lifetime A Retrospective of Soul, Blues, & Gospel 1956-1999*. 2000. Page 28. Quote from Don Davis.

Chapter 24

1   "Black Stars". *Ebony*. September 1971, Page 46.

2   Interview with Gregg A. Smith, May 12, 2023.

3   Interview with Pat Arnold, May 3, 2023.

4   Interview with T.J. Hooker, April 11, 2023.

5   Interview with T.J. Hooker, April 11, 2023.

Chapter 25

1   "Disco 9000". *imdb.com.* https://www.imdb.com/title/tt0219646/#:~:text
     =Storyline&text=Edit-,Fass%20Black%2C%20an%20accomplished%20
     black%20man%20in%20Los%20Angeles%2C%20is,it%20ain%27t%20
     groovy%20enough.&text=When%20He%27s%20In%20The%20
     Groove%20The%20Mob%20Better%20Move!. Accessed May 17, 2023.
2   "Disco 9000". *Chicago Tribune.* Saturday, July 2, 1977, Page 71.
3   "CBS stages benefit for Black Caucus". *Soul.* November 2, 1976, 1967, Page 12.
4   *Unsung 818 Johnnie Taylor.* October 30, 2018. Jonathan Taylor quote. https://
     vimeopro.com/user15889254/unsung/video/297999415. Accessed April 27,
     2023.
5   *Unsung 818 Johnnie Taylor.* October 30, 2018. Marcus Chapman quote.
     https://vimeopro.com/user15889254/unsung/video/297999415. Accessed
     April 27, 2023.

Chapter 26

1   Interview with Ernie Johnson, April 27, 2023.
2   Gordon, Robert. "Respect Yourself Stax Records and the Soul Explosion".
     New York. Bloomsbury USA, 1972. Page 367.
3   Hildebrand, Lee. Liner Notes *Johnnie Taylor Lifetime A Retrospective of
     Soul, Blues, & Gospel 1956-1999.* 2000. Page 27. Quote Deanie Parker.
4   *Unsung 818 Johnnie Taylor.* October 30, 2018. Alan Walden quote. https://
     vimeopro.com/user15889254/unsung/video/297999415. Accessed April 27,
     2023.
5   *Unsung 818 Johnnie Taylor.* October 30, 2018. Bettye Crutcher quote. https://
     vimeopro.com/user15889254/unsung/video/297999415. Accessed April 27,
     2023.
6   Interview with David Washington, April 16, 2023.
7   Hildebrand, Lee. Liner Notes *Johnnie Taylor Lifetime A Retrospective of
     Soul, Blues, & Gospel 1956-1999.* 2000. Page 26. Quote Al Bell.
8   Morthland, John. "Soul Survivor". *Texas Monthly.* Page 55. https://www.
     texasmonthly.com/articles/soul-survivor/. Accessed May 15, 2023.
9   *Unsung 818 Johnnie Taylor.* October 30, 2018. Ernie Johnson quote. https://
     vimeopro.com/user15889254/unsung/video/297999415. Accessed April 27,
     2023.

10 *Unsung 818 Johnnie Taylor*. October 30, 2018. LaTasha Taylor quote. https://vimeopro.com/user15889254/unsung/video/297999415. Accessed April 27, 2023.

11 *Unsung 818 Johnnie Taylor*. October 30, 2018. Jonathan Taylor quote. https://vimeopro.com/user15889254/unsung/video/297999415. Accessed April 27, 2023.

12 "Johnnie Tells How His Hits Are Tailored". *Jet Magazine*. March 2, 1972. Page 59.

13 Interview with David Washington, April 16, 2023.

14 Interview with Crystal Wright, May 4, 2023.

15 Brown, Geoffrey F. "Johnnie Taylor's Daughter Debuts At Sweet Sixteen:". *Jet Magazine*. July 24, 1975 Page 30.

16 "Johnnie Tells How His Hits Are Tailored". *Jet Magazine*. March 2, 1972. Page 60.

17 Wilonsky, Robert. "Mr. Somebody". *Dallas Observer*. https://www.dallasobserver.com/music/mr-somebody-6395133. Accessed May 5, 2023.

Chapter 27

1   "Taylor Says Cops Made Illegal Gun, Coke Search". *Jet Magazine*. July 17, 1980, Page 61.

2   "Disco singer sentenced to 2 years in prison". *The Dallas Morning News*. July 26, 1980, Page 40.

3   Interview with Kim Sanders, retired Dallas Police Department Detective, April 27, 2023.

4   Interview with Kim Sanders, retired Dallas Police Department Detective, April 27, 2023.

5   *Unsung 818 Johnnie Taylor*. October 30, 2018. T.J. Hooker quote. https://vimeopro.com/user15889254/unsung/video/297999415. Accessed April 27, 2023.

6   *Unsung 818 Johnnie Taylor*. October 30, 2018. Fonda Bryant quote. https://vimeopro.com/user15889254/unsung/video/297999415. Accessed April 27, 2023.

7   *Unsung 818 Johnnie Taylor*. October 30, 2018. Alan Walden quote. https://vimeopro.com/user15889254/unsung/video/297999415. Accessed April 27, 2023.

8   *Unsung 818 Johnnie Taylor*. October 30, 2018. L.C. Cooke quote. https://vimeopro.com/user15889254/unsung/video/297999415. Accessed April 27, 2023.

9   *Unsung 818 Johnnie Taylor*. October 30, 2018. Rodgers Redding quote. https://vimeopro.com/user15889254/unsung/video/297999415. Accessed April 27, 2023.

10 *Unsung 818 Johnnie Taylor*. October 30, 2018. Mae Young quote. https://vimeopro.com/user15889254/unsung/video/297999415. Accessed April 27, 2023.

11 *Unsung 818 Johnnie Taylor*. October 30, 2018. Gerlean Taylor quote. https://vimeopro.com/user15889254/unsung/video/297999415. Accessed April 27, 2023.

12 *Unsung 818 Johnnie Taylor*. October 30, 2018. Gregg A. Smith quote. https://vimeopro.com/user15889254/unsung/video/297999415. Accessed April 27, 2023.

13 "Johnnie Tells How His Hits Are Tailored". *Jet Magazine*. March 2, 1972, Page 60.

Chapter 28

1   Pitts, Leonard Jr. "Johnnie Taylor Tries". *Soul*. June 22, 1967, Page 17.

2   Pitts, Leonard Jr. "Johnnie Taylor Tries". *Soul*. June 22, 1967, Page 17.

3   White, Timothy. "Rock Lives Profiles and Interviews". New York. Henry Holt and Company, Inc., 1990. Pages 642-643.

4   "Johnnie Tells How His Hits Are Tailored". *Jet Magazine*. March 2, 1972, Page 62.

5   "Johnnie Taylor Suffers Heart Attack in Dallas". *Jet Magazine*. March 27, 1980, Page 15.

Chapter 29

1   Whiteis, David. "Johnnie Taylor". "Malaco Music Group "The Last Soul Company". https://www.malaco.com/artists/blues-r-b/johnnie-taylor/. Accessed April 18, 2023.

2   Interview with Rodgers Redding, August 2, 2023.

Chapter 30

1   Interview with Tommy Couch Sr., July 27, 2023.

2   *Unsung 818 Johnnie Taylor*. October 30, 2018. Marcus Chapman quote. https://vimeopro.com/user15889254/unsung/video/297999415. Accessed April 27, 2023.

3   Mehr, Bob. "The story of Malaco Records: An inside look at the 'Last Soul Company'". *Commercial Appeal*. https://www.commercialappeal.com/story/entertainment/music/2021/03/23/malaco-records-the-last-soul-company-rob-bowman-music-books/4735772001/. Accessed July 7, 2023.

4   Mehr, Bob. "The story of Malaco Records: An inside look at the 'Last Soul Company'". *Commercial Appeal*. https://www.commercialappeal.com/story/entertainment/music/2021/03/23/malaco-records-the-last-soul-company-rob-bowman-music-books/4735772001/. Accessed July 7, 2023.

5   Morthland, John. "Soul Survivor". *Texas Monthly*. Page 53. https://www.texasmonthly.com/articles/soul-survivor/. Accessed May 15, 2023.

6   "A Tribute To Johnnie Taylor". *Living Blues*. September-October 2000, Issue 153 vol. 31 no. 5. Pages 40.

7   Interview with Tommy Couch Sr., July 27, 2023.

8   Bowman, Rob. "The Last Soul Company The Malaco Records Story". Jackson, Mississippi. The Malaco Press, 2020. Page 92.

Chapter 31

1   Interview with Tommy Couch Sr., July 27, 2023.

2   Interview with Bobby Patterson, May 24, 2023.

3   Interview with Butch Bonner, December 29, 2023.

Chapter 32

1   Interview with Emmitt Hill, November 29, 2023.

2   Interview with Ernie Johnson, April 27, 2023.

3   Interview with Ernie Johnson, April 27, 2023.

4   Interview with Ernie Johnson, April 27, 2023.

5   "Stax History". "Stax". https://staxrecords.com/history/. Accessed June 30, 2023.

6   Davidson, Justin. "What Really Happens When A Singing Voice Gets Old". *Vulture*. https://www.vulture.com/2016/10/mysteries-of-the-aging-voice.html. Accessed July 17, 2023.

Chapter 33

1   "Little town is recording giant". *The Dallas Morning News*. May 29, 1978, Page 49.

2   "Little town is recording giant". *The Dallas Morning News.* May 29, 1978, Page 49.

Chapter 34

1   Gubbins, Teresa. "Yes, he's experienced - Guitarist picks his way to Jimi Hendrix competition". *The Dallas Morning News.* August 26, 1999, Page 5C.
2   Interview with Crystal Wright, May 4, 2023.
3   Untitled. *Chicago Tribune.* April 26, 1993, Page 16.
4   "Second Annual Blues Bowl". *Chicago Tribune.* July 13, 1994, Page 52.
5   Bowman, Rob. "The Last Soul Company The Malaco Records Story". Jackson, Mississippi. The Malaco Press, 2020. Page 92.
6   Interview with Bobby Patterson, May 24, 2023.
7   Interview with Bobby Patterson, May 24, 2023.
8   Untitled. *The Dallas Morning News.* March 10, 1978, Page 85.
9   Interview with Bobby Patterson, May 24, 2023.
10   Interview with Bobi Bush, December 22, 2023.
11   Interview with Gregg A. Smith, May 12, 2023.
12   Interview with Gregg A. Smith, May 12, 2023.
13   Interview with T.J. Hooker, April 11, 2023.
14   Interview with Bobby Patterson, May 24, 2023.
15   Interview with Tommy Couch Sr., July 27, 2023.
16   Gray, Leon. "Blues in the basement Johnnie Taylor vs Tyronne Davis". *Youtube. com.* https://www.youtube.com/watch?v=CUiXfIaKwEY. Accessed June 12, 2023.

Chapter 35

1   "Rhythm & Blues Foundation: Pioneer Awards". *davemusicdatabase.* https://davesmusicdatabase.blogspot.com/2012/11/rhythm-blues-foundation-pioneer-awards.html. Accessed June 3, 2023.
2   "Longhorn Legacy". *longhornballroom.com.* https://www.longhornballroom.com/history. Accessed May 29, 2023.
3   Bowman, Rob. "Soulsville U.S.A. The Story of Stax Records". New York. Schirmer Trade Books, 1997. Page 306.

Chapter 36

1   Interview with Bobby Patterson, May 24, 2023.

2 Interview with Rhonda Grimes, August 3, 2023.
3 Interview with Bobby Patterson, May 24, 2023.
4 Interview with Emmitt Hill, November 29, 2023.
5 Interview with T.J. Hooker, April 11, 2023.

Chapter 37

1 Hildebrand, Lee. Liner Notes *Johnnie Taylor Lifetime A Retrospective of Soul, Blues, & Gospel 1956-1999*. 2000. Page 30. Quote from Wolf Stephenson.
2 Interview with Gregg A. Smith, May 12, 2023.
3 Interview with Ernie Johnson, April 27, 2023.
4 Interview with Ernie Johnson, April 27, 2023.
5 Interview with Gregg A. Smith, May 12, 2023.
6 *The Will Parts 1 and 2. Facebook*. https://www.facebook.com/watch/?v=6070 29640075354 and https://www.facebook.com/watch/?v=166976931277956. Accessed August 13, 2023.
7 Interview with Irma-Jean Parker, May 4, 2023.
8 Interview with T.J. Hooker, April 11, 2023.

Chapter 38

1 Interview with Emmitt Hill, November 29, 2023.
2 Weitz, Matt. "Thousands turn out for Taylor's funeral - Singer remembered by fellow R&B stars". *The Dallas Morning News*. June 8, 2000, Page 25A.
3 Weitz, Matt. "Thousands turn out for Taylor's funeral - Singer remembered by fellow R&B stars". *The Dallas Morning News*. June 8, 2000, Page 25A.
4 Interview with Ernie Johnson, April 27, 2023.
5 Weitz, Matt. "Thousands turn out for Taylor's funeral - Singer remembered by fellow R&B stars". *The Dallas Morning News*. June 8, 2000, Page 25A.
6 Interview with Rhonda Grimes, August 3, 2023.
7 "Johnnie Taylor - Good Love A Biography, The Loving Memory of Johnnie H. Taylor". *Sandra Clark Funeral Home Obituary*. June 7, 2000.
8 "Johnnie Taylor - Good Love A Biography, The Loving Memory of Johnnie H. Taylor". *Sandra Clark Funeral Home Obituary*. June 7, 2000.
9 Weitz, Matt. "Thousands turn out for Taylor's funeral - Singer remembered by fellow R&B stars". *The Dallas Morning News*. June 8, 2000, Page 25A.
10 Interview with Pat Arnold, May 3, 2023.
11 "Johnnie Taylor - Good Love A Biography, The Loving Memory of Johnnie H. Taylor". *Sandra Clark Funeral Home Obituary*. June 7, 2000.

12 Minutaglio, Bill. "Remembering Johnnie - Taylor combined fervor and sophistication". *The Dallas Morning News*. June 8, 2000, Page 5C.

13 Ritz, David. "The Life of Aretha Franklin". New York. Little Brown and Company Hachette Book Group. 2014. Page 444.

Chapter 39

1 Interviews with Bobby Patterson, May 24, 2023 and Ernie Johnson, April 27, 2023.

2 Untitled advertisement. *Chicago Tribune*. June 8, 2000, Page 69.

3 *Unsung 818 Johnnie Taylor*. October 30, 2018. LaTasha Taylor quote. https://vimeopro.com/user15889254/unsung/video/297999415. Accessed April 27, 2023.

4 *Unsung 818 Johnnie Taylor*. October 30, 2018. Fonda Bryant quote. https://vimeopro.com/user15889254/unsung/video/297999415. Accessed April 27, 2023.

5 *Unsung 818 Johnnie Taylor*. October 30, 2018. Mae Young quote. https://vimeopro.com/user15889254/unsung/video/297999415. Accessed April 27, 2023.

6 *Unsung 818 Johnnie Taylor*. October 30, 2018. Mae Young quote. https://vimeopro.com/user15889254/unsung/video/297999415. Accessed April 27, 2023.

7 Interview with T.J. Hooker, April 11, 2023.

8 *Unsung 818 Johnnie Taylor*. October 30, 2018. LaTasha Taylor quote. https://vimeopro.com/user15889254/unsung/video/297999415. Accessed April 27, 2023.

9 *Unsung 818 Johnnie Taylor*. October 30, 2018. L.C. Cooke quote. https://vimeopro.com/user15889254/unsung/video/297999415. Accessed April 27, 2023.

10 Minutaglio, Bill. "Remembering Johnnie - Taylor combined fervor and sophistication". *The Dallas Morning News*. June 8, 2000, Page 5C.

11 *Unsung 818 Johnnie Taylor*. October 30, 2018. T.J. Hooker quote. https://vimeopro.com/user15889254/unsung/video/297999415. Accessed April 27, 2023.

12 *Unsung 818 Johnnie Taylor*. October 30, 2018. LaTasha Taylor quote. https://vimeopro.com/user15889254/unsung/video/297999415. Accessed April 27, 2023.

13 *Unsung 818 Johnnie Taylor.* October 30, 2018. Sabrina Taylor quote. https://vimeopro.com/user15889254/unsung/video/297999415. Accessed April 27, 2023.

14 Interview with Bobbie Patterson, May 24, 2023.

15 Ollison, Rashod D. "DALLAS' MR. SOUL - Legendary Johnnie Taylor isn't bitter about standing in the shadows." *The Dallas Morning News.* August 4, 1999, Page 1C.

16 Christensen, Thor. "Johnnie Taylor dies at 62". *The Dallas Morning News.* June 2, 2000, Page 36A.

17 Christensen, Thor. "Johnnie Taylor dies at 62". *The Dallas Morning News.* June 2, 2000, Page 36A.

18 Huey, Steve. "Johnnie Taylor Soul Heaven". *vermonthunter.com.* https://vermonthunter.mystrikingly.com/blog/johnnie-taylor-soul-heaven. Accessed May 15, 2023.

19 Minutaglio, Bill. "Remembering Johnnie - Taylor combined fervor and sophistication". *The Dallas Morning News.* June 8, 2000, Page 5C.

20 Minutaglio, Bill. "Remembering Johnnie - Taylor combined fervor and sophistication". *The Dallas Morning News.* June 8, 2000, Page 5C.

21 Minutaglio, Bill. "Remembering Johnnie - Taylor combined fervor and sophistication". *The Dallas Morning News.* June 8, 2000, Page 5C.

22 Minutaglio, Bill. "Remembering Johnnie - Taylor combined fervor and sophistication". *The Dallas Morning News.* June 8, 2000, Page 5C.

23 *Unsung 818 Johnnie Taylor.* October 30, 2018. Millie Jackson quote. https://vimeopro.com/user15889254/unsung/video/297999415. Accessed April 27, 2023.

24 Minutaglio, Bill. "Remembering Johnnie - Taylor combined fervor and sophistication". *The Dallas Morning News.* June 8, 2000, Page 5C.

25 Guralnick, Peter. "Sweet Soul Music: Rhythm and Blues and the Southern Dream of Freedom". New York. Back Bay Books, 1999.

26 Wilonsky, Robert. "Mr. Somebody". *Dallas Observer.* https://www.dallasobserver.com/music/mr-somebody-6395133. Accessed May 5, 2023.

27 Weitz, Matt. "Thousands turn out for Taylor's funeral - Singer remembered by fellow R&B stars. *The Dallas Morning News.* June 8, 2020, Page 25A.

28 Weitz, Matt. "Thousands turn out for Taylor's funeral - Singer remembered by fellow R&B stars. *The Dallas Morning News.* June 8, 2020, Page 25A.

29 Huey, Steve. "Johnnie Taylor Soul Heaven". *vermonthunter.com.* https://vermonthunter.mystrikingly.com/blog/johnnie-taylor-soul-heaven. Accessed May 15, 2023.

30 *Unsung 818 Johnnie Taylor.* October 30, 2018. Alan Walden quote. https://vimeopro.com/user15889254/unsung/video/297999415. Accessed April 27, 2023.

31 Ollison, Rashod D. "DALLAS' MR. SOUL - Legendary Johnnie Taylor isn't bitter about standing in the shadows." *The Dallas Morning News.* August 4, 1999, Page 1C.

32 Minutaglio, Bill. "Remembering Johnnie - Taylor combined fervor and sophistication". *The Dallas Morning News.* June 8, 2000, Page 5C.

33 Minutaglio, Bill. "Remembering Johnnie - Taylor combined fervor and sophistication". *The Dallas Morning News.* June 8, 2000, Page 5C.

34 Ollison, Rashod D. "DALLAS' MR. SOUL - Legendary Johnnie Taylor isn't bitter about standing in the shadows." *The Dallas Morning News.* August 4, 1999, Page 1C.

35 "Letters To The Editor". *The Dallas Morning News.* June 17, 2000, Page 28A.

36 Ollison, Rashod D. "DALLAS' MR. SOUL - Legendary Johnnie Taylor isn't bitter about standing in the shadows." *The Dallas Morning News.* August 4, 1999, Page 1C.

Chapter 40

Chapter 41

1 *The Will Parts 1 and 2. Facebook.* https://www.facebook.com/watch/?v=607029640075354 and https://www.facebook.com/watch/?v=166976931277956. Accessed August 13, 2023.

2 Interview with Fonda Bryant, June 11, 2023.

3 *The Will Parts 1 and 2. Facebook.* https://www.facebook.com/watch/?v=607029640075354 and https://www.facebook.com/watch/?v=166976931277956. Accessed August 13, 2023.

4 *The Will Parts 1 and 2. Facebook.* https://www.facebook.com/watch/?v=607029640075354 and https://www.facebook.com/watch/?v=166976931277956. Accessed August 13, 2023.

5 *The Will Parts 1 and 2. Facebook.* https://www.facebook.com/watch/?v=607029640075354 and https://www.facebook.com/watch/?v=166976931277956. Accessed August 13, 2023.

6 *The Will Parts 1 and 2. Facebook.* https://www.facebook.com/watch/?v=607029640075354 and https://www.facebook.com/watch/?v=166976931277956. Accessed August 13, 2023.

7   *The Will Parts 1 and 2. Facebook.* https://www.facebook.com/watch/?v=6070 29640075354 and https://www.facebook.com/watch/?v=166976931277956. Accessed August 13, 2023.

8   *The Will Parts 1 and 2. Facebook.* https://www.facebook.com/watch/?v=6070 29640075354 and https://www.facebook.com/watch/?v=166976931277956. Accessed August 13, 2023.

9   *The Will Parts 1 and 2. Facebook.* https://www.facebook.com/watch/?v=6070 29640075354 and https://www.facebook.com/watch/?v=166976931277956. Accessed August 13, 2023.

10   *The Will Parts 1 and 2. Facebook.* https://www.facebook.com/watch/?v=6070 29640075354 and https://www.facebook.com/watch/?v=166976931277956. Accessed August 13, 2023.

11   *The Will Parts 1 and 2. Facebook.* https://www.facebook.com/watch/?v=6070 29640075354 and https://www.facebook.com/watch/?v=166976931277956. Accessed August 13, 2023.

12   *The Will Parts 1 and 2. Facebook.* https://www.facebook.com/watch/?v=6070 29640075354 and https://www.facebook.com/watch/?v=166976931277956. Accessed August 13, 2023.

13   *The Will Parts 1 and 2. Facebook.* https://www.facebook.com/watch/?v=6070 29640075354 and https://www.facebook.com/watch/?v=166976931277956. Accessed August 13, 2023.

14   *The Will Parts 1 and 2. Facebook.* https://www.facebook.com/watch/?v=6070 29640075354 and https://www.facebook.com/watch/?v=166976931277956. Accessed August 13, 2023.

15   *The Will Parts 1 and 2. Facebook.* https://www.facebook.com/watch/?v=6070 29640075354 and https://www.facebook.com/watch/?v=166976931277956. Accessed August 13, 2023.

16   *The Will Parts 1 and 2. Facebook.* https://www.facebook.com/watch/?v=6070 29640075354 and https://www.facebook.com/watch/?v=166976931277956. Accessed August 13, 2023.

17   *The Will Parts 1 and 2. Facebook.* https://www.facebook.com/watch/?v=6070 29640075354 and https://www.facebook.com/watch/?v=166976931277956. Accessed August 13, 2023.

18   "Estate sale showcases blues singer's personal effects". *My Plainview.* https:// www.myplainview.com/news/article/Estate-sale-showcases-blues-singer- s-personal-8872240.php. Accessed May 21, 2023.

19   "Estate sale showcases blues singer's personal effects". *My Plainview.* https:// www.myplainview.com/news/article/Estate-sale-showcases-blues-singer- s-personal-8872240.php. Accessed May 21, 2023.

20   Interview with T.J. Hooker, April 11, 2023.

21 "Estate sale showcases blues singer's personal effects". *My Plainview*. https://www.myplainview.com/news/article/Estate-sale-showcases-blues-singer-s-personal-8872240.php. Accessed May 21, 2023.

22 *The Will Parts 1 and 2. Facebook.* https://www.facebook.com/watch/?v=607029640075354 and https://www.facebook.com/watch/?v=166976931277956. Accessed August 13, 2023.

23 Interview with T.J. Hooker, April 11, 2023.

24 Interview with T.J. Hooker, April 11, 2023.

Chapter 42

1 Bernstein, Jonathan. "He Scored the First Platinum Hit. 45 Years Later, His Family Is Fighting for Every Penny". *Rolling Stone*. https://www.rollingstone.com/music/music-features/johnnie-taylor-fonda-bryant-sony-royalties-1241773/. Accessed April 8, 2023.

2 Bernstein, Jonathan. "He Scored the First Platinum Hit. 45 Years Later, His Family Is Fighting for Every Penny". *Rolling Stone*. https://www.rollingstone.com/music/music-features/johnnie-taylor-fonda-bryant-sony-royalties-124173/. Accessed April 8, 2023.

3 Bernstein, Jonathan. "He Scored the First Platinum Hit. 45 Years Later, His Family Is Fighting for Every Penny". *Rolling Stone*. https://www.rollingstone.com/music/music-features/johnnie-taylor-fonda-bryant-sony-royalties-1241773/. Accessed April 8, 2023.

4 Bernstein, Jonathan. "He Scored the First Platinum Hit. 45 Years Later, His Family Is Fighting for Every Penny". *Rolling Stone*. https://www.rollingstone.com/music/music-features/johnnie-taylor-fonda-bryant-sony-royalties-1241773/. Accessed April 8, 2023.

5 Interview with T.J. Hooker, April 11, 2023.

6 Interview with T.J. Hooker, April 11, 2023.

7 Interview with T.J. Hooker, April 11, 2023.

Chapter 43

1 Interview with T.J. Hooker, April 11, 2023.

2 Interview with T.J. Hooker, April 11, 2023.

3 Interview with T.J. Hooker, April 11, 2023.

4 Interview with Pat Arnold, May 3, 2023.

5 "Floyd Taylor." *Malaco Music Group*. https://www.malaco.com/artists/blues-r-b/floyd-taylor/ Accessed December 24, 2023.

6   "Floyd Taylor." *The Great Black Music Project.* http://www.thegreatblackmusic project.org/floydtaylor.html. Accessed 12/24/2023.

7   *The Birmingham Times.* "Son of Soul Music Legend Johnnie Taylor, Floyd Taylor's New Deluxe Edition Album." *Birminghamtimes.com.* https://www.birminghamtimes.com/2014/09/son-of-soul-music-legend-johnnie-taylor-floyd-taylors-new-deluxe-edition-album/

8   Interview with Tommy Couch Jr. July 11, 2023.

9   Interview with T.J. Hooker, April 11, 2023.

10 "Floyd Taylor, blues singer and son of Johnnie Taylor, dies at 60." *Soultracks. com.* https://www.soultracks.com/floyd-taylor-dies. Accessed May 22, 2023.

11 Kshelby1. "Floyd Taylor (Johnny Taylor's Son) Dead at 60. *Lipstick Alley.* https://www.lipstickalley.com/threads/floyd-taylor-johnnie-taylors-son-dead-at-60.654488/. Accessed May 31, 2023.

12 Interview with Pat Arnold, May 3, 2023.

13 "Sabrina N. Taylor-Lewis". *Facebook.* https://www.facebook.com/sabrina.taylorlewis. Accessed August 1, 2023.

14 Interview with Fonda Bryant, June 11, 2023.

15 Interview with Peggye Bryant, August 1, 2023.

16 Interview with Peggye Bryant, August 1, 2023.

17 Yarborough, Chuck. "Johnnie Taylor's daughter: Put my dad in the Rock and Roll Hall of Fame." *cleveland.com.* https://www.cleveland.com/entertainment/2016/02/60s_singer_johnnie_taylors_dau.html. Accessed May 15, 2023.

18 *Unsung 818 Johnnie Taylor.* October 30, 2018. Fonda Bryant quote. https://vimeopro.com/user15889254/unsung/video/297999415. Accessed April 27, 2023.

19 Interview with Fonda Bryant, June 11, 2023.

20 Interview with Fonda Bryant, June 11, 2023.

21 "Three People Declared Children Of Famed Singer Johnnie Taylor". *Jet Magazine.* November 18, 2002, Page 39.

22 Email from T.J. Hooker, April 17, 2023.

23 Email from T.J. Hooker, April 17, 2023.

24 Interview with T.J. Hooker, April 11, 2023.

25 Interview with T.J. Hooker, April 11, 2023.

26 "Three People Declared Children Of Famed Singer Johnnie Taylor". *Jet Magazine.* November 18, 2002, Page 39.

27 Interview with Emmitt Hill, November 29, 2023.

28 "Jon Harrison Taylor Biography". *IMDb.com.* https://www.imdb.com/name/nm6354401/. Accessed July 24, 2023.

29 "Jon Harrison Taylor". *Linked In.* https://www.linkedin.com/in/jonharrisontaylor. Accessed July 24, 2023.

30 "Jon Harrison Taylor". *Apple Music.* Accessed July 24, 2023.

31 Interview with Emmitt Hill, November 29, 2023.

32 "Tasha Taylor". *allmusic.com.* https://www.allmusic.com/artist/tasha-taylor-mn0001473056/biography. Accessed July 24, 2023.

Chapter 44

1 Interview with Crystal Wright, May 4, 2023.

2 Interview with Crystal Wright, May 4, 2023.

3 Interview with Crystal Wright, May 4, 2023.

4 Interview with Crystal Wright, May 4, 2023.

5 Interview with Crystal Wright, May 4, 2023.

6 Interview with Shaquanta and Helen Myles, May 11, 2023.

7 Interview with La Shawn Webb, May 12, 2023.

8 Interview with La Shawn Webb, May 12, 2023.

9 Interview with Raheem Mackey, May 25, 2023.

Chapter 45

1 "Gold & Platinum". *riaa.com.* https://www.riaa.com/gold-platinum/?tab_active=default-award&se=Johnnie+Taylor#search_section. Accessed May 31, 2023.

2 *Rock & Roll Hall of Fame.* https://www.rockhall.com/inductees/classes. Accessed July 19, 2023.

3 Guralnick, Peter. "The Triumph of Sam Cooke Dream Boogie". New York. Back Bay Books / Little Brown and Company, 2005. Page 570.

4 Hildebrand, Lee. Liner Notes *Johnnie Taylor Lifetime A Retrospective of Soul, Blues, & Gospel 1956-1999.* 2000. Page 26. Quote from Al Bell.

Chapter 46

1 "Discography Johnnie Taylor". *allmusic.com.* https://www.allmusic.com/artist/johnnie-taylor-mn0000198162/discography. Accessed June 2, 2023.

2 "Johnnie Taylor". *discogs.com.* https://www.discogs.com/artist/158399-Johnnie-Taylor. Accessed June 2, 2023.

3 "Johnnie Taylor". *wikipedia.com.* https://en.wikipedia.org/wiki/Johnnie_Taylor. Accessed June 2, 2023.

4   "Who's Making Love, Johnnie Taylor." *rateyourmusic.com.* https://rateyourmusic.com/artist/johnnie-taylor. Accessed June 2, 2023.

5   Hildrebrand, Lee. Liner Notes *Johnnie Taylor Lifetime A Retrospective of Soul, Blues, & Gospel 1956-1999.* 2000. Pages 39-40 and 43-44.

ABOUT THE AUTHOR

Gregory Hasty graduated from the University of Texas Arlington with a communications degree. He wrote for the Texas Tech paper, The University Daily, and also wrote articles for American Dawn Magazine and Lit Monthly. Hasty was an FM DJ in college and worked at an ABC affiliate station in Lubbock, Texas, where he was a DJ and music director. He's interviewed numerous notable musicians and has written several other books.

Visit him online at: www.navajoslim.com.

INDEX

Crutcher, Bettye 65, 66, 115, 237, 238, 246
Cunningham, Eddie 24, 39

D

Dallas African American Genealogy Interest Group 226
Dallas Chaparrals 162
Dallas, City of 44, 177
Dallas Convention Center 160
Dallas Federal Courthouse 184
Dallas Morning News 43, 44, 175, 178, 229, 234, 235, 243, 244, 245, 247, 249, 250, 251, 252, 253, 254
Dallas Observer 118, 247, 253
Dallas Police Department 73, 119, 226, 239, 247
Daltry, Roger 143
Damn Yankees 203
Dante's Inferno 6
Davidson, Justin 143, 249
Davis, Don 60, 62, 64, 65, 66, 78, 88, 93, 99, 100, 101, 103, 105, 106, 118, 121, 126, 240, 245
Davis, Melvin 83
Davis, Tyrone 80, 150, 171
DeBurgh, Chris 148
Deer, Bennie 172
Delfonics, The 87
Denson, Paul 172
Derby Records 39, 41
DeShazo, Judge Nikki 184, 185
Deyo, Dean 216
Diamond Club 152, 158
Diggs, Andre 172
Disco 9000 110, 111, 112, 157, 161, 216, 220, 222, 246

Disco Lady (tour bus) xi, 70, 100, 101, 102, 103, 104, 105, 106, 108, 109, 110, 116, 117, 118, 119, 135, 136, 148, 152, 154, 157, 158, 188, 202, 207, 215, 221, 244, 245
Dismas House 193
Dorsett, Tony 140
Dorsey, Thomas A 6
Dozier, Lamont 124
Dramatics, The 99, 160
Duke Records 57, 58
Dunn, Duck 58, 64
D'Urville, Martin 110
Dusable High School 193

E

Earth Wind & Fire 100
Eastwood Country Club 109
Ebay 194
E Company Rockett 203
Edwards, Gene 110
Emmanuel Baptist Church 172
Emotions, The 85, 89, 99, 178
Empire Room 43, 53, 54, 73, 151
Evans, Rev. Clay 20

F

Fairfield Four 8
Fairmont Hotel 222
Fair Park 73, 150, 151, 160
Family Matters 179, 204
Fantasy, Inc. 143
Farley, J.J. 27
Fellowship Baptist Church 28
First Independent Bank of Detroit 121
Five Blind Boys of Mississippi 32
Five Echoes, The 11, 12

K

Kansas City 3, 4, 5, 6, 7, 8, 9, 10, 11,
    13, 29, 33, 40, 43, 53, 70, 89,
    108, 128, 154, 158, 172, 173,
    181, 192, 193, 199, 200, 201
Kansas City Blues Society 193
KC and the Sunshine Band 127
KC Clouds 201
KDFW 162
Keen Records 16, 21
Kennedy, Barbara 170, 177
Kennedy, John F. 40
Kentucky Derby 192
King, Albert viii, 52, 56, 84, 89, 160,
    161, 217
King, B.B. viii, 142, 157, 160, 177
King, Claretta Scott 111
King Faisal 92
King, Freddie viii, 139, 217
King, Martin Luther 47, 63
King Records 15
King, Wanda ix
KKDA 125, 167, 176
Klein, Allen 47, 48
Knowbody Else, The 75
Kool and the Gang 193
Kool Jazz Festival 160
Kozmic Blues Band 72
KPRT 33
Kudlicki, Bart 138, 226

L

LaBelle, Patti 149
LaSalle, Denise 36, 131, 150
Latimore, Benny 131
Laurel, Mississippi 168
Leadbelly 18
Lee, Bernard 172
Lee, Laura 40, 234

Leo's Casino 61
Lewis, Harriet 13, 33, 195
Lewis, Jimmy 133
Light the Way for a Better
    America 162
Lit Monthly x
Little Milton 36, 52, 80, 85, 124, 131,
    142, 151, 162, 171, 176
Little Richard 15
Little Shop of Horrors 203
Little Willie John 35, 63, 217, 218
Longhorn Ballroom 43, 108, 124,
    125, 128, 137, 157, 158, 166,
    168, 174, 222
Lopez, Lance 148
Los Angeles 15, 23, 29, 30, 32, 41, 42,
    44, 48, 84, 86, 146, 202, 203,
    210, 211
Los Angeles Memorial Coliseum 84
Los Angeles Sentinel 42
Lundvall, Bruce 104, 114
Lynyrd Skynyrd 145

M

Mackey, Raheem (Rodney) 54
Macon Municipal Auditorium 61
Madison, Stewart 146
Mad Lads 60
Magruder (Mr.) 151
Malaco European Tour of 1989 142
Malaco Records 28, 128, 130,
    131, 146, 173, 176, 191, 226,
    249, 250
Malcolm and Eddie 204
Malcom X 47
Malouf, Mitchell 130
Manhattans, The 160
Mann, Herbie 146
Mar-Keys 64

Printed in the United States
by Baker & Taylor Publisher Services